MINING, DISPLACEMENT, AND MATRILINY IN MEGHALAYA

This book studies how Development-Induced Displacement (DID) radically restructures gender relations in indigenous tribal societies. Through an in-depth case study of the Indian state of Meghalaya, one of the few matrilineal societies of the world, it analyses how people cope with conflicts in their perception of self, family, and society brought on by the transition from traditional modes of living to increased urbanisation, and how these experiences are different for men and women. It looks at the ways in which this gendered change is experienced inter-generationally in different contexts of people's lives, including work and leisure activities. The book also investigates people's attitudes towards matrilineal structures and their perception of change on matriliny where mining has played a role in building their view of their matrilineal tradition.

Drawing on extensive interviews with individuals directly affected by this phenomenon, the book, part of the Transition in Northeastern India series, makes a significant contribution to the study of DID. It will be useful for scholars and researchers of urbanisation, gender studies, Northeast India studies, development studies, minority studies, public policy, political studies, and sociology.

Bitopi Dutta is an Assistant Professor at the School for Liberal Studies at the University of Petroleum and Energy Studies(UPES), Dehradun, India. She has a PhD from the School of Law and Government, Dublin City University, Ireland (2020), her Master of Arts in Social Work from the Tata Institute of Social Sciences (TISS), Mumbai and her BA Hons. in Sociology from Lady Shri Ram College for Women, University of Delhi. She has been an Irish Research Council Awardee Scholar by the Government of Ireland and has four books on displacement studies including one on one traditonal method of conflict resolution to her authorship. Prior to joining UPES, she has taught in TISS and continues to be associated with film-making with her production house called Vortex Films, whose first feature film production has won the National Films Award in 2021. She is one of the pioneers of the Queer Movement in Northeast India and was the co-organiser of the first Queer Pride walk in Assam which took place in 2014. Her research interests include Gender and sexuality, Indigenous people, displacement studies, qualitative research.

TRANSITION IN NORTHEASTERN INDIA

Series Editor: Sumi Krishna,
Independent scholar, Bengaluru, India

The uniquely diverse landscapes, societies and cultures of northeastern India, forged through complex bio-geographic and socio-political forces, are now facing rapid transition. This series focuses on the processes and practices that have shaped, and are shaping, the peoples' identities, outlook, institutions, and economy. Eschewing the homogenising term 'North East', which was imposed on the region in a particular political context half a century ago, the series title refers to the 'northeastern' region to more accurately reflect its heterogeneity. Seeking to explore how the 'mainstream' and the 'margins' impact each other, the series foregrounds both historical and contemporary research on the region including the Eastern Himalaya, the adjoining hills and valleys, the states of Arunachal Pradesh, Assam, Manipur, Meghalaya, Mizoram, Nagaland, Sikkim, and Tripura. It publishes original, reflective studies that draw upon different disciplines and approaches, and combine empirical and theoretical insights to make scholarship accessible for general readers and to help deepen the understanding of academics, policy-makers and practitioners.

LEGAL PLURALISM AND INDIAN DEMOCRACY
Tribal Conflict Resolution Systems in Northeast India
Edited by Melvil Pereira, Bitopi Dutta and Binita Kakati

CONSERVATION LANDSCAPES AND HUMAN WELL-BEING
Sustainable Development in the Eastern Himalayas
Edited by Siddhartha Krishnan
Associate Editors: Soubadra Devy and Neha Mohanty

MINING, DISPLACEMENT, AND MATRILINY IN MEGHALAYA
Gendered Transitions
Bitopi Dutta

For a full list of titles in this series, please visit www.routledge.com/Transition-in-Northeastern-India/book-series/TNI

MINING, DISPLACEMENT, AND MATRILINY IN MEGHALAYA

Gendered Transitions

Bitopi Dutta

Routledge
Taylor & Francis Group
LONDON AND NEW YORK

First published 2022
by Routledge
2 Park Square, Milton Park, Abingdon, Oxon OX14 4RN

and by Routledge
605 Third Avenue, New York, NY 10158

Routledge is an imprint of the Taylor & Francis Group, an informa business

British Library Cataloguing-in-Publication Data
A catalogue record for this book is available from the British Library

Library of Congress Cataloging-in-Publication Data
A catalog record has been requested for this book

ISBN: 978-0-367-67850-0 (hbk)
ISBN: 978-0-367-71128-3 (pbk)
ISBN: 978-1-003-14946-0 (ebk)

DOI: 10.4324/9781003149460

Typeset in Sabon
by SPi Technologies India Pvt Ltd (Straive)

Dedicated to my late mother Anima Dutta, who taught me courage and resilience; my late sister Karabee Dutta, who taught me to dream and fly; and my father Kusheswar Dutta, who always believes in me more than myself.

CONTENTS

ACKNOWLEDGEMENTS

I was carrying the idea of this research for few years although I did not know that I would end up doing a PhD on it! This research would not have been possible without the constant support and guidance of my supervisor Prof. Eileen Connolly. Thank you so much Prof. Connolly for pushing me to keep exploring the significance of my research question, to critically engage with my theoretical framework, and most importantly to never give up on the highest of expectations of how this research project could be shaped. Your guidance and high expectations encourage me to give my best and keep pushing my limits as an academic, and this is something that will always inspire me for the rest of my life.

My deepest gratitude to Prof. Maura Conway for her valuable feedback on the research throughout this journey, Prof. John Doyle for his constant support, and Prof. Ian MacMenamin for his constant encouragement. DCU's Ireland India Institute has been the most welcoming space and I am grateful to all my colleagues for all the wonderful memories that they have gifted me.

I am extremely grateful to Dr. Dolly Kikon (Melbourne University) for pushing me to write, and for her generous comments on my research questions. My sincere thanks to Jennifer Shahneen Hussain, for looking through my reference/bibliography file and helping me organise it!

My friends have been my treasure! Thank you Sweta, for having my back, reading through my chapters and sharing your comments. Thank you Hari, Vidushi, Jonathan, Joe, Inga, Clark, Joe, Rachna, Liridona, Arpita, Denise, Veronica, and Miraj for always being there.

My deepest gratitude to my sister Bornita Dutta and brother-in-law Abhijit Saikia for always being my rock support, for taking me all around the UK and Ireland numerous times in those travels, and for those countless celebrations we had whenever I landed up in your house in Brighton.

Last but not the least, my thanks to spouse Prakash Deka for his utmost love, care, and support that makes my life meaningful and beautiful, and especially for accompanying me around those fieldwork days when I felt I needed someone to travel through those distant roads.

ABBREVIATIONS

AIDS	Acquired Immunodeficiency Syndrome
APHLC	All Party Hill Leaders' Conference
CPR	Common Property Resources
DID	Development-Induced Displacement
DLHS	District-Level Family Health Survey
DJ	Disc Jockey
HALC	Hynniewtrep Achik Liberation Council
HIV	Human Immunodeficiency Virus
INR	Indian Rupee
KHADC	Khasi Hills Autonomous District Council
KSU	Khasi Students Union
NCPR	National Commission for Protection of Child Rights
NEI	North East India
NFHS	National Family Health Survey
NGT	National Green Tribunal
PAP	Project-Affected Person
SHG	Self Help Group
SRT	Syngkhong Rympei Thymmai
ST	Scheduled Tribes
STI	Sexually Transmitted Infection
USA	United States of America

INTRODUCTION

This research project grew out of my work as a researcher of Development-Induced Displacement (DID) in North East India and in particular, the state of Meghalaya. Meghalaya has been severely affected by unrestricted and illegal coal mining, as well as other forms of mineral extraction. While I was sympathetic to the local groups that opposed mining, I was also aware of how socially complex the situation was, as local indigenous people were both complicit in the mining project and victims of that project. While mining was undermining the traditional fabric of the tribal society of Meghalaya as a whole, women were suffering multiple disadvantages as a result of this mining dominance. I wanted to understand the nuances of how this process operated. As a feminist, I was aware that, although mining was undermining the traditional status and rights of the women in Meghalaya, it did not mean that the women had a high status in the society before the advent of mining. Rather, the advent of mining had radically restructured the gender relationships in the region in a very short period of the mining economy boom, leading to increased disadvantage of women. As an academic, I wanted to understand this process of rapid gender restructuring that has happened over a 30–40-year period that Meghalaya as a case study provided me the opportunity with. It is this reordering of gender relations that is the primary focus of this study.

In the case of Meghalaya, not all those experiencing the impact of displacement have been physically displaced or relocated, yet, the social and cultural displacement unravelled by mining has had an equally strong impact as physical displacement. I wanted to capture how ordinary people experienced this cultural displacement and how they made sense of their current situation. One purpose in doing this is to address the shortcomings in the policy-influential academic literature on DID and to improve its capacity to inform policy in this area. Much of the existing DID research has remained limited to analysing the general impact of displacement on subaltern groups without a substantial engagement with the role of DID in reordering gender relations. Gender either has been treated as an add-on in the dominant DID narrative or subsumed under it. This is true for the standard works of displacement such as those of Parasuraman (1993); Koeing (1995);

DOI: 10.4324/9781003149460-1

Srinivasan (1997); Cernea (1997); McDowell (1997); Colson (1999); Mehta and Srinivasan (2000a, b); Deka (2013); Fernandes et al. (2016). Although this set of literature has looked at the impacts of displacement on women, none has systematically investigated the process through which these changes come about. Also, this literature has treated the people, including women affected by DID, as objects rather than as subjects of enquiry while treating displacement as the central category of analysis.

The seriousness of the impact of DID on vulnerable populations has been widely acknowledged internationally, and women have been identified as the most vulnerable category of those affected (Mehta, 2009; Fernandes, 2009; Haksar, 1998; Kumar and Mishra, 2018). However, a detailed gender analysis of displacement has not yet been undertaken. This research project aims to bridge this gap in the existing literature on DID by doing a gender analysis of the experience of displacement in the tribal indigenous societies of Meghalaya. It makes gender the central category of the analysis while treating the people that it studies, including women, as the active subjects of research whose narratives form the basis of its analysis. This will contribute to the DID literature and enable an enhanced contribution to the understanding of sustainable development and gender justice in situations of displacement.

This book also draws on the literature on the gendered impacts of mining (Ahmad and Lahiri-Dutt, 2006; Hill and Newell, 2009; Kotsdam and Tolonen, 2016). The gender and mining literature provide an account of the impact of mining on the gendered structure of society, on women's experience, and on the gendered nature of the mining industry internationally. The experience of the people in Meghalaya provides a point for comparison with the international experience of mining settlements. The literature on the social impacts of mining has analysed women's experience of the social, cultural, and economic impacts of mining with greater detail as compared to the DID literature. In this research, these two literature studies are brought together to analyse the case of Meghalaya.

This research asks, how does DID reorders gender relations in tribal indigenous societies? Using Meghalaya as a case study, this research treats gender as the central category of analysis, and therefore, it not only analyses the gendered impacts of DID in Meghalaya but also examines the processes that produce this gendered transformation and also the way in which these processes operate.

Meghalaya is a good case study as the purpose of this research is to fill the gap of an insufficient gender analysis in the DID literature and also to critique the existing dominant theories of DID through a gender lens. To do this, it is necessary to focus on peripheral narratives that are outside the framework of dominant narratives which can engage and critique the gender perspectives of the dominant DID theories. Meghalaya presents a peripheral region where a majority of the population are tribal indigenous people. It has been established that indigenous people, as a subaltern group, have suffered most from processes of displacement globally. Meghalaya has a matrilineal social structure which makes the unfolding of the process of gender dislocation sharper, with women moving from a position of comparative advantage to a situation of comparative disadvantage in DID. The case study in this research puts a central focus on the experiences of indigenous women which is important because indigenous women represent the most vulnerable group in DID even among the indigenous people.

Taking the gendered dislocation of Meghalaya as a case study, the research analyses the way in which the displacement experienced in this state due to mining has introduced changes in traditional gender roles and relations in the matrilineal society. The Jaintia Hills of Meghalaya which represents the hub of mining activities in the state is the primary focus for this research, although references to other parts of Meghalaya such as the Khasi Hills are also made. The research investigation looks at how this gendered change has been experienced inter-generationally in different contexts of people's lives including work and leisure activities, and how individuals perceive the impact of mining on their lives; it looks at changing life aspirations of women and men from the past to the present and the processes that have driven this change; it also looks at how people cope with the conflicts with perception of self, family, and society in the transition between traditional modes of living and increased urbanisation and how those conflict and experiences are different for men and for women; it also investigates people's attitudes to matrilineal structures, and their perception of change on matriliny where mining has played a role in the building of people's perception of their matrilineal tradition.

The research is based on life narratives of individuals who have been affected by mining. This approach was chosen as it provides a way to draw in-depth analysis out of individual's experience. It also allows for a nuanced comparison of experience across the generations by incorporating different age groups of respondents. This is an important aspect of the research design as it allows for a discussion of the nature of change over time.

In this way, the research aims to make explicit the micro-politics of gender and also to place this micro-gendered analysis in a macro-analysis of the structure of the gender transitions induced by mining displacement. The micro-politics of gender is revealed by capturing the nuances of people's lives. The discussion throughout the research treats people as the central protagonists in whose lives the impact of DID unfolds. In this way, the research frames the process of DID with a gender analysis derived and guided by people's life narratives.

This work gives centrality to people's narratives, and to women in particular, which is missing in the current DID literature. Through the nuances of people's lives collected through the narratives, the discussion also uncovers how these gender transitions translate into the daily lives of people, especially women. The dailyness of women's lives has been captured from the totality of the life cycle of the women, beginning from their experiences of childhood, marriage, labour, leisure, mobility, and reproductive health. It also uncovers the nexus of gendered impacts that have been experienced by people of different social status and how that operates to produce a particular gendered experience for women. In this discussion, how mining has restructured and re-gendered indigenous society and how individuals have also internalised these changes or resisted them are also analysed.

The book structure

Chapter 1. A gender analysis of development-induced displacement

This chapter provides an analytical framework that guides the discussion in the book. It discusses the international literature on the gender impact of mining and presents a critique of the dominant theories of DID. It discusses the issues around researching indigenous or subaltern societies in a way which gives them voice and places them at the centre of the analysis in the context of the critique of the current literature. It discusses the idea of "relationality" and importance of "women's narrative" in countering the eurocentrism inherent in displacement theories that colour their understanding of indigenous societies.

Chapter 2. Reinventing narratives of displacement: Methodological considerations

Drawing from the arguments of Chapter 1, this chapter presents a discussion on the suitability of Meghalaya as the case study and on the selected method of data collection for this research. In doing so, this chapter discusses the choice to employ life history narratives as the method of data collection that informs this methodological innovation of the book and how it is systematically designed in a way that makes women's narrative guide the analysis of this book and not vice versa.

Chapter 3. The context of Meghalaya

This chapter begins with an introduction to the demography, governance, and administration of Meghalaya. It discusses the historical background of inward migration and early settlement of different ethnicities in Meghalaya from South East Asia and presents an account of the history of modern-state formation in Meghalaya. It also discusses the immigration history of Bangladesh and Nepal to Meghalaya and how that configures in the state-making process of the state. The chapter then goes on to explain the matrilineal structures and discusses the impact of Christianisation and presents a brief history of mining in Meghalaya and how that overlaps with the Meghalaya as an indigenous community. The discussion ends by introducing the implication of the overlaps of mining proliferation into the matrilineal tradition of Meghalaya which is of particular interest to this book.

Chapter 4. Gender, mining, and matriliny in the Jaintia Hills

This chapter analyses men's and women's perceptions of matriliny and compares their points of contention (or cooperation) on how they view their lives in the matrilineal culture. It asks if matriliny in Meghalaya is disintegrating with the intrusion of mining or has matriliny been resilient in spite of the changes accompanying mining. The chapter discusses the grounds on which men resist or support matriliny and how they envisage the ideal matrilineal structure. It explores women's perspective on the changing nature of the matrilineal structures, discussing their reasons for supporting, or resisting matriliny.

Chapter 5. "Growing up in a mining area": Gendering labour, leisure, and mobility

This chapter discusses the shift that has taken place from a women-centred economy to the masculinised occupational culture of mining and how this transition has reduced the status of indigenous Khasi/Jaintia women. In doing so, it maps the gendered socio-economic, cultural, and political transitions that women in this matrilineal society have witnessed across generations and how their experiences of changing ideas of labour, leisure, and mobility reveal the changing content of their status. The chapter does this through a description of childhood of the older generation in the pre-mining era where childhood for the older generation was coterminous with hard work, few or no time for leisure and lot of responsibilities towards the household. It discusses how the idea of social mobility was engrained in the nature of work that they did and how the habit of roaming around for work gave the tribal women a sense of ownership of the public space. It then goes on to discuss how the older generation started migrating for better working opportunities with the arrival of mining and how their first exposure to consumerist good like TV and radio happened. Basically, through these descriptions, this chapter traces the gradual shift in life from a very traditional lifestyle to a modern one that was subsequently offered a very different experience for the next generation of people, especially women, who came to live very different lives from the older generation of women.

Chapter 6. Intimacies and violence in the mines

This chapter discusses the intersection between domestic violence against women, the instability of heterosexual relations, and the growing sex work industry associated with mining. The chapter engages with the complex idea of moralities that characterises the discourse on abandonment, domestic violence, and sex work. The sex work industry introduced new notions of sexual moralities and unconventional sexual relationships in the state against the backdrop of a monstrous coal boom while it also absorbed a lot of women deserted by their husbands who were looking for financial support. The chapter argues that these issues are tied together by a common popular discourse on morality that is shaped by the socio-cultural as well as the politico-economic history of Meghalaya.

Chapter 7. Gendering love, marriage, and reproductive health: The question of continuity and change

This chapter argues that while on one hand sexual autonomy, stigma-free divorce, progressive marital arrangement characterises the Khasi/Jaintia people, on the other hand, it also characterises a lack of control by the woman of her body. It does this through a discussion on the changing narrative of love, marriage systems, and reproductive health across the generations in Meghalaya. The chapter discusses how the nature of love stories has changed across time in Meghalaya which has been accompanied by a change in the nature of marriage systems. It also discusses the intercultural love stories that happened between migrant non-tribal mine workers and indigenous tribal women and how these marriages ignited different debates on the desirability or non-desirability of these cross-cultural marriages. The chapter discusses the idea of sexual freedom for women that the traditional matrilineal culture offered to the women of Meghalaya and how the expression of freedom has changed with time as the mining industry bloomed in the region. It discusses the religious and cultural taboos on contraception and abortion which simultaneously existed with a lot of sexual autonomy of women's bodies. It discusses how the rates of teenage pregnancies have gone up in Meghalaya recently with the mining boom and how the matrilineal culture is often blamed for this crisis.

1

A GENDER ANALYSIS OF DEVELOPMENT-INDUCED DISPLACEMENT

Mining-induced displacement: The magnitude

The Bankwide Review of Projects 1986–1993[1] involving Involuntary Resettlement stated that mining was the cause of 10.3% of DID worldwide and yet, the literature on mining displacement is scarce and limited to contemporary India and a few African states (Terminiski, 201). What is unique about mining displacement is that unlike other forms of DID, the number of people who are affected by the environmental effects of mining regularly exceeds the number of people who are physically displaced by mining projects (Terminski, 2013). The "Social Disruption theory" of the 1970s and 1980s emphasised that the huge negative social and economic impacts of a fast-growing mining industry erodes local culture and structures (Smith et al., 2001; Ennis et al., 2014) and this has been reportedly true for Asia, Africa and, Southern and Central America.

In Asia, countries like China, Indonesia, Papua New Guinea, and the Philippines have recorded high incidence of mining displacement (Terminski, 2013). The Grasberg (Freeport) gold mines located on the Indonesian part of Papua Island have caused displacement of more than 15,000 people. Coal mining in India has displaced more than 2–2.5 million people between 1950 and 2000. Around 3.2 million hectares of land have been contaminated in China along with displacing thousands of people, according to a 2004 estimate. The expansion of OK Tedi mine in Papua New Guinea caused huge environmental damage in surrounding areas and forced 4,000 people to relocate. In Africa, the mining of coal, copper, iron, gold, bauxites, and diamonds has led to highly visible environmental degradation and DID. Mining in the Tarkwa region displaced about 30,000 people between 1990 and 1998, destroyed forest land and farms, and contaminated rivers. Mali, Namibia, Botswana, RSA, and Zimbabwe have a high rate of mining-induced displacement. Yet, according to the official report of the Southern African Development Community, mining-induced displacement was one of the most underreported causes of displacement in Africa despite its likelihood of increase, since mineral extraction has remained a key economic driver in the whole region (Criekinge, 2001). Among the Southern and

DOI: 10.4324/9781003149460-2

Central American countries experiencing mining displacement are Peru, Venezuela, Guyana, Argentina, Suriname, Chile, Honduras, and Venezuela must be mentioned (Terminski, 2013). Displacements in Chile have resulted from copper-mining development which led to the resettlement of over 3,000 families from the mining town of Chuiquicamata to the nearby city of Calama situated in Northern Chile. The most famous example of involuntary resettlement associated with mining in Bolivia concerns the Ayllu Jesús Machaca indigenous community in the La Paz Department (Terminiski, 2012).

Gender and mining

The impact of mining on women and gender relationships is fundamental to the process of cultural displacement. A mining industry typically reinforces patriarchal power relationships through an expression of human dominance over nature (Lozeva and Marinova, 2010). Since the success of mining is purely dependent on an extensive exploitation of nature, it stands in an absolute anti-thecal relationship to tribal indigenous societies who derive their primary identity and survival from nature and especially to tribal women, who enjoy a relatively higher status for their direct association with nature through land that is commonly owned and not specifically by men (Fernandes, 2001). Scott (2007) articulated how mining has contributed to a special type of hegemonic white masculine ideology that operates in different contexts to uphold the sex and gender system in society that completely ignores or overrules the connections that women and indigenous people have with their land. Feminist political ecology that emerged in the 1990s also argues that gender as a meaning system is produced not only through economic relations and cultural and social institutions but also as a result of ecologically based struggle (Wangari et al., 1996). Mining, in that sense, presents a case of rigorous struggle of indigenous people where they are faced with not only an ecologically based struggle but also an incomparable penetration of capitalist consumerism and ideas of a monetised economy, and a deepening patriarchy that accompanies a mining economy.

The gender and mining literature worldwide has established a detailed account of the extreme masculine and gendered implications of mining on women and gender relations. This section discusses the impact of mining on women and then gender relations as has been elaborated by the existing gender and mining literature.

Impacts of mining on women

Global evidence suggests that while the benefits of extractive industry projects are captured primarily by men, women often bear a disproportionate share of social, economic, and environmental risks (World Bank, 2013). An

Oxfam Australia Report (2009) based on experiences from South East Asia and Australia, provided an overall assessment of the multiplier impacts of mining on indigenous women. It discussed how the environmental damage and displacement caused by mining introduces a shift from subsistence to a cash-based economy, encourages male employment in the mines, lack of formal employment for women coupled with limited choice in job opportunities, poor working conditions, low wages and unequal pay for equal work, and on the overall, diminishing women's status in society. Men's direct access and control over the money earned from the mines increases economic dependence of women on men. Increased alcohol consumption, domestic violence, sexually transmitted diseases, and prostitution are other common impacts of mining worldwide (Hill and Newell, 2009). Evidence from Africa has shown the marginalisation that women experience in job and occupational prospects in mining. With the structural shift caused by mining in Africa, women shifted from agricultural work to the service sector and eventually out of the labour force. It is estimated that more 90,000 women get service sector jobs as a result of industrial mining in Africa, while more than 280,000 women left the labour force (Kotsdam and Tolonen, 2016). This established that the decline in agriculture far outweighs the increase in service sector jobs which reduces overall female employment in the mining industry. This leads to greater financial dependence of women on men. Failure to consult women while negotiating access to land and royalties for the mines not only disempowers women but also breaks the gender-friendly traditional decision-making structures.

In India, lack of reliable figures of displaced people due to mining continues to remain an issue. The reason for this data deficit is the remoteness of the affected areas that cut across administrative units, and also due to the project to project basis of the mining explorations that have shorter gestation periods (Ahmad and Lahiri-Dutt, 2006) making them hard to track. Homelessness, loss of livelihood, food insecurity and marginalisation, illness, psychological trauma, and various social and cultural risks are the common impacts of mining on women in India (Ahmad and Lahiri-Dutt, 2006). Feelings of uncertainty in life situations increase psychological pressure and increased alcohol consumption among men whereas women become the soft targets of domestic violence as a means to release men's frustration (Ahmad and Lahiri-Dutt, 2006, p. 327). Age-old social and cultural networks are disrupted which further aids to the collapse of social network and support structure for women (Ahmad and Lahiri-Dutt, 2006, p. 327). Hence, mining displacement means not only physical relocation but also social and cultural displacement, accompanied by the loss of livelihoods derived from subsistence resources offered by the local environment (Ahmad and Lahiri-Dutt, 2006). People lose not only their farming land but also their forests, rivers, pond, grazing land on which their lives are dependent. The social bonds between people are destroyed. This is followed by displacement from resource-based traditional occupations that happen across a longer duration of time (Ahmad and Lahiri-Dutt, 2006) leading to a complete transformation which is gendered.

Impact of mining on gender relationship

The impact of mining on gender relationships is fundamental to the process of cultural displacement. The range of the existing gender and mining literature has discussed that the dynamics of gender relationships in mining sites are maintained by perpetuating the mining space as dominantly masculine, even though the shades of that masculine dominance may vary (Lozeva and Marinova, 2010; Zanzani, 1997; Murphy, 1997; Kotsdam and Tolonen, 2016; Klubock, 1998; Ballard and Banks, 2013; Heemskerk, 2000; Mayes and Pini, 2010; Cuvelier, 2014). What is unique about a mining situation is that each mining context provides very different insights into the same theme of masculine dominance, the nuances of which are important to understand how patriarchy in mining finds numerous ways to penetrate into the socio-cultural diaspora of mining settlements. This subsection discusses the multiple shades of this masculine dominance as they have unfolded in several mining contexts across the world that is relevant for this research.

The mine sites of Leonara of Western Australia present a very interesting account of male dominance of the public sphere that is maintained not only through an exclusive male access of the mining town but also through a conscious segregation between the mining workforce and the local residents, including the local male residents (Lozeva and Marinova, 2010). The poor conditions of the mining settlements make it very unfavourable for women to raise their children and they live away from the mine sites. Because of this exclusion, women never thrive as mineworkers even though they might survive in the mines for some time (Lozeva and Marinova, 2010). Restrictions on the workers from the mining companies prohibit them from interacting with the local residents, which has created a visible segregation between the mineworkers and the local residents, and their meaning of public space. While the mine workers drive through and roam around in the streets of Leonora in their work-provided vehicles, the local residents, both from Aboriginal and non-Aboriginal background are seen walking and interacting with each other in a variety of public spaces, like parks, footpaths, outside of shops, etc. For the male miners, the point of contact for each other is few pubs which further goes to establish that Leonara is a men's town', far away from any woman's access (Lozeva and Marinova, 2010).

Even in mining spaces that are de sex-segregated, the masculine dominance continues to operate in a different form, as is evident in the mining settlements in Butte of the United States. In Butte, even long after the mining settlements were de sex-segregated, they continued to remain a men's space because, the mineworkers replicated their leisure spaces with the sexually segregated environment that they worked in (Murphy, 1997). Male miners from Butte preferred to "go out with the boys" and they resisted women's attempts to break into their carefully guarded social world. Private amusements like brothels and gambling halls had more support from the Butte residents than efforts to establish parks and public recreation programmes. This state of affairs was also maintained by the fact that the mining companies found it easier and cheaper to keep the male miners happy when prostitution, drinking, and gambling were unregulated. The money that was earned in the mines by the workers was spent in these leisure activities, which compelled them to come to work the next morning and thus the cycle continued, and Butte remained a men's world with men drinking, gambling, or doing any of these "men's" stuff for a long period of time, until women broke into the male domain and got themselves served in the bar, even if they weren't entirely welcomed (Murphy, 1997).

It is not only through men styled leisure and work in the public sphere that this masculine dominance is maintained but also through private sphere of the family. Klubock's (1998) work in the copper mines of El Teniente in Chile indicates this. The North American copper companies (with the state) actively encouraged and monitored the creation of working-class nuclear families in the mining settlement of El Teniente which was in accordance with North American gender roles that established the man as the head of the household. Unlike Butte, male miners in Chile were discouraged from socialising or gambling with other men but were encouraged to make families, which could help in establishing a nontransient workforce. However, the wage was always small enough to ensure that men kept coming to work, in order to maintain their families with the limited income that they earned, in a similar way like how in Butte, the miners kept coming to work for the limited income that they spent on leisure. Creation of this kind of a male-headed extremely heterosexual family also meant increased authority and dominance of the men in their families and increased control of women's sexuality by the men by way of masculine coercion. Klubock (1998) documented men who responded to the pressure to marry by marrying twice and maintaining two families at the same time, and single women who tried to secure economic independence in order to escape male violence and state coercion by falling into sex trade. At the same time, men and women also supported each other through these hard times and women's unpaid domestic work covered for the times when men's wage did not suffice to keep up with the cost of living (Klubock, 1998; Kanpur, 2004).

Even in mining contexts where women have been integrated into the workforce and have seen successful women mineworkers, the idea of the mining space as dominantly masculine does not cease to exist. The gold mining settlements in California are an example of this. Tracing a long period of time through 1850–1918 and 1918–1950, Zanzani's (1997) has discussed how successful women workers in the California mines who rose up their career ladder despite many obstacles and challenged the gendered nature of the mining spaces yet could not dismantle the dominant idea of the mining spaces as a masculinised terrain. The female prospectors, to be treated as equal, had to be twice as strong and self-reliant as the men and even though they might be admired by the men for their capability, their occasional success was seen as luck or divine intervention. Zanzani (1997) has also discussed the ambivalence of the men in the mines who could not treat the female mineworkers as "ladies" because they worked with their hands like the men, nor could they categorise the women in the conventional roles of mother, wife, or even prostitute.

Another crucial reason for this masculine dominance in mining can be attributed to the fact that a mining economy provides and reinforces the opportunity for the formation of a tough and superior heteronormative masculine identity for the menfolk. Cuvelier (2014)has examined the relationship between work and masculinity among artisanal miners, or *creuseurs*, in Katanga and highlighted the dynamics, diversity, and complexity of processes of masculine identity construction in the artisanal mining areas. This process of different masculine identity construction, according to Cuvelier (2014), is not only an economic survival strategy but also an attempt to experiment with new ways of being a man in a context of economic crisis and changing gender relations. Cuvelier (2014) discusses how the industrial mining sector established the image of an ideal man who can provide for their families in Creuseurs and how with the downfall of the industrial mining sector in the region, men were called out for not being men enough for their incapability to provide for their families. With the coming in and legalisation of artisanal mining in Katanga, the men used the mine site to construct different types of masculinities to regain the status of being a man that they had lost in the downfall of industrial mining in the region, and also in the process created a counter-culture to the wide rejection they faced from the mainstream society for not being men enough during the downfall. These different shades of masculinity consisted of the "Meza Moto" (heat swallower) who is a daredevil in fond of dangerous situation, or a "Pomba" meaning a big digger who behaves like a wrester with great power, dynamism, and stamina, or a "Mubinji" who is a successful miner with lots of money and always inviting his friends for a drink. One could also be "Bakubwa" (adult) who advocates for an ascetic and responsible lifestyle that makes him less generous or a "Boxeur" (miser), or a "crane" who is believed to be a very knowledgeable person in the mining business and has little trouble coping with unexpected events; a "Bouliste" is someone who can hold his ground in negotiations with the mineral buyers and government officials and is able to grab a better deal than is originally offered. Through his work in Creuseurs, Cuvelier (2014) argues about the coexistence of several competing ideals of masculinity in a mining situation which are characterised by different masculinity practices (Cuvelier, 2014).

The primary theoretical insights that can be borrowed from the different experiences of these various mining diasporas across the world boils down to three major points- First, women suffer increased marginalisation as a result of industrial mining; Second, mining increases male power and privilege by deepening patriarchy that further reinforces the marginalisation of women; Third, mining leads to a male dominance in gender relationships at different levels of the public and the private domain. This includes: (a) the mining workplaces, including those that are sex-disaggregated; (b) "men only spaces and towns" that are maintained by a transient unmarried unorderly male dominated mining workforce population. These sections of men are generally free from family responsibilities and their greater accesses to male friends help them construct and perpetuate these male-dominated public spaces; (c) the domestic sphere of the family. Here, a settled orderly male workforce perpetuates this masculine dominance with the support of mining work structures that prize male authority not only in their workplace but also in their family spheres. What is common to the reality of a mining space is that it prizes a strong heterosexual and heteronormative masculinity and directly or indirectly aids in creating very heteronormative male-centric public sphere "dominated" by men and or strong heteronormative private spheres of families "ruled" by men.

Gender- and development-induced displacement

A rapid infrastructural boom and wealth maximisation led to an exponential rise in DID in the 1970s and 1980s in North East India and many other regions globally. This was followed by the rise of a series of popular resistance movements against displacement in the 1990s (Dwivedi, 2002). The academic debate on DID can be divided into two schools of thoughts. While one school view development as a given and see displacement as an inevitable outcome of it (Cernea, 1990, 1999; Cernea and Guggenheim, 1993; George and Sabelli, 1994; Cernea and Maldonado, 2018; Sheikh, 2009; Sánchez and Urueña, 2017; Rew et al. 2000; Stanley, 2004), the other critiques the idea of development by arguing that displacement represents a development crisis (Parasuraman, 1996b, 1999; Fernandes, 2009, 2014, 2016). For the former school of thought, the resettlement of displaced people is of pivotal importance which can minimise the impact of displacement while also securing the fruits of development. The latter is, however, interested in the larger issue of political rights and governance that sees development not as a well-meaning process but as something which is loaded with structural inequality.

However, what remains a constant to both this school of thought is their lack of a sufficient gender analysis and their failure in treating gender as the central category of analysis in DID, which is why, they fail to sufficiently discuss the embeddedness of gender in the displacement process (for example, Thukral, 1996; Mehta, 2002, 2011; Parasuraman, 1993; Fernandes and

Khatso, 2007; Fernandes and Raj, 1992; Sen, 1992; Benjamin and Fancy, 1998; Gururaja, 2001). This section discusses the inadequate gender discussion on both schools of thoughts in the DID literature.

Resettlement literature in DID

What remains consistent with all of the standard works on displacement that see resettlement as the solution to DID is that they view displacement as an inevitable and unfortunate by-product of the modern development paradigm and therefore advocate for just resettlement and rehabilitation of displaced people so that the people can adapt to the reality of a post-displacement situation. Since its inception until now, this body of work remains a top-down policy and legislation centric account that aims to minimise the damage that displaced persons suffer in DID. Although the resettlement perspective has analysed the series of impact that women as a category suffer under DID, the gendered complexity that produces those impacts continue to be insufficiently researched (for example, Cernea, 1990; Cernea and McDowell, 2000; Picciotto et al., 2001; Kanpur, 2004; Cernea and Maldonado, 2018; Sheikh, 2009, Sánchez and Urueña, 2017, Rew et al. 2000; Stanley, 2004). This subsection discusses the evolution of the Resettlement literature in the dominant DID discourse and highlights the inadequacy of its engagement with gender.

Kulischer (1943) coined the term " displaced persons" to refer to all kinds of categories of forced mobility in Europe during the Second World War. As such what displaced persons meant for Kulischer (1943) differs greatly from what displaced people means in contemporary times. The early debates of contemporary displacement studies were centred on the importance of resettlement of people displaced by development projects. American Social Anthropologist Elizabeth Colson and Thayer Scudder (1971) marked the beginning of the studies on resettlement, in their study of the impact of the Kariba Dam on the Zambezi on the situation of 57,000 resettled Gwembe Tonga People. Their work became a fundamental text in applied anthropology of resettlement and impacted the evolution of development studies worldwide (Terminski, 2013). Scudder and Colson (1982) also later proposed a four-stage model to analyse how people and socioeconomic systems respond to resettlement namely: (1) labelled recruitment, (2) transition, (3) potential development, and (4) handing over or incorporation.

Since the 1950s, further research on resettlement following economic development had been undertaken in other parts of the world, including Asia and America (Dobby, 1952 and Villa Rojas, 1955 cited in Terminski, 2013). It was, however, the first half of the 80s that saw rapid development in studies on DID and resettlement and towards the mid and late 80s the term "development-induced displacement and resettlement" first started to appear in scientific publications (Terminski, 2013). The volume *Putting People First: Sociological Variables in Rural Development* edited by Cernea

(1985) played an important role as the initiator of more advanced studies in this area. Influenced by Cernea's work, World Bank adopted its first Involuntary Resettlement policy in 1980.[2]

Much of these works of research during this period was shaped by the controversies over the consequences of two particularly well-known development projects of that time: The Three Gorges Dam in China and the Sordar Sarovar Dam on the Narmada river in India. Academic institutions and research centres saw an upsurge of resettlement studies in the 80s and 90s. The extensive studies of this problem in India by Walter Fernandes (2001, 2004, 2006, 2007, 2011, and 2016) also explored effective methods for the rehabilitation of displaced persons and people affected by development projects which influenced the displacement literature worldwide. Chris McDowell (1995) presented another in-depth study of the displacement problem compiling from a famous conference on DID by the Refugee Studies Programme, University of Oxford called "Understanding Impoverishment: The Consequences of Development Induced Displacement." The debate on ethics of development had become an important topic in these growing strands of literature and was discussed by Peter Penz, Jay Drydyk, and Paolo Bose (2011) in their "Displacement by Development: Ethics, Rights and Responsibilities."

In the displacement and resettlement literature, Cernea's (1997) Impoverishment Risk and Reconstruction (IRR) model has been influential in shaping policy and research and is considered as path-breaking for its contribution to policy. The IRR model explained that impoverishment as a result of displacement has a high probability of occurring in eight ways as landlessness, joblessness, homelessness, marginalisation, increased morbidity and mortality, food insecurity, loss of access to common property, and social disarticulation, which if given attention, Cernea believes these impoverishments can be prevented (Cernea, 1997). However, the IRR model has received passionate critiques from scholars such as Dwivedi (2002). Dwivedi (2002) critiqued Cernea's (1997) IRR model for its diagnostic and predictive nature and for uncritically advocating a top-down approach from a planning perspective without giving any voice to the people whose life it aims to restore. Crucial issues like consent, terms of participation, dispute resolution are left out of the model's purview (Dwivedi, 2002). Dwivedi (2002) argued that the IRR model failed to realise that while some losses such as assets and material losses can be computed, other losses like communities, institutions, networks and values, loss of customary rights to resources, ways of life, and traditional institutions cannot be restored (Dwivedi, 2002). Dwivedi (2002) also raised questions on the incapability of the IRR model in considering the subjective perception of risks that might vary among affected people depending on the nature of threat that they receive from DID and how other factors like class, gender, ethnicity, caste, region, etc., mediate risk-responses of people. Since perceptions of risk are always changing due to political influences, may it be the state or the grass-root movement, risk is not a single event that occurs in a linear fashion but as a process that must take into account the complex unfolding of systemic factors in a sequence of events, which is another reality that, Dwivedi (2002) argued, the IRR model was unable to address (Dwivedi, 2002). As such, although Cernea and the scholars from a similar standpoint of resettlement have tried to advocate for the rights of displaced people, their top-down policy-centric approach still treats people as objects whose interests need to be safeguarded by mercy of policies that lack nuance.

This focus on the importance of planning and resettlement continues to prevail in the contemporary resettlement literature. For example, it is only recently that Cernea and Maldonado (2018) have discussed the formulation of a new paradigm that they call "resettlement with development" which is inclusive of the social, economic, and cultural dimensions of resettlement and is grounded in the recognition and protection of human rights. This latest body of work by Cernea and Maldonado (2018) critiques the substantial knowledge deficit that continues to prevail in the resettlement policies leading to absence of legislations or one-sided legislations and poor implementation of these policies. Another contribution resettlement literature is that of Vanclay (2017) who argues that the key issues facing resettlement today are increasing competition for land, widespread lack of capacity of resettlement practitioners who give inadequate attention to social issues, corruption in land acquisition and project development, inadequate compensation arrangement, a sole dependence on cash compensation and a failure to adequately consider the issues experienced by displaced communities, which if taken care of, Vanclay (2017) argues, resettlement can be an opportunity for development. Vanclay (2017) proposes the need to pay attention to restore and improve livelihoods and well-being through a negotiated resettlement process that would ensure that people in traditional communities without legal land titles are entitled to compensation. The focus on adequate compensation and resettlement to solve the displacement problem also echoes in the recent work of Sánchez and Urueña (2017) who has emphasised the nonexistence of government policies to recognise DID in Columbia and urges the Columbian government to develop laws and effective policies to ensure that displacement must not be the price of development.

Hence, the focus on planning and resettlement has been viewed as the most ideal way of dealing with a DID in the resettlement literature, probably because getting tangible interventions in place is far more important for grassroots interventions. However, as well meaning this perspective of thought is its concentrated focus on policy is problematic because it is blind to the plethora of social complexities on which the policies must be grounded to be effective. Even though majority of the scholars arguing from the resettlement perspective do mention locating resettlement in the social and cultural paradigm of the displaced people, there is little engagement with the complexity of the social and cultural that fails to acknowledge that a detailed engagement with the socio-cultural complexities might alter and even deconstruct the idea of resettlement policy altogether. This inability to engage with the cultural milieu of displacement has been reflected in Cernea's IRR model in which each of its eight categories of understanding impoverishment are complex and multi-layered and can't be treated only as "one of the many components" of DID in the way that Cernea proposes.

In this literature, Gender does not feature, other than as a very simple variable presented as an add-on in the milieu of the social and cultural. Hence, there is little scope to engage on the question of gender within this body of literature as they do not see the complexity and potential of gender as category of analysis. This is also true for the critiques of Cernea, like that by Dwivedi (2002) who mentions gender as "one of the factors" that gives DID a complex shape along with caste, class, ethnicity, etc., but fails to acknowledge that gender itself can be the central category of analysis. Treating gender as the sole category of analysis, with a focus on gender relations and people and women as active subjects (who are not only the receivers but also the actors who negotiate with the displacement experience in complex ways), could radically deconstruct the whole idea of DID not only from a planning point of view but also in discursive ways.

Displacement as a development crisis

Although the Displacement as a development crisis school of thought provides a radical critique to the resettlement literature of DID by arguing that displacement itself as a development crisis, it shares the same drawback in its treatment of gender – especially in its failure to embed gender in its analysis and its inability to go beyond than arguing for a gender mainstreaming of the DID literature (for example Thukral, 1996; Mehta, 2002, 2011; Parasuraman, 1993; Fernandes and Khatso, 2007; Fernandes and Raj, 1992; Sen, 1992; Benjamin and Fancy, 1998; Gururaja, 2001). This subsection engages with the arguments of the "displacement is development crisis" set of literature and their insufficient gender analysis.

The "displacement is a development crisis" school of thought originated in people's protest and resistance to development projects that threaten or displace people. The international anti-dam movement is an example of this protest forum where thousands of environmentalists, human rights and social activists, and indigenous people's organisations across the world have built alliances with each other and worked together to stop disastrous dam-related impacts on people and the environment. Dam opponents advocate for sustainable, equitable, and efficient technologies and management practices, which can be established by political and structural changes.[3] This school of thought gradually entered academia and research and continues to interrogate the failures of the resettlement perspective, although it has not been as prolific as the resettlement perspective. The work that can be identified from this perspective is that of Parasuraman (1999), Baviskar (1995), and Fernandes (2009, 2011, 2016).

The primary argument of the "displacement is a development crisis" school hold that the structural biases inherent in development projects favor a few elites at the cost of the vast majority of others, especially the minority groups, who pay the price for development. Through six case studies in India, Parasuraman (1999, p. 35–39) substantiated this argument. The intersection of the caste, class, and gender angle that shapes the impact of DID and the way in which the impacts filter through these intersections to create varying views among affected people concerning their quality of life in the post displacement reality finds major focus in this set of literature (for example, Parasuraman, 1996a). This set of literature also argues that Resettlement and Rehabilitation policies in themselves do not guarantee justice because it is the interest of the dominant groups in the development projects that determine the nature of development politics (Parasuraman, 1996a) which confirms that "displacement is inherent in the ideology and policy of development" (Parasuraman, 1999, p. 41). As such, it is not a question of compensation and rehabilitation, but of legal pattern of the dominant development paradigm that impoverishes people in the name of a "public purpose" declared by the state while acquiring land that needs to be debated and redefined (Fernandes and Khatso, 2007) to ensure which, there is a "need for radical changes in the dominant model of development" that encourages such large-scale displacement (Parasuraman, 1999, p. 265).

Because of the structural inequality maintained by elite control that does not care about infringement upon people's right (Parasuraman, 1999, p. 47), the "displacement is a development crisis" set of literature argue that it is not state policies but other factors like ethnic characteristics and political power, and the nature and intensity of collective action of the affected people that alone play significant roles in securing justice in a displacement crisis the loss of people's right is only realised when resistance and protest movement occurs (Parasuraman, 1996a, p. 1532).

This school of thought also questions the approach of the state that treats the displaced people as citizens without rights who are deprived of their livelihood without their consent (Fernandes and Khatso, 2007). The question of indigenous people's rights feature very strongly in this set of literature, especially in the state's approach of treating tribal people based on common property resources as criminals in order to acquire unnecessary excess land for development projects (Fernandes and Khatso, 2007, p. 205). It also questions the skewed land laws which ensure that the benefits of development projects do not reach the affected people even when the projects might have rehabilitation and resettlement policies and the disposition of the land laws that does not even count the displaced people whose lives are based on common property resources in countries like India (Fernandes and Khatso, 2007, p. 204).

The arguments of the "Displacement as a Development crisis" school of thought in DID indeed introduced a very critical perspective into the DID literature, where the intersectionality of caste, tribe, gender, and class were taken into consideration to elaborate the impacts of DID that were determined by a combination of all these factors. Their work also exposed the inadequacy and power politics that shaped the legal pattern of resettlement policies on which the resettlement perspective laid huge faith on. However, no matter how critical this sets of work are, they are still concentrated on the impacts of DID without providing much details on the process of displacement and they continue to see gender as an add-on to their analysis, with little or no focus on gender relations.

Fernandes's work (2007; 2011; 2016) has also argued about the rights of displaced people to share benefit from the development projects, which he believes a radical change in the legislations on the development paradigm could ensure. This work could also be placed in the "resettlement" school of thought, as for him, resettlement is legitimate provided the legalities of it encompass respect the affected people's rights. In this sense, this work is only a small advance on Cernea, as he does not really unpack the nuances and contradictions of the social and cultural complexities that even a legally reformed displacement and resettlement paradigm would have to address.

The importance of understanding the contradictions within an indigenous tribal society was argued on by Baviskar (1995) through her anthropological work in a village called Anjanwara of Madhya Pradesh in India which raises important questions on both "resettlement" and "displacement as a development crisis" schools of thoughts in the DID literature. Baviskar (1995) challenged the innate conservationist ethics shared by tribal dwellers and explored the contradiction of the movements for tribal rights. In exploring the movements for indigenous rights, Baviskar (1995) argues, "It is adivasis[4] who have ideas, whose subjective understanding guide their collective action and gives it meaning and shape their world" (p. 237). By arguing in this line Baviskar (1995) not only brings the centrality back to the indigenous people through a bottom-up approach, but also an in-depth insight that these movements of tribal rights are not always necessarily representative of real hopes of indigenous people, nor are they always the bearers of tribal culture and hence need not always represent an alternative to the dominant development paradigm. While Parashuraman's and Fernandes's work critiques displacement as a development crisis, Baviskar (1995) takes the discourse to a further level to also highlight the layers of contradictions in subaltern communities that also shape people's experiences of displacement. Considering the fact that the resettlement literature had been highly focussed on a linear argument of resettlement in the 1990s, Baviskar's (1995) account that advocated this radical perspective is significant and way ahead of its time, considering the fact that a bottom-up DID narrative continues to be a rare occurrence in contemporary literature on DID even today.

Gender critique of the DID literature

The body of literature that has critiqued the insufficiency of a gender angle in the existing literature of DID, however too, does not go much beyond than indicating the inadequacy of the resettlement initiatives or beyond arguing for the necessity of mainstreaming gender into the displacement literature (for example, Thukral, 1996; Mehta, 2002, 2011; Parasuraman, 1993; Fernandes and Khatso, 2007; Fernandes and Raj, 1992; Sen, 1992; Benjamin and Fancy, 1998; Gururaja, 2001). This section discusses the gender critiques of the DID literature by arguing that the gender critiques of DID, too, have reduced gender into an impact analysis framework and have not engaged with gender as the primary analytical category in the totality of lives of the displaced and affected population.

The gender critique of the DID literature has critiqued the dominant DID literature for its narrow view on the housel-hold as a site of convergent homogenous interests which are shared equally by all of the family members (Agarwala, 1988). It also raises questions on the marginalisation that women face in development policies despite international recognition of rural women's contribution to food production and their rights to land and land distribution (Sharma, 1989). In the Indian context, the fallacy of Indian land laws that reinforce the issue of women's lack of ownership of land and property and the land laws' blind eye to the loss of women's access to fuel, food, fodder, and other minor forest produce due to displacement has received sufficient importance in these critiques (for example Thukral, 1996). The gender critiques of DID also argue about the gender biases in the rehabilitation policies and urges for policies that accord equal status to husbands and wives, pay special attention to displaced women and treat women in women-headed households as the head for post-displacement consultation (Thukral, 1996; p. 1503).

A detailed description of the nature of impoverishment that women suffer in a DID situation holds significant space in the gender critique of the DID literature. For example, Thukral (1996) has elaborated the difficulty faced by women in the transition period in a post-displacement scenario when the displaced families find it difficult to transit to a new place, putting women to the burden of maintaining two homes in this transition period (p. 1501–1502). It is not just lack of skills but rather to make way for the men, Thukral (1996) argues, that women lose their jobs so that men could make their way into the scarce jobs given by the development projects after displacing them. Discussions on displacement-induced morbidity, break up of traditional networks, high rates of breakdown of marriages that causes greater harm to women than the men in a DID situation also consist of Thukral's (1996) gender critique of displacement (Thukral, 1996).

The impact analysis emphasis of the gender critique of the DID literature, however, saw a shift to a structural mode of analysis when it emphasised on the gendered power play that puts women into a double bind of oppression in a DID situation (for example Mehta, 2002, 2006, 2009, 2011). The double bind, Mehta (2009) argued, operates in such a way that while male biases in society help perpetuate gender inequality in terms of unequal resource allocation and distribution and legitimise silencing of women's interests in forced displacement processes, biases within state institutions, structures and policies exacerbate these inequalities. Mehta (2009) also argued about the necessity to redefine certain concepts that are core to the displacement and resettlement process. Like Thukral (1996), Mehta too emphasised developing a gender-sensitive understanding of the household. While Mehta (2009) did emphasise the need to reconsider the understanding of the nature of loss after displacement through a gender lens of cost and benefit analysis, she also maintained that certain components cannot be reduced to a simple cost and benefit component (p. 8). While discussing the nature of loss of assets and income, Mehta (2009, p. 9) argued about the need to record the losses suffered by women, when they lose their customary rights. The fact that these losses do not make it into the tangible list of losses prepared by the resettlement policies, it skewed up the understanding of well-being for women by promoting a simplistic understanding among the resettlement workers that modern amenities of relocation places are doubtlessly beneficial for women as they reduce the drudgery of women's labour (as compared to the traditional pre-displacement society). In order to challenge such simplistic perspectives, Mehta (2009) argued about the need to understand landlessness from the women's point of view (p. 12), since the loss of common property resources is experienced differently by women than the men. Although Mehta was critical of the "displacement followed by resettlement paradigm" and termed resettlement and gender justice as an oxymoron, she still argued on the need for gender mainstreaming in resettlement and rehabilitation policies which could have the potential to create institutional structures to address gender inequalities and ensure better the lives for women (Mehta, 2011, pp. 2, 17). Gururaja (2001) too stressed the importance of application of global norms in order to secure gender justice in displacement which could be implemented through an understanding of the social structure of displaced population.

Internalisation of the patriarchal ideology by the women due to DID has been an important insight provided by the gender critiques of displacement (Fernandes, 2006; Menon, 1995). Often, the few men from displaced families who manage to get absorbed in formal employment opportunities in the development project, do not want their wives to do domestic or other unskilled work as they consider it against an office worker's dignity to have his wife doing menial work. With time, women internalise this ideology of their place being in the kitchen and of not being intelligent enough for skilled work (Menon, 1995, p. 101). The few women who hold permanent jobs are forced to "voluntarily" give up their jobs and accompany their husbands, after the husbands have lost their jobs to mechanisation in the development projects, compelling the men to seek other permanent jobs far away (Sen, 1992, pp. 392–394).

These gender critiques of DID falls between the "resettlement" perspective and the "displacement is a development crisis" perspective because, on one hand, they are critical of the "resettlement" perspective and speak of radically altering the idea of resettlement, but on the other hand, they are also hopeful that once radically altered, resettlement could be a feasible solution to DID. However, the gendered account in this set of literature shares the limits of a policy-oriented impact analysis framework, as they do not sufficiently engage with the complexities of structural changes in gender relations in the affected communities in the totalities of the lives of the people as subjects. On the positive side, this literature makes "women" visible as the most vulnerable category of people in a DID situation; but it treats gender primarily as a descriptive variable in the process of resettlement. Hence, this literature engages with women's experiences only as a by-product of displacement and does not unveil an understanding of women's lives in totality in women's personal experience as well as their socio-cultural context.

Bisht (1999) contributed to the DID literature by addressing these theoretical limitations to some extent in an account of the lives of the displaced communities of the Tehri Dam in India. This work elaborates how prior to displacement, the natural environment supported the subsistence economic practices of the indigenous people (Bisht, 1999). Men brought money into the household, but women had economic freedom due to their access to the natural local resources that they sold and allowing them to raise money of their own (Bisht, 1999, p. 306). Dependence on money was low since daily lives were maintained by the locally available resources. Women reported having a sense of control and happiness over their lives and work prior to displacement because they felt their labour had value (Bisht, 1999, p. 307). The relocation sites had no common property resources, the local governing bodies were rendered irrelevant, and women were left with no work. The women that Bisht (1999) interviewed, shared how in the past even though the work was hard, they were happy; whereas in the present life, their physical burden of household tasks was diminished because of modern amenities in the relocation sites but they live in anxiety and a sense of a lack of purpose (p. 309). The cultures of new relocation sites practised "purdah" (the practice of veiling) which, if the indigenous women did not follow, they were treated as inferior mountain dwellers by the host community (p. 312). The situation of widowed women worsened because unlike the traditional society where widowed women had access to land and livelihood opportunities this did not exist in the relocation site (p. 313). So, from being active workers, women became passive onlookers. Bisht's (1999) account of the displaced people of the Tehri Dam adds substance to what the gender critiques of displacement have argued for in principle but has not dealt with the subject with detailed empirical research, that is the "why and how" of women's experience of DID. In the body of work by Fernandes (2001), Kumar and Mishra (2018), Parasuraman (1993), Modi (2004) and Mehta (2009), the question of the experiences of women in general and indigenous women's experiences in particular, surfaces to the extent in their discussion on the importance of customary rights and the supplementary income from the common property resources that women lose as a result of displacement; but that analysis remains subsumed within an impact analysis framework limiting its insight and policy usefulness.

The DID literature, including that which deals with gender, has viewed the displacement discourse, as a serial, more or less unilateral, and causal disruption that has been analysed more from a managerial and infrastructure planning and service-oriented and impact-oriented focus. The gender critiques of displacement unveil in an impersonal structural change approach, where people are more objects of enquiry or largely passive receivers with limited agency, who are trying to adapt to the systemic disruption introduced by displacement. Even though certain literatures do make the differences of caste, class, and ethnicity visible, yet people even in these categories are homogenised to a large extent. As such it does not unveil the erratic and tumultuousness of experiences that could be varied across different personal and domestic contexts. Marginalised cultures are largely seen as blending into the larger established reality of an aftermath of displacement, and the experiences of the people of the marginalised culture are homogenised. This is a problem because affected people in this account of displacement are treated as components of their cultures who were in balance and harmony with their original cultures that they lost in displacement. In reality, however, people are not just components of their cultures but have their own voices, contradictions, and their own worldviews which need not always be in accordance with an ideal traditional culture or society. Unlike the mining literature, the displacement literature does not deal sufficiently with the possibility of this kind of a variety of experience and it does not speak about how people interact and play a role in shaping their own lives in this process of social and cultural disruption.

Modernisation, eurocentrism, and the weakness of the DID literature

The influence of modernisation theories on the literature of displacement explains the reason why gender as an independent category does not feature significantly in the DID literature. The period when the world saw a massive displacement caused by development projects in the 1960s–1970s, was also the time when modernisation theory emerged in the 1960s which equated development with massive infrastructural growth. The modernisation theories were seen as not just abstract analytical theories in themselves but as a blueprint for praxis. Modernisation theory emphasised democracy, industrialisation, rational and scientific knowledge, welfare centrism, equalitarian values, revolution in technology, industrialisation, higher standard of living, universal education, etc., and it was believed that modernisation was a process that was undoubtedly desired by postcolonial nations themselves too (Gilman, 2003). The process of modernisation that is capable of transforming traditional societies to become modern, according to the classical modernisation theorists, was directly proportional to the theory of evolution; hence, this kind of a progress was believed to be unidirectional and humanity was taken to be progressing from a primitive to a more advanced state (So, 1990). Heavily Eurocentric in its vision, modernisation theory also emphasised that the modernisation process experienced by the USA and several Western European countries could be also replicated in developing countries to develop along this path (Kreutzmann, 1998). Western liberal feminism walked hand in hand with modernisation theory by presenting a similar problematic homogenisation of third world women as typical housewives restricted to the four walls of the private sphere under masculine diktats, to bear the brunt of tradition and patriarchy (Chowdhry, 1995). Western liberal feminists believed that equal access to work and economic rewards through necessary legal and administrative changes would significantly reduce the problem of women's subordination in developing countries, like it has done for the first world white women (Chowdhry, 1995).

Ronal Ingleheart and Pippa Norris (2003) argued that in the first phase of modernisation, agrarian societies progress to industrial societies, herald dramatic gendered transformations in terms of altering the traditional family structure thereby empowering women with greater control over their reproductive lives and family planning, and by increasing women's access to privileges as administrators and managers. Gaining access to a wide range of occupational choices, women not only excel in their economic value in the marketplace but are also able to double their literacy rate via increasing access to modern education which, in turn, facilitates social and cultural empowerment of women. The second phase, according to Ingleheart and Norris (2003) is the shift from an industrial to a post-industrial society where greater gender equality in cultural terms is magnified. The second phase in a post-industrial society witness women's increased influence in political participation, decision-making, and leadership, greater educational access of higher education in universities, and a higher rate of women occupying elite positions in managements and other white-collar professions. However, Ingleheart and Norris (2003) maintained that these shifts in gender attitudes do not occur in isolation but correspond to broader social and cultural shifts occurring in this transition from traditional to secular rational values (as seen in the decline of the traditional family) and in shifts occurring from survival to self-expression values (as reflected in the rise of gender equality). Not cultural change alone can guarantee women's progress in this scenario but is largely facilitated by structural reforms at the legal and policy levels coupled with public support for women's right movements. It is important to note the way Ingleheart and Norris (2003) contrasted the idea of traditional society with that of a secular rational – the traditional society with values of traditional families, deference to authority, and absolute moral standards of patriotism and nationalism, dismissive of divorce, abortion, euthanasia, etc., are attributed to agrarian societies. The secular and rational societies with values exactly opposite to the traditional values, on the other hand, have been largely attributed to modern and post-industrial societies. While explaining the desired shift from a traditional to a modernised secular and rational society, Ingleheart and Norris (2003) contrasted western countries like Europe and USA (representing the secular) with the Asian, African, and Middle Eastern countries (representing the traditional, with the exception of developed countries like Japan).

However, towards the later 60s, a limited set of literatures critiqued the classical modernisation theory. Theorists like Joseph Gusfield (1967), Reinhard Bendix (1967), Rudolph and Rudolph (1967), Eisenstad (1967), Rajni Kothari (1968), Heesterman (1963), Whitaker (1970), many of whose empirical work focussed on India, challenged the dichotomy attributed to tradition versus modernity by classical modernisation theories. The theory of reflexive modernisation by Ulrich Beck, Wolfgang Bonss, and Christoph Lau (2003) offered a further radical critique saying that when societies reach a certain point of modernisation, it radicalises itself which alters the principle base of a modern society (Beck, et al., 2003). As such, no attributes of the modern societies in that sense are permanent but are in a constant process of flux and change.

The centre stage that a neoliberal model of development achieved in the modernisation theories in the 1960s–1970s continues to remain in the development paradigm of today, including the displacement literature. The resettlement school of thought on displacement advocated by scholars like Cernea and Mcdowell, clearly believed in the fruits of development in resonance with the Eurocentric beliefs of the modernisation theory, provided resettlement policies were taken care of. The IRR model of Cernea (1997) echoes the belief of modernisation theories that saw the necessity of adequate infrastructure support required by traditional societies to modernise and develop. On the other hand, in the "displacement is a development crisis" school of thought represented by scholars like Parasuraman (1996a, 1999) and Fernandes (2011, 2016), the dominant development paradigm occupies the centre-stage too, even if in a negative light. The later modernisation theories (like that of Heesterman, 1963) that critiqued the classical modernisation theories for their Eurocentrism and insufficiency in understanding traditional societies, however, did not develop an independent narrative of indigenous or traditional societies in their own context. Indigenous societies were studied as objects to broaden the understanding of the main subject which is "modernisation theory" which can also be seen as a different form of Eurocentrism that denies voices to the people that it studies. The development crisis school of thought too falls into the same Eurocentric trap of treating indigenous societies as objects of enquiry to broaden or alter the idea of the "subject" of their interest i.e. "development." While they play the role of spokespersons of the displaced communities, people's lives are their objects and content of analysis on whose "behalf" they speak rather than people speaking for themselves. Communities are constructed in reference to development and displacement and not vice versa. As a consequence, they end up using a Eurocentric approach to counter that very eurocentrism. This is an unending loop and a vicious trap that the existing displacement literature is stuck in.

The way in which gender was treated as an add-on in the modernisation continues to remain a characteristic in the current dominant development paradigm, including in its gender critiques. For example, Ingleheart and Norris (2003) did feature gender as the core variable of analysis in their modernisation theory but this did not make gender an independent analytical category. They talked about what modernisation can achieve in terms of changing gender relations and not how gender can shape modernisation. In their writing, they argue that patriarchy in societies that modernise has to counter the impact of modernisation, but they fail to consider that patriarchy in modernisation theories too imposes its Eurocentric vision on what it considered as regressive traditional societies. Ingleheart and Norris (2003) argued that women's lives are made better through modernisation, but their cross-cultural analysis had its own implicit patriarchal underpinnings because their analysis is subsumed in a Eurocentric fascination of what modernisation has achieved. This is evident in the way that their cross-cultural analysis did not challenge the basic premises of a dichotomous division between the traditional and modern societies on which the classical theories of modernisation rested. They were convinced that that "women needed saving" by modernisation without being aware of the highly masculine disposition of the modernisation theory itself. Hence, gender was a by-product of Ingleheart and Norris's (2003) analysis of modernisation, even if it was the primary by-product that they discussed. A similar criticism can be made of the gender critique of displacement by Fernandes (2001), Parasuraman (1998), Mehta (2009), Gururaja (2001), and Thukral (1996) because gender is subsumed into their metatheories of DID. As such, these body of work do not imply a structural shift in understanding gender from that of Ingleheart and Norris (2003) work, because these whole set of literature fails to embed gender as an independent category or treat women as subjects rather than as objects of analysis and have failed to argue beyond the mainstreaming of gender in development, and displacement and resettlement policies.

The critique of Eurocentrism inherent in the dominant development paradigm cannot be rooted in Eurocentrism or derive its language from a Eurocentric perspective. It must derive its language and voice from those cultures which Eurocentrism fails to understand, rather than treating those cultures as mere objects of enquiry; and if a gender analysis wants to stand outside of a Eurocentric intellectualism, it has to embed gender into its analysis and treat women as primary subjects in their own independent cultural context and not just as a counter to the vision of a dominant development and displacement paradigm. Even in treating women as subjects, it should be grounded in a lens of indigenous feminism which has vehemently resisted the western, white, and Eurocentric appropriation of women's experiences (like that by Ingleheart and Norris).

Indigenous people as the subjects of analysis

Non-western and indigenous feminists have long argued about the omissions of indigenous women's world views and oral literatures by Western feminists and how western female based structures of language, concepts, theories, and models has been used as a criterion against which experiences of all non-western women as well men, can be known and written about (Ashcroft, et al., 1989) (Spivak, 1988). This othering of the indigenous cultures is a hierarchical way of looking at non-western, indigenous societies (Mohanty, et al., 1991).

The main task of this research is to bring the centrality back to the indigenous people and indigenous community structures in their own context, with a perspective that is not loaded with Eurocentric concepts. In order to avoid this drawback of western feminism, this research requires a pathway that can capture, through its analysis, Meghalaya's own unique context of the matrilineal society. However, it must also be noted that there is no one perfect blueprint for understanding indigenous societies in general or the gender dynamics of indigenous communities in particular. Nonetheless, in the same way that women as a category are heterogeneous and intersectional, yet individual women share similar experiences of being women, indigenous communities across the world share a similarity of a relational culture despite the differences of how that relationality operates in each context.

The idea of *relationality* can be understood in the worldviews of other indigenous societies like that of the South African Bantu, where "being" is intimately bound up with others (Oyewumi, 1998). Escober (2011) described relationality as that which eschews the divisions between culture, individual, and community, as well as between us and them. This is what Black feminist Patricia Collins (2000) meant when she wrote "the voice that I know is individual and collective, personal and political reflecting the intersection of my unique biography within the larger meaning of my historical times." Unlike the western self that is described in terms of "I think therefore I am," an indigenous self is described in terms of "I am we; I am because we are; we are because I am" (Goduka, 2000). Goduka (2000) argued that the western self is in tune with a mono-lithic and one-dimensional construction of humanity', which is not true for indigenous societies because, in the latter, the group has priority over the individual without necessarily erasing the individual. *Existence-in-relation* and *being-for-self-and-others* sum up the African conception of life and reality (Oyewumi, 1998) which could be indicative of other indigenous societies across the world. African feminists have argued how importance of the relational worlds that indigenous women live and derive their agency from has been negated by western feminists (Fennell and Arnot, 2008). For example, African women's role as "mothers" has not only provided them a site for their resistance to patriarchal oppression in local power relations but has also acted as a unifying site for sisterhood, friendship, and solidarity (Nnameka, 1997) (Oyewumi, 2001) (Collins, 1991). Nnameka's emphasis upon the importance of relational gender roles recasts the domestic sphere as an active site for small acts of resistance (Nnameka, 1997 quoted in Fennell and Arnot, 2008). It is in this context that Spivak (1988) emphasises "decentring" the individual and removing the geographical imperialisms that lurk behind the western style of gender analysis of indigenous societies.

The importance of the production of knowledge by *theorising from the lived experiences and cultures* of indigenous women has also been long argued by indigenous feminists to understand how indigenous women build relationships heals the self and the community in their larger (and specific) socio-cultural and historical context. The necessity of theorising in spaces that are often not deemed as "theoretical enough" from a western academic perspective, holds a centrality in indigenous feminism (Saavedra and Nymark, 2008) because it is the lived experiences of indigenous women reflected in their sayings, rituals, folklores, and worldviews that makes the palpable agency of indigenous women visible in their life experiences, yet which mostly remains absent in mainstream academic debates.

Datta's (2015) idea of *Relational Ontology* provides a very relevant blueprint for understanding indigenous societies from their regular lived experiences and worldviews that not only enables one to understand indigenous societies in their own relational contexts but also helps deconstruct dominant pre-conceived western ideas of land, management, and sustainability. The core idea of relational ontology is that actors including their actions can be understood in terms of their diverse and continuous relations and not in a dualism between management and culture, mind and body, humans and nonhumans, and science and society. Banuri's (1990) work on personal maps of culture emphasised a similar relational aspect where everything exists in meaningful relations to each other. Unlike the modern which conceives of everything from material goods to family members as a source of gratification, yet replaceable, in a relational culture everything is perceived as unique and irreplaceable (Banuri, 1990). This also means that a relational culture remains silent on the meaning of roles, rights, and preferences independent of their cultural contexts.

An example of the relational culture can be seen in the human and nature relationship which is fundamental to the basic structure of indigenous societies. The meaning of *Nature* in an indigenous worldview is a part of everyday culture which in intricately related to people's experiences. For example, in some indigenous cultures like that in Assam in India and also in West Bengal, trees are not only objects or symbolic metaphors but also material actors who are married to a woman – this ability of the tree to act as material actors (and other similar traditional knowledge and practices) breaks down the Western nature–culture dichotomy or the western nature management concept (Escobar, 1996, 1999, 2011; Ingold, 2011) and refutes the western static view of nature (Datta, 2015). Similarly, land in indigenous societies, as an actor, can have various identities, like god, animal, woman, man, etc., in its complex relationships with other actors. *Land* like trees also offers a space which involves multiple relational practices with people. This kind of a relationality of indigenous people with nature engages humans and nonhumans in a deep connection, often seen in spiritual terms. It is this spiritual rather than objective viewing of nature, land, and trees by indigenous people is what made them responsible actors with reference to the environment. Hence, *Sustainability* in indigenous societies means holistic livingness or regular living practices, rather than merely a management of ecological balance as proposed by modern development theories (Datta, 2015). Berkes (1999) defined this kind of an indigenous idea of Sustainability as "a cumulative body of knowledge, practice, and belief, evolving by adaptive processes and handed down through generations by cultural transmission, about the relationship of living beings (including humans) with one another and with their environment". As such, the idea of *Scientific knowledge* sees both "science" and "traditional experiences" often expressed as mythical experiences, as equally valid forms of knowledge since traditional experiences, like science, can lead to prediction of the future (Levi-Strauss, 1968). For example, if a plant is found to be poisonous in a traditional indigenous society, people might become cautious to use this specific plant which in fact, through time and storytelling can become a myth that functions to avoid danger in the future (Datta, 2015). A traditional indigenous community does not look up to nature only for a livelihood or material benefit, but nature also shapes their experiences, worldview, ethnic identities, social organisation, and most significantly spiritual worldview that involves a respectful surrender to the forces of nature and to the land where their ancestors rest in the afterlife.

However, it is important to note here that, since the neo-liberalisation era beginning in the 1980s, and for India especially from the 1990s, the indigenous diasporas have been exposed to an incomparable force for change where capitalist consumerism and ideas of a monetised economy have penetrated many of the indigenous societies. This penetration has been compelling as the global order itself is based on the idea of a formal market economy, a desire to exist outside of this hegemony calls for range of struggles for minority groups like indigenous communities. When a market economy characterised by a highly commodified, anti-nature, and patriarchal income generation work like mining is introduced into an indigenous land, the community becomes divided between their belongingness with nature vis. a vis. the need to destroy nature for their personal survival. In this way, the emergence of capitalist interests in the indigenous communities has led to a range of contradictions and disruption in the traditional socio-cultural system of the indigenous societies across the world where the indigenous people are struggling between the gains and losses that result from the conflict between tradition and modernity.

The result of this transformation has not been positive for indigenous people because urbanisation and rural de-agriculturalisation are intimately linked processes in tropical countries (Fry, 2011). For example, the Perote valley of Mexico has seen an increase of mine surface area from 181 to 706 hectares between 1995 and 2005, even in the least accessible areas (Fry, 2011). Factors like increased prices for aggregates, consumerist desires for new homes, and declining returns from agriculture convinced the farmers to convert their farm fields to mines. While deep mines were always more likely to be completely abandoned, farmers believed that they could re-cultivate in the less-deeper mined land once extraction was over. Yet a large amount of 202 hectares of land of the 482 hectares were not re-cultivated by 2006, which is almost 45% of the mined land (Fry, 2011). This diminishing agricultural potential led farmers to migrate to cities for employment. A cycle, that ironically, met the economic needs of the relationship between the urban demands for construction labour and mining of the agricultural fields because, the growth of the construction industry depends on labour and materials from rural and peri-urban areas, which also is a key component of rural–urban interactions (Fry, 2011).

Erosion of collective land or protests against external mining industries but support for one's own mining activities is becoming a frequently common phenomenon across different indigenous communities in the world which indicates the penetration of capitalist world views into indigenous societies. This is evident in the case of indigenous communities in the Philippines where land as home and carrier of cultural identity eroded in the face of poverty (Watzlmaier, 2012). The indigenous people in the Philippines had raised strong opposition against mining companies for preserving their environment and culture from the gold and copper mining industries, yet favoured small-scale mining that they conducted themselves. That's because mining proved to be a viable alternative occupation at a time when farming did not suffice to feed their families, the river water had become insufficient for better irrigation requiring more forests to be cleared to plant vegetables. They took to mining even with their awareness that in the long term, the impact of small-scale mining will be as disastrous as large-scale mining. The degree of benefit that one could avail from their mining activities determined his or her opinion on if mining benefits the community in general or not, even though complaints about miners from outside provinces polluting their ancestral land continue to exist (Watzlmaier, 2012). Even though an indigenous mine labourer might support small-scale mining as a livelihood, they do not receive much profit from their employment in the mines. That is because the shares first go to the financer, the mill operator, the land owner, and to the maintenance of the equipment, and then at the end the indigenous labourers. This is coupled with the unsafe working conditions of the mine labourers, which had caused deadly accidents due to gas poisoning in the tunnels (Watzlmaier, 2012).

Similar is the story of alienation of common land in Africa. A report submitted to the United Nation Human Rights Committee by The Women and Law in Southern Africa Research and Educational Trust and The Global Initiative for Economic, Social and Cultural Rights argued about massive alienation of common land through sales in Malawi of South Africa. According to the report, the chiefs have sold off common land to the buyers in return of money or gift. Such land alienation has increasingly marginalised women's land rights not only in the informal set up of family and lineage negotiations but also in the wider formal processes of land reform policies and programmes, despite the existence of a progressive Malawian National Law that protects women's right to land and property and despite the fact that customary land in Malawi is collectively owned by the community and prohibits any form of its permanent alienation (WLSA-Malawi and GIES-CR, 2014). The indigenous people of Ghana too have witnessed an increase in poverty and a reduction in agricultural productivity as a result of gold mining, the effects of which are greatly suffered by the rural households located nearer to the mines, while the urban centres in the mining areas reap the benefits (Aragón and Rud, 2012). The importance of mining has substantially increased in the last few decades in Ghana and according to the Ghana Chamber of Mines, mining activities generated around 45% of total export revenue, 12% of government's fiscal revenue and attracted almost half of foreign direct investment in 2008. The gold mining sites in Ghana are located in the fertile grounds of the Western region known for its Cocoa production - the primary agricultural export of the region. With the expansion of mining, the mining areas witnessed an increase in poverty between 1998–1999 and 2005, making the mining areas poorer than nonmining areas.

Drawing from this body of work, this research captures the socio-economic disruptions and displacement that the relational culture of Meghalaya might be witnessing as a result of monetisation and capitalist interest introduced by the emergence of the mining economy. The research bases its gender analysis, first, on the lived experience of the indigenous women (and men) that can bring out the similarities and heterogeneity in the gendered experiences and ideologies of indigenous men and women in Meghalaya and places those heterogeneity (or similarities) in the broader common framework of a "strong relational culture" in Meghalaya that is undergoing change. By doing so, this research attempts to make it easier for the reader to relate the reality of Meghalaya with the broader reality of indigenous people across the world while treating people as the subjects of this analysis.

A framework for investigating the changing gender relations in DID

This research aims to understand the changes in gender relations in a DID situation by drawing from the critiques of the DID literatures and the findings of the gender and mining literature, substantiating its arguments through the case study of Meghalaya in North East India. A comparison between the "gender and mining literature" and the "gender and DID literature," as discussed in this chapter, reveals that there is a gap between these two bodies of literatures. While the gender and mining literature has captured the complexity of how gender unfolds under a stressed situation created by mining, the displacement literature (other than mining) has been a linear account of the impact of DID on gender and women and does not go beyond arguing for mainstreaming gender into the displacement discourse. The gender literature on mining unravels the chaos and anarchy in socio-cultural disruptions that indigenous societies encounter. It unveils an account of the transformations that the traditional societies encounter in mining displacement, both structurally and organically through detailed descriptions of how people act and what they become in that transformation. The personal is not lost in this account but unfolds in the structural changes. However, this complexity of how gender reveals itself in mining can show further insights if they are integrated with a systematic understanding of the broader political and socio-cultural context in which they take place. The DID literature, on the contrary, provides a macro and structural explanation of the phenomenon of displacement but fails to capture the details and contextual complexities and also fails to view the displacement paradigm by taking gender as the central category.

This insight pinpoints the necessity of putting both the perspectives that emerge from the mining and displacement literature together. An enquiry such as this, require understanding lives of women and the operation of gender relations in their original context independent of displacement, and at the same time, uncover the vulnerable gendered aspect of the cultural structure through which the structural impact of a DID restructure women's (and men's) lives.

This book presents a gender analysis of DID in Meghalaya of North East India by maintaining a focus on the people on whose lives DID unfold and not vice versa. An independent focus on people means that this study not only derives its analysis from the voices of people's experiences but brings out the totality of their lives from childhood to old age, with all their contradictions, struggle, and agency in shaping their lives, both irrespective of DID or within a DID situation. Understanding the contradiction and agency between and among women (and men) automatically breaks the possibility of a linear gender analysis of DID and brings out the diversity in opinion, ideologies and practices of how people operate in a DID situation. It also brings out the gendered complexities of the socio-cultural context that shapes people's lives and vice versa. This approach makes this research a detailed analysis of how people's lives unfold in a DID situation that is integrated into the socio-cultural structure of where it occurs, which in turn, contributes to further humanising the DID discourse. Voices of people primarily guide this investigation instead of people being added into a dominant framework of analysis. This keeps the possibility open that, beyond predicting an expected outcome of a DID situation, any unexpected occurrence of a social reality in Meghalaya might (or might not) challenge the existing perspectives of the DID literature. While discussing how external forces (in this case mining) restructures and re-genders indigenous structures, this research also discusses how those external forces are internalised, processed, resisted, or coped with by community consciousness across genders, time, and different generation. My argument for treating people as subjects rather than objects of displacement is also to make a political statement that, as important as it is to engage with the DID literature so that it includes the changing experiences of people, it is also essential that the affected people be acknowledged as "living subjects with their own voices" around whom the discourse is centred and not vice versa. Apart from these theoretical considerations that this research wishes to contribute to the general DID literature, it also wishes to contribute newer insights to the global mining literature, that Meghalaya as a case study has the potential to contribute.

The experiences of women in the Meghalayan mining experience echo the accounts of negative impact of mining has been discussed by the international literature on mining. However, this plethora of negative impacts of mining on women in Meghalaya is also accompanied by a contrary sense of empowerment that women derive from the mining economy in terms of higher income, access to modern amenities and consumption behaviour, meeting newer needs in an era of speeding urbanisation that have replaced traditional survival needs and so on. Kuntala Lahiri-Dutt (2012) has argued about the importance of viewing mine spaces not only as sites of masculine dominance but also as feminist spaces where women play active roles in supporting, resisting, and negotiating the base of a mining economy (Lahiri-Dutt, 2012). Going beyond a linear impact focus narrative of mining on women, this research too brings out the complex ways in which women have negotiated with the mining economy of Meghalaya.

The next chapter discusses the methodology that this research has used in the effect of what it aims to capture.

Notes

1 The Bankwide resettlement review was initiated in 1992, to encompass all projects with resettlement in the Bank's portfolio between 1986 and 1993 and to assess consistency between policy and operations.

Check here, https://documents1.worldbank.org/curated/en/130891468136498228/pdf/multi-page.pdf (accessed on August 2019).

2 See, Michael M. Cernea. 1995. Social Integration and Population Displacement. Available at https://documents1.worldbank.org/curated/en/624861468739784522/pdf/multi0page.pdf (accessed on September 2018).

3 See https://archive.internationalrivers.org/the-international-anti-dam-movement (accessed on June 2019).

4 Adivasi is an Indian term for indigenous tribal people.

2

REINVENTING NARRATIVES OF DISPLACEMENT

Methodological considerations

Selection of case study

I wanted this book to not only bridge the existing gender gap in the DID literature but also to contribute, inform, and critique the existing dominant theories of DID through a gender lens. In order to critique and inform the dominant mainstream, I use the peripheral narratives that lie outside the ambit of dominant narratives and that offer not only invaluable insights but can also challenge the core ideas of the dominant narrative. I wanted to pursue the gender-culture dimension of DID from a peripheral context that can de-stabilise and also speak straight to the gender perspective of the dominant DID theories. Hence, for this research, I wanted to build a gender narrative from a peripheral region not only because a periphery is often left voiceless, invisible, or at best subsumed in meta-narratives of culture, history, society, and politics; but also because a peripheral context can help me discover unusual situations and social realities that are often missed out by a "mainstream DID analysis" and that could destabilise the idea of the "mainstream and centre" itself. In that sense, Meghalaya provides a suitable case for this research.

While North East India is itself a peripheral context in terms of the social, political, and cultural marginality that the region has experienced compared to the rest of India,[1] Meghalaya in North East India has been exposed to a force of drastic socio-economic and cultural change in the last 35 years as a result of the displacement induced by an emerging mining industry. Meghalaya's location in the DID discourse in the North East India is interesting because it is one of the eight states in the North East India with a dominant (almost 95%) tribal population. Also, the whole state of Meghalaya enjoys a special right to self-governance under the Sixth Schedule status of the Indian constitution, which aims to protect its indigenous culture.[2] Despite this safeguard, the region has had a controversial history of displacement and other human rights violations caused by a history of illegal coal mining; and this is despite the fact that no non-tribal is allowed to buy and own land in Meghalaya nor is any native indigenous resident of Meghalaya is allowed to sell land to outsiders. Irrespective of

DOI: 10.4324/9781003149460-3

such strict land law, most of the entrepreneurs of the mining business are non-tribal and non-resident of Meghalaya.[3] Most importantly, Meghalaya is famous for its matrilineal culture practised by some of its major tribes like Khasi, Garo, and Jaintia who trace the lineage from the female side, and this is often cited as a fundamental reason for the relatively higher status enjoyed by women (although their status is not equal to men) in this region compared to the other parts of India.[4] Interestingly, some recent literature has argued about a gradual shift in these matrilineal societies to a patrilineal social structure[5] which is indicative of a sharp gender narrative of transition in its traditional culture. Also, the mining history in Meghalaya is argued to have played a very significant role in this transition in gender relations which has occurred over a relatively short time frame of around 30–40 years. The matrilineal tribes like Khasi, Garo, and Jaintia in Meghalaya also have a strong tradition of Common Property Resources (CPRs)[6] that are communally owned. CPRs form an important component in the lives of indigenous women because, as long as the CPRs are community owned, women exercise a partial control over it, irrespective of the fact that the administration of the CPRs might differ from tribe to tribe. The control of the CPRs lies with the village council, which consists of men. As such, the men in the village council play a strong role in decision-making concerning the CPRs even though they are not the direct owners. CPRs are managed by a gendered division of work and control between the social and family spheres and what makes a difference in the lives of women is the difference in their family relations due to their role in CPRs. Unlike societies characterised by individually owned land and settled agriculture where the men control both the private and the public domain, in tribal societies such as Meghalaya, the women control the family economy and agricultural production (Fernandes, 2009). This in turn gave women some control over the community resources and a relatively higher status. Although it did not make her an equal to the men (Menon, 1995, p. 110), one reason why women were seen as economic asset in a tribal society is a combination of all these factors. However, as a result of the coal economy rapidly encompassing the entire socio-political and cultural landscape of Meghalaya, not only the CPRs have been destroyed but the entire traditional gendered fabric of the matrilineal communities continues to undergo massive structural and socio-cultural displacement including irreversible ecological destruction.

Meghalaya is an ideal case study for this research because it provides a peripheral narrative to the dominant discourse of development-induced displacement where the indigenous communities have been drastically transformed by the mining economy in the region. The nature of change the Meghalaya has witnessed speaks to the DID literature in general and the mining literature in particular and offers an opportunity to integrate non-western and indigenous perspectives to the wider body of literature while maintaining gender as the central analytical category. In terms of contribution to the gender in mining and displacement literature, Meghalaya offers a specially case to analyse gender transitions because of the comparatively higher status that women enjoyed in the region before encountering the impact of mining.

I was born and brought up in North East India and this personal experience grants me the privilege of a close familiarity with the history and culture of the region. I have also been academically engaged with North East India and have already conducted research in the area and this gives me an additional advantage of an understanding of its social complexities and the process of change that it is undergoing. It is from this knowledge base that I chose Meghalaya as the ideal case for this research.

Why life narratives

The indigenous culture of the tribes in Meghalaya, including matrilineal tribes, is based on oral history. Unlike modern societies that produce knowledge in a compartmentalised system, knowledge and experiences produced under a tradition of oral history exist in a continuum. Hence, life narratives of women and men collected through unstructured in-depth interviews fit with this oral tradition. An interview guide designed around specific themes rather than specific questions was used to ensure the flow of narratives from the interviewee. As such, although the interview mode for this research is not purely based on an oral history methodology, it does take inspiration from oral history and incorporates it into its own mode of enquiry.

Atkinson (1995) defines life history as a personal account in the teller's own words which are selective, contingent upon remembered events and which provide a clear and ordered record of a personal truth that consists of both fact and fiction. According to Casey (1993), life history is a life story or a form of oral history with additional dimensions. Shacklock & Thorp (2005) discusses how by locating experiences and descriptions on the contexts of where they occur, life history enables one to understand how lives are socially constructed in a way that is not limited to just one individual cohesive identity but also informs the greater complexities that exist across societies and between individuals. Life narratives enable the subjective mapping of experience and the working of a social and cultural system that are often missed in other forms of research (Behar, 1990).

Oral history has the possibility of changing both the terms and content of history (Thompson, 2003). It has already been generally argued how history has been mostly about men's history.[7] There have also been several attempts to integrate the voices of women in the history written mostly by men. As Thompson (2003) argues, while there are voices that are spoken, there are also voices of minorities that are silenced or pushed to the periphery. This is because there are different ranges in which history is written which serve different purposes. The local history of a town or a village enables a sense of meaning of its changing character, in which one can find one's roots of their personal historical knowledge, while family history offers a person a sense of a much longer lifespan that will survive even their deaths (Thompson, 2003). Oral history redirects the focus of history by engaging with the underclasses, unprivileged and in doing so opens up new avenues of enquiry, asks questions that were left unasked or unimportant. It also challenges the accepted myths of history to the authoritarian judgement inherent in its tradition. It provides a means for radical transformation of the social meaning of history and offers a sense of belonging to a place or in time (Thompson, 2003).

Beyond pragmatic considerations, the concern of this research resonates with the argument of Thompson (2003). This research collects life narratives of women (and men) and investigates aspects of their experience that remains insufficiently researched in the existing DID literature, and by doing so, it aims to bring out under-represented narratives of people's reality through people's own voices as subjects. By doing so, this research attempts to uncover silences and transform both the content and purpose of history. It aims to give a voice to the people who are marginalised among the marginalised – the ordinary tribal women. At the same time, this research explores gender – and hence it integrates both men's and women's experiences into its analysis which goes beyond the existing impact analysis framework. This is a significant departure from the displacement literature in general which is limited only to the big impacts that tribal communities suffered in general or that suffer women in particular. The research also attempts to capture the daily-ness of gendered experiences and how it translates into the lives of people on a day-to-day basis. Going beyond traditional and state-centric facts and statistical figures on land acquisition, often presented in a vacuum and disconnected from the discourses of customary rights and indigenous systems (let alone women), this research focusses on personal accounts of women and men and as Thompson (2003) argues, captures information embedded in family histories which are often left unexplored. This is not to say that local archives have not contributed to understanding such complexities of displacement and modernisation processes in Meghalaya – indeed they have made substantial contributions. This research draws inspiration from such existing knowledge and attempts to highlight how different approaches can be applied to the understanding of the same issue (in this case gendered transition), and by doing so, it attempts to integrate women's voices into the local archives that continue to be dominated by men. In doing this, it makes a deliberate decision to interview a particular subject – the women (primarily) and men – and ask questions that have not been yet been asked. A juxtaposition of the findings of this research with the existing literature opens up new areas of enquiry and also informs existing theory on displacement and gender and also on how gender operates under conditions of stress.

Since this research collects women's life narratives and histories, it is important to reflect on what is special about the oral histories of women.

Gluck (2008) argues that oral history not only leads us to "any woman," but it also raises a different set of questions to be explored. It asks about clothing and physical activity, menstruation, knowledge, and attitudes about sex and birth control, childbirth, economic functions in the household, household work, the nature of relationships among women, the magazines and books they read, the menopausal experience, and the relationship of the private life to the public life. Thus, not only is the political base of women's oral history different but also the content is special, and a common thread of experiences links all women irrespective of their differences. This allows the research to move beyond written record that primarily describes elite women's experiences and enables one to understand the lives and experiences of ordinary women who have not gained prominence (Gluck, 2008). Sangster (1994) believes that asking women how explained their past and why women choose to rationalise it in particular ways can provide insights into the social and material structure in which they operate, the choices they make, and the cultural patterns that shape the individual consciousness of women. Julie Stephens (2010) goes a step ahead of this to say how life history is capable of unfolding inconsistencies and cleavages inherent in already existing women's histories and narrative including that of feminist movements thus enabling one to delve into the varieties of accounts, which are often oppressed even within progressive scripts of history.

The aim of this research is in line with the ideas of Gluck (2008) and Stephens (2010). This research attempts to uncover gendered contents and experiences of women that have not been explored so far. It also attempts to capture the dynamics of emotions and perception and meaning perceived by women in the gendered transition that they experienced – many of which are missed or neglected by dominant narratives, including those with a state-centric neoliberal perspective, as well as those with a progressive resistance discourse that support indigenous rights.

Memory

The use of life narratives in an oral tradition requires awareness of the nature of memory and its complications. The first thing concerns the distance of the oral narrative from the event and consequently information coming from a faulty memory. Whereas there are also situations where memories are aided by practices within their respective cultures, certain stories are repeatedly told in the form of a formalised narrative that preserves a typical textual version of the event. In addition, the positionality of the narrator with reference to their social standing colours the narration. Certain acts that were validated in the past may be presently seen as outdated or even unacceptable. However, what holds true for all of these different complications is the fact that memory is a constant process of creation of meanings and is never static. Precisely this is the reason why most of the precious information often lays hidden in the narrator's narration. Oral history in this sense is not objective but is partial, variable, and artificial and is a potential resource only when the researcher calls it into existence. As Portelli (2003) says, "The condition for the existence of the written source is emission; for oral sources, transmission." This is what makes oral history always a work in progress because no oral testimony is the same twice, and it is told from multitude points of views that it is never possible to exhaust the memory of a single informant. The reason why Benison (1995) emphasises the importance of detailed interviews since the possibilities of revealing varying information on the same topic via oral history is immense.

For the purpose of this research, multiple oral narratives of women have revealed common as well as contradictory narratives not only vis-à-vis men but also among women. Some of these contradictions are a result of the comparative social standing of individual women even though they might belong to the same ethnic group. Memory in that sense does not only uncover the varieties of experiences but also the varieties of "cracks" in tradition that has operated differently and brought about unique gendered change for people with reference to their different social standings. Hence, a common cultural thread has the possibility of revealing dialectical narratives of how gendered changes introduced by displacement heralded different worlds in different socio-political circles although they are all holding onto the common cultural thread of ethnicity.

The life narratives collected for this research has also attempted to uncover ideologies as it has attempted to uncover untold stories. As Warren Susman (1964) says, "the historical vision of the past does not replace a mythic vision; rather, in historical societies they exist in dialectical tension with one another and by combination and interaction, they produce a variety of historical visions." Such mythical dialectics that exists in the gendered history of the matrilineal tribes of Meghalaya is a pivotal interest of this research. The interview guide has been structured by this interest in mythical dialectics to understand the constantly evolving structure and function of the gendered ideology of Meghalaya that informs its transitions. It is this ideology that shapes the conceptions and consciousness of the interviewee in terms of how they relate to their state of existence as gendered beings. Portelli (2003) argues that the articulation by the interviewee of their views of historical change, causality, the evolution of institutions, and their view of the way in which the past has been ordered and rationalised, and upon which the future predicted, explains the particular ideological context of the interview and to what extent has the interviewee accepted the hegemonic view of the culture. However, understanding ideological structures that shape narratives also means that the researcher and the interviewee are aware of a larger context and history under which the narratives exist; otherwise, there is a huge possibility of misunderstanding of what is being said and why. This enables consciously articulating the ideological prerogative of the interviewee through the information that is shared in a particular cultural context and thus transforms an individual story into a cultural narrative.

This research is more concerned with meaning than facts, which also resonates with the spirit of oral history. That oral history emphasises on meanings rather than on the facts and events does not mean that oral history has no factual validity, it rather means that they reveal hidden and untold or silenced aspects of facts that are already known. As such, oral history reveals not only just what people did, but also why they did what they did, what were the underlying beliefs that guided what their actions then, and what they currently think about what they did in the past. Hence, the importance of oral history transcends the conventional idea of credibility in the sense that, it goes beyond factual validity and credibility to the departure from facts revealed in imaginations, symbolism, and desires of individuals which is why there are no false oral sources, as Portelli (2003) argues, "the diversity of oral history consists in the fact that "wrong" statements are still psychologically "true" and that this truth may be equally as important as factually reliable accounts." Hence, interviewees are selected because they typify historical processes and are not in line with conventional statistical representative norms.

Data collection

This research has attempted to uncover the history of gender transition in Meghalaya, not only in the spoken narratives of men and women but also that which exists between the gaps and in the spaces and silences between woman's and men's narratives and also between and among generations of men and women in Meghalaya. This is what makes this research a study of silences along with things said, about changes happening unanimously and also changes happening despite resistances, changes happening without a conscious plan or a need for "*that*" change, and also about changes that have been accepted by the matrilineal society as a matter of changing times. From the data collected, this research also tries to understand how certain changes that happen gradually over a period of time in the subtleties of the daily-ness of lives, that often may or may not register in the mind of the individual, whereas how many other transformations come to be accepted as a quest for development or a civilising mission under the promises of neoliberalism, which might be considered imposed yet desirable. This is not to say that there is no resistance against such mainstreaming of the tribal cultures in the region, indeed there are many. But at the same time, these resistances coexist with increasing popularity of a modern lifestyle that is deemed more "*developed*" by many community members; and in this quest of balancing tradition with modernity, something changes the dynamics of gender relations, either consciously or unconsciously, either forcefully or with consent, either as inevitability or as an essentiality. The interest of this research lies in such nuance that makes it an investigation of processes that are not only policy driven but also culture driven.

As such, the data collected traces the gendered transitions that happened in Meghalaya in such a short period of approximately 30–40 years, both at the structural level as well as at the micro level. Acknowledging the fact that the mining-induced changes happening at the micro level of gendered lives and the structural level of changing traditional structures may not directly coincide at certain juncture, but could also show intricate connections between both at certain other junctures, the mode of enquiry has tried to ensure both levels of investigations of the micro and macro blend interconnectedly while also granting enough space for independent enquiry. As such, the framework of this research has addressed two levels of inductive analysis. Firstly, by trying to understand the processes of gendered transition investigated through memories of people at the micro level and how the changes in micro level is reflected in the mining-induced macro-structural changes in Meghalaya. It is by putting both of these levels of micro and macro analysis of changes together that this research uncovers not only the gendered transitions that the matrilineal communities in the Jaintia hills of Meghalaya have undergone but also the nuances of how these changes occurred and why they occurred the way they occurred.

Selection of interviewees

In-depth personal interviews to collect people's life narratives were the main method of data collection through which people's (especially women's) experiences of the gendered transitions in the Jaintia hills of at least 30 years of coal boom to the present times have been documented. As such the upsurge of coal mining in the Jaintia hills in the 1990s was treated as the main reference point in comparison to which people's memory of their changing lives throughout the pre-mining days until the present time has been recorded. The research focuses more on the experience of women than that of men since women as a subaltern group have experienced increased disadvantage as a result of DID. The data collected through the life narratives were supplemented and contextualised through documentary research using Government Data, and local media sources of the region.

A total of 35 in-depth interviews and 4 Focus Group Discussions (FGD) were conducted. Of the 4 FGDs, the first was with older women, the second with men from different generations, the third was with men and women together, and the fourth was a family FGD where three generations participated together. The primary reason behind conducting FGDs was that group discussion could ignite memories of the overall culture of the tribe in the past vis-à-vis the present which might not be captured effectively only through personal accounts. Of the 36 interviews, 23 were women and 13 men. Interviewees were divided across age and income and marital status, the age criteria being a major criterion of categorising interviewees. The older generation consisted of the age group of 55 years and older, the middle-aged represents the age group between 35 and 55 years old, and the younger generation represents the age group of 15–35 years old. The 55 and above age group of interviewees, who had been roughly in their 20s when coal mining in the Jaintia hills saw a boom, were expected to reveal information on the gendered status of the community prior to the launch of the mining projects and the changes that they had witnessed throughout the 25–30 years of their lives. The 35–55 years age group of respondents, who were born in and around the beginning of the coal boom, represent a transitory generation who have seen and grown up in a period of dynamic change in the Jaintia hills with the exposure of the mining boom. As such, they are the bridge generation between the old and the new. The younger than 35 years old generation were born at a time when the major changes brought in by mining were more or less established. As such the younger generation were expected to reveal information on the contemporary gendered fabric of the Jaintia hills. Narratives from across these three generations have provided an account of the intergenerational changes that Meghalaya has witnessed from the pre-mining era till the present times, where mining has proved to be pivotal factor in changing the content of their experiences and worldview. As such, this research has covered people's changing experiences of childhood, love, marriage, divorce, labour, leisure, violence, etc., since the pre-mining era to contemporary times.

The oral testimonies of women have explored women's experiences in detail and in subtleties. The queries have primarily targeted the structural socio-cultural context from which men and women's narratives (with reference to their location in that specific historical juncture) have emerged while the analysis has been derived from regular lived experiences. The broader points of queries were centred on the journey of the community from the past to the present, before and after displacement.

Fieldwork

The fieldwork was conducted in three phases:

Pilot interview phase, conducted from August to September 2017.

Major Fieldwork, phase 1, conducted from March to May 2018.

Major Fieldwork, phase 2, conducted from November 2018 to February 2019.

Since this research is an exploratory research, heavily derived from the empirical realities of Meghalaya existing literature on which empirical context is rare, the pilot fieldwork was conducted to test the efficiency of the method of data collection and to gain a better understanding of the region as well as making contacts. Taking insights from the experiences and learning from the pilot phase, the methodology of the interview guide was modified for data collection for the major phases of fieldwork.

Ethical issues

Being born and brought up in the state of Assam in North East and due to my prior experience as a researcher on displacement in the region, I had access to local support networks from local people and members from civil society organisations of Meghalaya who were aware of my research and extended their help in conducting my fieldwork. The changes in gender relations that were investigated have occurred in the past 30–40 years. Many of the people voluntarily shifted from traditional agriculture and embraced the livelihood of coal mining since they consider it improved their lifestyle, i.e. increased income and purchasing power, etc. Hence, unlike a refugee situation induced by displacement, the people in Meghalaya are not living in a vulnerable situation which ensures that this research did not ignite any traumatic experience. Moreover, the focus of the research is on restructuring of gender relation in the wider social fabric of the tribe due to changes induced by coal mining and any discussions on the shift from the past to the present in terms of gender relations is seen as a matter of change in time while progressing to a modern society. As such, the research did not pose any external or internal threat to the respondents.

Interviews were recorded with permission from the respondents. No minors were interviewed, and every respondent was at least 18 years of age. All interviewees were explained the aim and purpose of the research before conducting the interviewees. Anonymity of the interviewees was maintained, except for the interviewees who are comfortable in being published with their real name. The idea of a plain language statement and consent form was discarded after few interviews during the pilot phase since taking signatures of interviewees appeared too intimidating for the people who have already been battling with various official and documentary intimidations considering the political atmosphere of Meghalaya. As such, verbal consent was preferred by the interviewees which was respected. While taking verbal consent from the interviewees, the following aims and objectives of the research were communicated to the interviewees.

(a) Interviewee's right to provide, refuse or withdraw from providing information at any point of time while conducting the interview or at any stage of conducting the research.
(b) Potential benefits of the research.
(c) Details of dissemination strategies of the research.
(d) Interviewee's right to decide on what should be written for publication and what should be kept for information.
(e) Interviewee's right to confidentiality and anonymity while participating in the research.
(f) My contact details, if required.

In order to ensure that the findings of this research were directly communicated to the general public, I had conducted several workshops in North

East India and taken feedback from the attendees of the workshop. This proved very useful, not only for me but also for the community, allowing them to reflect on the abrupt processes of change undergoing in North East India in a more nuanced way.

Limitations of the research

Language

Since I had to rely on translators as I did not know the local language of the community, I might have missed out on the cultural subtext that is hidden in the spoken narrative of the interviewees or the subtle meaning that might have accompanied in some narratives, apart from the obvious statements made. This also means data loss, since the nuances of spoken narratives are important for this research.

Accounts of daily-ness

As there is not enough literature available on the everyday gendered politics in Meghalaya, I had to solely rely on the narratives of women to discover their daily lives. As such, although I had tried to capture as many micro details on the women's everyday lives, I did not know if I have missed any significant aspect that might introduce other extraordinary dimension to the analysis that I have done in this research. This is especially true for the narratives that I collected from the older generation of women because the daily lives of the older women, as it occurred in the past could only be discovered from their memory. This is unlike the privilege that I had of "seeing" the daily lives of the old, middle, and younger generation of women as they operate in the present. As such, although I could collect data on the past of Meghalaya on thematic grounds, for example, say narratives of love stories in the past, I could not always collect an account of how the love stories were conducted in daily lives with sufficient details. Lack of enough details of the dailyness of the period prior to 1980 posed a limitation for this research in doing a comparison between the past and the present in the most nuanced way possible. This also prevented me from drawing more interlinkages that might exist between different areas of life of the women in Meghalaya that speaks about their freedom and un-freedom (like the interlinkages that I have drawn between labour, leisure, and mobility in Chapter 6).

Volatile situation in Meghalaya

While I was conducting the fieldwork for this research, I was frequently pushed into unpredictable situations of being or not being able to conduct interviews or getting people to speak up because of the volatile situation in Meghalaya. For example, the tragedy the miners who lost their lives after getting stuck in the mine shafts in the Jaintia hills of Meghalaya in December 2018 made the political atmosphere of Meghalaya very volatile which prevented me from speaking to anyone about mining for part of my final fieldwork phase. The elections in March 2018, before which the mining ban was temporality lifted for few months, also made the political atmosphere of Meghalaya very unstable, which again compelled me to postpone the fieldwork for a period until the state returned to normalcy, at least in relative terms.

Before discussing the empirical findings of the research, the next chapter provides a context to Meghalaya in which the research can be understood. It also explains the matrilineal structure which is at the heart of the traditional culture of the region.

Notes

1 See Preeti Gill (ed.). The Peripheral Centre: Voices from India's Northeast.

2 Sixth Schedule. http://lawmin.nic.in/olwing/coi/coi-english/Const.Pock%202Pg.Rom8Fsss(34).pdf (accessed on September 2016).

Patricia Mukhim.2013. "Sixth Schedule and Tribal Autonomy." http://www.thestatesman.com/news/5573-sixth-schedule-and-tribal-autonomy.html (accessed on September, 2016).

3 Bengt G. Karlsson. 2011. "Unruly Hills: A political Ecology of India's North East." Berghahn Books, p. 164.

4 Thomas Laird. "A woman's world- Meghalaya, India; matrilineal culture http://lib.icimod.org/record/9474/files/3602.pdf (accessed on February 2016).

5 Bengt G. Karlsson. 2011. "Unruly Hills: A political Ecology of India's North East." Berghahn Books, p. 164.

6 Deigracia Nongkynrih. 2014. "Land Relations in the Tribal Societies of Meghalaya: Changing patterns of land use and ownership. http://www.okd.in/downloads/jr_14_july/Deigracia.pdf (accessed on 1 and 05 and 2016).

7 June Hannam. Women's History, feminist history. http://www.history.ac.uk/makinghistory/resources/articles/womens_history.html (accessed on September 2017).

3

THE CONTEXT OF MEGHALAYA

Meghalaya is one of the eight States in North East India, with a predominant tribal population of 95%. Previously a part of Assam, Meghalaya attained statehood in 1972. The name "Meghalaya" means "Abode of the Clouds" which also reflects the nature of the climate of the state. With an area of 22,429 square kilometre and a population of 2,964,007 (2011 census), Meghalaya has predominantly hilly terrains with foothills and some plains (D'Souza, 2013). Meghalaya has seventeen tribes notified as Scheduled Tribes by the Government of India. The largest tribe is Khasi, followed by Garo and Jaintia. Prior to the coming in of mining, agriculture, the people of Meghalaya were primarily engaged in agriculture. Two distinguishing features of the population compared to other states of the North East is that a large proportion of a tribal population is Christian, and the matrilineal nature of its traditional society.

The population of Meghalaya, as per the latest Census of India 2011, is 2,966,889 as opposed to the all India population of 1,210,854,977. The projected population of Meghalaya by 2020 is 3,772,000. With a growth rate of 27.95% in 2011, the decadal population growth in Meghalaya decreased by 2% as compared to 2001 when it recorded a growth rate of 29.94%. However, the decadal population growth in Meghalaya has been higher than the national growth rate by 10% in 2011 and 9% in 2001. However, all through the 20th century, the population growth of Meghalaya was higher than the national average. It rose from 304,525 in 1901 to 2,318,822 which is a 761.46% rise. Even in 1911–1921 when the All India population declined by 0.31%, that of Meghalaya grew by 7.21%. After a decline in 1941–1951 it rose again mainly because of immigration during that period (Fernandes et al., 2016).

In 1999, the per-capita income in Meghalaya was Rs. 12,083 against Rs. 15,562 in India as a whole which is lower than the national average by 22.35%. At Rs. 13,114 at current prices, the per capita income of Meghalaya in 2001 was 20.46% lower than that of India. Per capita State Domestic Product (SDP) in 1993–1994 was as low as Rs. 6,894 but rose to Rs. 9,003 in 1999–2000. It is indicative of a poor SDP growth. In 1980, the GSDP of Meghalaya was Rs. 200 crores whereas during 2000, it was Rs. 3,728 crores.

DOI: 10.4324/9781003149460-4

Table 3.1 Demography of Meghalaya

Year	*Meghalaya*		*India*	
	2011	*2001*	*2011*	*2001*
Population	2,966,889	2,318,822	1,210,854,977	1,027,015,247
Male Population	1,491,832	1,176,087	623,724,248	531,277,078
Female Population	1,475,057	1,142,735	586,469,174	495,738,169
Population Growth	27.95%	29.94%	17.70%	21.15%
Sex Ratio	989	972	943	933
Child Sex Ratio	970	973	919	927
Density/km per square	132	103	382	324
Literacy	74.43%	62.56%	74.04	65.38
Male literacy	75.95%	65.43%	82.14	75.85%
Female literacy	72.89%	59.61%	65.46	54.16
Per Capita Income	35,932	141,910	35,993	16,487

Source: Census CDs 2001 and 2011; Director of Economics and Statistics, Meghalaya, 2003 and 2017; http://pbplanning.gov.in/pdf/Statewise%20GSDP%20PCI%20and%20G.R.pdf) http://pbplanning.gov.in/pdf/Ranking%20of%20States%20Constant.pdf

According to this estimate, Meghalaya's GSDP is 19.13% slower than the All India growth (Directorate of Economics and Statistics, 2004, p. 71; Fernandes et al., 2016). The reason for this could be attributed to slow industrialisation and/or low agricultural productivity in the state. Though more than 75% of Meghalaya's population depends on agriculture, the contribution of this sector to the State GDP is only 22.32% (Director of Economics and Statistics, 2004, p. 71; Fernandes et al., 2016).

As per census 2011 records, female literacy in Meghalaya is around 10% higher than male literacy, whereas by the NFHS4 survey the female Literacy rate in Meghalaya is almost 25% higher than the national average (NHHS4, 2015–2016). However, 91.4% of married women (15–49 years) participate in household decisions and 57.3% own a house/and or land, almost 20% higher than the national average (NHHS4, 2015–2016). While 2011 census data shows a sex ratio of 989 in Meghalaya vis-à-vis the national average of 943 (census 2011), the latest NFHS4 shows a further improvement in child sex ratio of 1,009 females per 1,000 males (for children born in the last 5 years), making women more than half the state voters (NFHS4, 2015–2016; Priyanka Shah, 2018).

However, in terms of health indicators, Meghalaya records a 39 IMR per 1,000 live births as opposed to the national IMR average of 34. However, the percentage of institutional births has improved from 29% in 2005 to 51.4% in 2016. Although this denotes improvement in access to healthcare service in the state, the state has been the second worst performing state in terms of institutional deliveries in the entire northeastern region, according to the "Healthy States, Progressive India" report by the NITI Aayog, and lags behind the national average of institutional births by 27.5%. High fertility and prolonged child bearing have an adverse impact on the mother's and child's health as seen in their low body weight and high anaemia (Fernandes et al., 2016). There is a dearth of Medical officers and nurses in the Primary Healthcare Centres and Community Health Centres (CHCs) in the state (Priyanka Shah, 2018).

This chapter discusses the social, political, and economic structure of Meghalaya and particularly the Jaintia hills of Meghalaya where the fieldwork for this research was carried out. It first gives an overview of the history of state formation of Meghalaya and a brief introduction to the Khasi, Garo, and Jaintia hills that form the state of Meghalaya. It then goes on to discuss the history of migration, ethnicity, and conflict in Meghalaya followed by a discussion on Christianisation in Meghalaya. It then has a discussion on the matrilineal tradition in the state, followed by an outline of the history of mining in Meghalaya. The aim of this chapter is to provide a contextual understanding of the Meghalayan society, which is crucial to understanding the empirical realities of Meghalaya as discussed in this research.

The history of state formation in Meghalaya

The history of state formation in Meghalaya explains its ongoing peripheral nature within the State of India. Under British rule, the administration of Meghalaya was carried out through a three-tier system based on treaties with the native rulers which ensured the isolation of the hills from the plains. The tribal chief acted as agents of the Colonial rulers. British supremacy existed independent of the traditional institutions and the much-professed policy of non-intervention was bypassed if it was convenient for the colonial rulers. After the whole of India was taken over by the British in 1858, the District Deputy Commissioner carried out the administration in these areas as the Government's political officer (Syiemlieh, 1989). Later, the Khasi, Jaintia, and Garo hills were included in the administration of Assam when Assam was constituted into a Chief Commissionership.

In 1947, when the British made an announcement that it would leave India, the then representative of the Khasi hills in the Assam Legislative council Nicholas Roy wanted to bring the Khasi states within the framework of the Sixth Schedule of the draft constitution of free India whereas the federation of the separate Khasi states demanded that the region be a separate state (Marbaniang, 2009, p. 24). However gradually, most Khasi chiefs decided to accede to the Indian Union and the administration of these areas was finally brought under the Indian Government. After the Indian constitution was adopted, the Khasi states became part of the United Khasi-Jaintia Hills District within the State of Assam. Accordingly, hill areas were constituted into two Autonomous District Councils – the United Khasi-Jaintia Hills Autonomous District Council and the Garo Hills Autonomous District Council under the Sixth Schedule of the Constitution (Ladia, 2004, pp. 42–44). Under the sixth schedule, these districts were given a taste of self-governance with district councils operating in accordance with their customary laws; however, this self-governance was subject to the regulation of the Governor of Assam (Ladia, 2004, pp. 47–48).

The formation of the district councils in 1953–1954 under the sixth schedule proved inadequate to safeguard the interest, customs, and traditions of the hill states leading to a demand for separate statehood for Meghalaya (Lyngdoh, 1966, pp. 306–307). Movements of tribal solidarity among the Khasi, Jaintia, and Garo hills that existed before the transfer of power from the colonial rule to the Indian union, had already started deepening roots in the post-independence period and the demand for a separate Hill State was spearheaded by the Khasi National Durbar. By 1952, this movement had gained momentum in all the Khasi-Jaintia hills districts. In the general elections of 1957, the Eastern India Tribal Union party swept the polls with its demand for a separate state in its manifesto (Ray and Agarwal, 1996, p. 62). The victory of the Eastern India Tribal Union made the movement even more vociferous. The movement further accelerated with the introduction of the Assam Official Language bill in 1960 in the Assam Legislative Assembly which faced strong opposition from the hill districts and the Eastern India Tribal Union pulled out of its coalition from the then ruling party of Assam. The exit of the Eastern India Tribal Union from the coalition pulled all the leaders of all political organisations in the region under the leadership of Eastern India Tribal Union making the demand of a separate state for the hill states even stronger (Ray and Agarwal, 1996, pp. 62–63).

Later, The Eastern India Tribal Union was disbanded with the formation of the All Party Hill Leaders' Conference (APHLC) who resolved to adopt peaceful and constitutional methods for the achievement of a hill state (Sten, 1971, p. 62). In November 1960–1962, the first prime minister of India Jawaharlal Nehru offered his own plan to the hill states as an alternative to the separate state demanded. The Central Government initiated various proposals to resolve the rift between the Assam Government and the hill districts. These include a proposal for a loose federation with certain autonomy (Ray and Agarwal, 1996, p. 63), the "Nehru Plan" of 1963, which offered "full autonomy for the Hill Districts" subject to the preservation of the unity of the State of Assam (Ray and Agarwal, 1996, p. 63), the District State Plan and the Vishnu Sahay Plan that suggested a federation of the hill districts (Ray and Agarwal, 1996), and the Tilak Singh commission that suggested a union territory (Lyngdoh, 1966, pp. 63–64). During this period the hill state movement continued to put pressure on the Assam Government and the Government of India to come to a settlement of the issue (Chaube, 1973, pp. 122–123). These developments were considered of paramount importance keeping in view of the strategic location of the entire North East which shared international boundaries with China and then East Pakistan (which is present day Bangladesh).

On January 1967, the Government of India announced its decision to reorganise the State of Assam into a federal structure which conferred equal status to the hill districts with the rest of Assam. This proposal was welcomed by the people from the hills but met with stiff resistance from the plains (Rao and Hazarika, 1984, pp. 55–56). In these increasingly polarised situations, the All Party Hill Leaders' Conference (APHLC) launched programme of a non-violent direct action on September 1967 and urged the Government of India either to implement its decision or create a separate State for the hill areas (Lyngdoh, 1966, pp. 398–412). The effort of the Government of India to facilitate a joint discussion between the APHLC and the Assam Government did not lead to a solution but only resulted in deepening bitterness between both parties in the confrontation. In December 1967, the APHLC threatened to launch direct action if the demand for a separate state was not granted, since the Government of Assam had already failed to accept the federal plan (Hussain, 1987, p. 1330). As the APHLC was consolidating its roots in the hill districts, the voice of the APHLC had become the unanimous voice of the hill district people.

Finally, in September 1968, the Government of India announced the reorganisation of Assam which offered the formation of an Autonomous State within Assam, with jurisdiction over the two existing districts – the Khasi-Jaintia hills and Garo hills. The Autonomous State Plan was finally approved and accepted by the APHLC in January 1969 and the creation of the state of Meghalaya was passed by the Indian Parliament on 2nd of April 1970 (Lyngdoh, 1966).

The Khasi, Garo, and Jaintia hills of Meghalaya

Presently, Meghalaya consists of three mountainous regions of the Khasi, Jaintia, and Garo hills, which have been divided into 11 districts. The Khasi hills have a dominant population of the Khasi tribe of Meghalaya, the Garo hills have a dominant Garo tribal population, and the Jaintia hills have a dominant Pnar tribal population. This research focusses on the Jaintia hills of Meghalaya, which consist of two districts: namely the East Jaintia district and the West Jaintia district. However, this research also refers to the Khasi hills of Meghalaya, wherever necessary.

The social history of Meghalaya is shaped by the emergence of these three major tribes: the Khasis, the Jaintias, and the Garos. The Jaintias are also referred to as the Pnars. The Khasis and Jaintias share many similarities, speak the common dialect of "Khasi," and are also physically similar. Scholars hold different interpretations on the meaning of "Khasi"; however, the most common interpretation of the meaning of the word Khasi is "born of Mother" where "Kha" means born and "Si" means ancient mother (Bareh, 1967). Today, the Khasis reside in the centre of the state, the Jaintias in the east, and the Garos in the west. Both the Khasis and the Jaintias are related to the Mon-Khmer-speaking people of the Austro-Asiatic race (Batra, 2013). It is argued that that Mon-Khmers were one of the first people to settle in the Indian sub-continent (Reddy and Reddy, 2007).

It is a general belief that originally the Khasis were spread across a large part of North East of India but later they were confined to the Khasi and Jaintia hill districts of undivided Assam which is the present state of Meghalaya. For those who settled in the Khasi and Jaintia hills, their culture changed very little with later invasions, whereas those outside the Khasi and Jaintia hills saw a significant change in their culture due to assimilation with other cultures. Some refer to the Jaintias as a sub-tribe of Khasi. However, a large section of the Pnar people from the Jaintia hills has strong objections to being termed a sub-tribe of the Khasis and argue that Khasi is also a sub-tribe of the pan "hynniewtrep" tribe of Meghalaya, which means all these tribes, including the Khasis, the Pnars, Wars, Maram, Lyngam, and Bhois, are a sub-tribe of the pan "hynniewtrep" tribe. However, the term "Khasi" is frequently used to refer to both the Khasis and the Jaintias and some also insist on using "Khasi" as a pan tribe identity for all the sub-tribes. In essence, Pnars do not see themselves as separate from the Khasis, as all the tribes in Meghalaya share common culture and language and hence are in many respects one community, but they also maintain that each tribe of this community have their own distinct history and identity which cannot be just homogenised or subsumed into one (Mohrmen, 2011). Other tribes of the Jaintia hills include the War, Bhois, Lalungs, Biate, Hmars, and the Hadem. Such as the Pnar, the War tribe also shares the same culture and language with the Khasis (Pakyntein, 2011).

Migration, ethnicity, and conflict in Meghalaya

Since the post-independence period, Meghalaya has seen a series of inter-ethnic and conflict between tribal and non-tribal people. The reasons for these conflicts are multifaceted and are based on a complex diasporic history defined by social, political, and economic relations among the conflicting groups. First, the huge influx of migration (both legal and illegal) into Meghalaya from Bangladesh and Nepal has created contention among the indigenous people over the years which can be attributed to the fear of the indigenous tribes being outnumbered demographically, and culturally as well as economically by the non-tribal people (Lyngdoh and Gassah, 2003, p. 5024). Second, the inter-ethnic tension between dominant tribes and other smaller tribes has taken the struggle for self-determination into an even more complicated terrain. These layers of conflict have often been appropriated for political gain by different political parties which have further engineered the divide between peoples and contributed to deepening tension. The latest attempt by the Government of India to introduce the Citizenship Amendment Act of 2016, which supports the immigration into India of non-Muslim religious minorities from Bangladesh, Pakistan, Afghanistan, led to an outbreak of unified protests across the northeast (Agarwala, 2019). This resistance is based on what the local community perceives to be the bills anti-indigenous spirit which has, it is argued, betrayed several accords that promised to respect the historical struggle of the North East for self-determination (Mukhim, 2019).

Migration from Nepal to Meghalaya

This intercommunal tension has a long and deep history. The migration of Nepalese to Meghalaya began in the colonial period, especially after the Indo-Bhutanese war in 1864. During the colonial period, the Nepalese were either appointed as recruits to the Gurkha army of India or as labourers to open up forestlands, dairy farming, tea-plantations, etc. Following retirement from the Gurkha army, the Nepalese were encouraged to settle down in strategic locations on the frontiers. This led to the creation of small pockets of Nepali settlements in Jowai, Laban, Bishnupur, and in the Assam Rifles Quarter in East Khasi hills (Sinha, 1990, p. 227). During the colonial period, the experience of indigenous and settler communities were one of common trade, friendship, and cultural exchange (Dev, 2006). After independence, the scenario gradually changed to contention, especially after 1950. Nepali migration to Meghalaya accelerated after the Indo–Nepal Friendship treaty in 1950 and the Tripartite Delhi Agreement of 1951 which gave Nepali migrants the right to engage in business, acquire property, settle and seek employment, and move freely anywhere in India. The Nepalese migration inflow to Meghalaya saw its peak post-1975 with the beginning of the coal mining industry which led to an influx of Nepalese migrants in the Jaintia and, the East and West Khasi hills. From almost no migrants from Nepal pre-1951, Meghalaya saw 32,288 Nepalese migrants in 1961 which further increased to 44,445 in 1971 and 61,259 in 1981 (Timsina, 1992). Prior to mining, the migrants were mostly engaged in cattle rearing and tending cows for milk supply. From 2001 as the internal armed conflict in Nepal intensified, the flow of migrants from Nepal to India has increased (Bhattrai, 2007). A large number of workers from Nepal are illiterate or have low levels of literacy; they are also unskilled and belong to marginal population of rural Nepal (Bhattrai, 2007). The earlier migrants were welcomed if they assimilated the language, culture, and customs of Meghalaya. But the second phase of migration, especially from Bangladesh, invoked a sense of insecurity among the local populace. With the discovery of many electoral identity cards obtained fraudulently, many local NGOs have demanded the scrapping of the 1950 Indo-Nepal Friendship Treaty, or at least to make it non-applicable in Meghalaya to stop influx from Nepal (Haokip, 2013, p. 310).

Migration from Bangladesh to Meghalaya

Migration from East Pakistan (now Bangladesh) also dates back to the British rule in India when the Bengali migrants came along with the British between 1863 and 1866 to serve as clerks in the colonial administration (Haokip, 2013, p. 305). However, it did not create any tension among the local people in Meghalaya, until the Bangladesh Liberation war of 1971 (Dev, 2006), when the two North Eastern states, Assam and Tripura, saw an influx of migrants during 1961–1971. Many earlier Bengali migrants from Sylhet had been given land to settle in different parts of Shillong in Meghalaya by the ruling Government (Mukhim, 2007b, p. 7).

Meghalaya's experience with migration was very different until the British annexation of North East India. The Khasi and Garo hills shared cordial trade relations with East Bengal (which later became East Pakistan after the partition of India) without any population transfer issues. However, the partition of India changed the entire meaning of borders which consequently destroyed the age-old trade ties between these regions. The immediate impact was felt in terms of large-scale migration influx from Bangladesh leading to demographic changes in these regions. Eight years after the creation of the state of Meghalaya, the state witnessed a violent riot between the non-tribals and dominant tribal groups in 1979 (Haokip, 2013, p. 306) (Baruah, 2004). 1987 saw another riot when the Nepali coal mine workers were expelled from Meghalaya by the Khasi Students Union which led to a series of clashes between the Khasis and Nepalese (Dhar, 2002). The years 1991 and 1992 again saw violent clashes between the Khasis and Nepalese on issues of trade licenses to non-tribals when the Federation of Khasi, Jaintia, and Garo demanded a closure of more than 1,500 non-tribal establishments and suspension of trade licenses of non-tribals in the wholesale trade (Haokip, 2013, p. 306).

Shrinking employment opportunities in government services over the years has further aggravated tribal versus non-tribal animosity. There is also a general belief among a large section of the local populace that the non-tribal population is depriving the tribals of their rights and privileges. This belief has been strengthened by political parties who play the tribal versus non-tribal card for electoral gains which has further widened the animosity between the tribal and the non-tribals. It is often argued that the irregular migrant workers provide labour for dirty, dangerous, and low-skilled jobs that the indigenous workers will either never do or will command a higher wage than the irregular migrants who provide the needed labour at very cheap costs, largely associated with the production of coal. Hence, the local indigenous workers fail to secure their place in the labour force due to their higher cost as low-skilled labour. A study conducted by Aman Panchayat argued that indigenous workers were consistently underrepresented in the coal mine industry, especially in the top two managerial categories and overrepresented at the low end of the occupational categories. From a total pool of 78 workers in four coal mines from Jaintia and West Khasi hills that the study analysed, there were seven migrant workers in managerial positions such as Sordar as opposed to three indigenous workers, four Sordars as opposed to no indigenous Sarders, 23 migrant team leaders against three indigenous team leaders and 13 general migrant workers against 25 indigenous workers.[1] The flip side of this story is the increased marginalisation of the unorganised migrant workers in the coal mines. These workers suffer economic exploitation in terms of wages, long working hours and hazardous working conditions, physical and psychological tortures in various forms and are increasingly marginalised in many parts of the region.

However, the Khasi-Jaintias and non-tribals in Jaintia hills districts and in the interior parts of Khasi hills have been living together in harmony (Haokip, 2013, p. 306). Even in Jowai, the administrative headquarters of West Jaintia hills district, the native locals and non-tribals share a relatively cordial relationship. The reason for this peaceful co-existence could be because of a relatively small number of non-locals and the economy being controlled by the local people in terms of trade and commerce (Haokip, 2013, p. 306). In fact, many of the Nepalis and Biharis employed in the coal mines of Jaintia hills have married native-local girls. Some migrant Bangladeshis have also permanently settled in these places where they have been accepted by the native locals without any conflict.

Christianisation in Meghalaya

Another key factor in the relative uniqueness of this region compared to the rest of India is the high proportion of the population that is Christian and almost the local population there is a division between Christians and non-Christians. The Traditional religion in the Jaintia hills is called "Niamtre." The word "Niam" means "religion," and "tre" means "origin." Thus, the people who follow the original religion are called *Niamtre*. The traditional religion does not have any written script it is based mostly on oral tradition (Tangvah, 2015). The *Niam* is believed to have been given by God from the beginning of time. However, over the years a number of the *Hynniewtreps* have adopted other religions such as Hinduism and Christianity. Hinduisation has not had any significant impact on the tribal population, although many traditional Niamtre believers also identify themselves as Hindus. However, under the present Indian government, there is more active collaboration between dominant Hinduism of India and Niamtre Hinduism.[2] This blending of Hinduism and Niamtre has been possible by drawing certain lifestyle similarities that Niamtre believers share with Hinduism because of a range of similarities between Niamtre and Hindu religion. For example, beef is forbidden meat in both religions.

The Christianisation in Meghalaya has a long history, and not only Meghalaya but the entire Northeast India represents a major Christian population in India. According to 2011 census, North East India consists of 78 million of Christian concentration of the total 27 million Christian populations in India. Meghalaya was the earliest of the states in North East India to have witnessed the conversion to Christianity.

At the beginning of the twentieth century in 1901, there were already 21,000 Christians in Meghalaya, 6.2% of the Meghalaya population.[3] With the handing over the entire management and responsibility of education in the North East to the Christian missionary in the middle of the 19th century, the expansion of Christianity in Meghalaya was very successful.[4] People educated in the government schools run by Christian missionaries at that time frequently converted to Christianity. In fact, during that period the school education and conversion came to be so profoundly identical in the imagination of the tribal people of Meghalaya that schooling was frequently equated with baptism. The number of Christian concentration increased to 75,500 (15.7%) from 1901 to 1931. It reached to 24.7% in 1951 and in 2011 it was 74.6%.[5]

The Christian missionaries under Thomas Jones developed the first written script for the Khasi-Jaintia dialect and began the publishing of books in Khasi language written in Roman script (Sharma, 2004). The roman scripted Khasi language could be considered as a significant break from tradition which accelerated the change in traditional customs of the Khasi-Jaintias. There was an absence of any organised stand taken by the village durbar or any such traditional institution in support of the oppositions raised by the general tribal people against conversion to Christianity in order to protect their old customs and beliefs (Sharma, 2004). Most of the resistance to Christian missionaries were from individuals, and families in a particular village coming together oppose conversion, however, there is also no record of the villagers going to any organised authority to stop missionary conversion. Organised resistance by the traditional authorities such as the Dollois against the missionaries was more noticeable in villages that were mostly Hindus, even though such resistance was the exception rather than being the norm (Sharma, 2004).

Christianisation has changed the traditional structure of the Khasi-Jaintia people considerably, for example, as opposed to a present-day Niamtre household that continues to maintain a powerful clan house system where all the traditional rituals on important events of Rights of Passage are still being followed, a Christian Khasi-Jaintia household more resembles a western-styled nuclear household with a lesser emphasis on the clan's role. Christianity along with exposure to other patriarch social systems have contributed to the shift in perspective in present-day Meghalaya, especially men, who are advocating for an increased role of the father and a weakening of the position of the maternal uncle, as well as a subordinate position of women in the family. This influence can be seen in the present debate in which groups who oppose matriliny in Meghalaya are seeking to replace it with a patriliny.

Given the extent to which matriliny is under attack, the next section discusses the basic ideas of a matrilineal system that forms the basis of the culture of Meghalaya, while also drawing a comparison of the matrilineal system of Meghalaya with other matrilineal communities across the world.

Meghalaya and matriliny

A matrilineal system in its simplest term is societies characterised by a matrilineal descent, where the descent or the family name is traced through the mother's side. This establishes the primary kinship affiliation of both men and women to the women and mother's side. The argument of early evolutionist who claimed that the earliest societies of the world have eventually evolved from matriliny to the present system of patriliny (Fox, 1967, Divale and Harris, 1976 quoted in Das)[6] has been now discarded (Chacko, 1998) and it has come to be argued that both patrilineal and matrilineal systems have developed and flourished independently (Chacko, 1998).[7]

Cross-cultural evidences suggest that in societies where war exists amongst the neighbouring communities, residence is almost always matrilocal (Ember and Ember, 1971). The origin of the matrilocal system is traced back to the time when the sole purpose of men was to participate in warfare and protect their land which was considered to be the most important, honourable, and noblest of purpose. Lesser important tasks such as family, succession, children, and economic resources were left to the women to be taken care of primarily because the priorities of men at that time were different (Sebastian, 2016). As such, the earliest philosophy that established a matrilineal society was not essentially based on a superior status of women to men, it rather was the opposite. However, lack of male interference and authority in their daily lives did provide a relatively better status for women as compared to patrilineal societies where men controlled both family and socio-political domains. As such, matrilineal systems are not necessarily matriarchal, which means, women are not the primary authority figures in a matrilineal system. In a patrilineal and patriarchal system where descent is traced through the men, men exert the greatest control over the social, cultural, and political realms of society and also enjoy direct primary authority over women and children. In matrilineal societies too, even though descent is traced through the women, men still have greater power and women may be subject to the power of their maternal uncles and brothers.[8] Hence, even though it might be argued that women in a matrilineal system are relatively better off than women in a patrilineal system, they are still subject to a patriarchal matriliny to say the least.

All children of a woman in a matrilineal system take the family name of their mother (Kapadia, 1966) and only the children of the female of the family can become members of the matrilineage. The children cannot be the member of their father's matrilineage as they cannot take the family name of their fathers. A number of tribes in Africa, some part of Southeast Asia, and three groups of India are based on a matrilineal system. The Minangkabaus of West Sumatra, Indonesia, comprises the largest matrilineal ethnic group in the world (Tanius, 1983). In India, the matrilineal system is found only in small pockets of South India such as the Nairs and Mappilles in Kerala, the tribal groups of Minicoy Island, and among the Khasis, Jaintia, and Garos of Meghalaya in Northeast India. However, it must be noted that the matrilineal systems of each of these communities across these communities differ greatly from each other and even from one group to another in the same region and county (Kapadia, 1966). There are a variety of matrilineal residence patterns and the difference in residence system post-marriage is a significant marker of what distinguishes one matrilineal group and community from another. These different residence systems are – "a man residing with his wife's matrilineal kin," "a wife residing with her husband's matrilineal kin," "couples settling down together in a new residence," or the "two living with their respective natal groups following the duolocal pattern," etc. (Richards, 1950) (Dube, 1969). For example, among the Ashanti of the Gold Coast of Africa, the pattern of duo-local residence exists, the Minangkhau of Sumatra and the Nayars of Central Kerala follow a duo local residence system. The Khasis of Meghalaya follow a "matrilocal residence" where the husband resides with his wife's matrilineal kins or settle down together in a new residence in and around his wife's maternal place generally termed as neo-local residence. After the birth of one or two children, the couple may move to a separate house to form a neo-local family. In most cases, the mother of the bride gifts the house where the couple settles down to form a neo-local household (Sinha, 1970). Property is transferred through the female line and is held by the females. Whatever a male member of the family earns belongs to or is contributed to his maternal family and goes either to his mother or inherited by his sister and her female descendants.

Matrilineal system in Meghalaya

The matrilineal tribes in the Jaintia hills of Meghalaya including the Pnar of the Jaintia hills and also the Khasis of Khasi hills follow almost identical matrilineal structures and operate on the same matrilineal principles, although the terms that they use for significant aspects of the structure, the youngest daughter, maternal uncle, clan, etc., may differ. Since this research is focussed on the Jaintia hills, this section primarily, but not exclusively, discusses the Jaintia hills' structure of matriliny with a focus on the Pnar tribe.

The **Kur**, that is, the clan is a primary category on which the social organisation of the Jaintias (Pnar) is based. Each clan consists of a number of sub-clans, known as **Jaids**. The Jaids represent a number of lineages or descent lines called **kpoh** (meaning the womb) consisting of different family groups referred to as **Chi Lung. Lung** means a family, the smallest unit of this social organisation (Pakyntein, 2011). Each Pnar individual, especially for those who follow the traditional Niamtre religion, belongs to the family and clan in the present life and also in the afterlife. The clan holds primary importance around which the Pnarand Jaintia society revolves with all of its social, economic, religious, and political administration. For each Clan, there is an ancestral mother of the clan called **ka Iawbei**, her husband called **Thoolang** who is the progenitor of the clan, and, **U Suidnia** meaning the orator and mediator who is the maternal uncle or brother of ka Iawbei. Dr. Pakyntine (2011) calls the composition of these three authority figures "the symbolic triad" (Pakyntein, The Pnar Trilogy: Explicating Pnar Society and Culture through the Lahoo Dance, 2011). Matriliny in the Jaintia hills is reinforced by a belief in the ancestral clan mother and clan members trace their descent from the same clan-mother. The kinship affiliation to the father's descent group remains temporary for about three to five generations at the most. The traditional Pnar and Jaintia society was characterised by a matrilocal family with visiting husbands and primarily and consisted of the woman, her married or unmarried children, grandchildren from the daughters as well as her uncle or brother. In present times, even though the man relocates to the wife's house after marriage, he continues to remain an active part of his own clan and matrikins. Relationships between brothers and sisters in the matrikin were and are encouraged and maintained through common socio-economic and socio-religious duties. This ensures the maintenance of a strong matrilineal bond in the family (Pakyntein, 2011).

The youngest daughter inherits the ancestral property from her mother. She is the custodian of the property and is bound to the advice of her maternal uncle and other sisters over the management, production, and disposal of the ancestral property. However, for any self-acquired movable or immovable property, the owner holds the right to dispose-off the property at their sole discretion. However, it is customary for the woman to pass on such self-acquired property of hers to any of her daughters, or to a male member of her maternal kin. Presently, self-acquired properties are also passed on to sons by their mothers. According to tradition, the wife does not have a right over her husband's property, except for a portion of the husband's income (Pakyntein, 2011), while his maternal family can also make a strong claim over his income (Lamare, 2005, pp. 27–28 quoted in Pakyntein, 2011). In the traditional subsistence economy too, the woman or the mother, her maternal uncle or brother, and her children played the most important roles. The agricultural land which belongs to the mother is cultivated by her sons and daughters as well as by the maternal uncles or brothers. The husband of the married daughters may provide minimal labour to the cultivation process, but provides most of his labour to the economy of his mother's household (Pakyntein, 2011). Thus, the family duties are divided three-way – the women are responsible for the hearth, the father should provide for the essential necessities of his wife and children. The maternal uncle looks after the family matters related to property, religion, birth, naming ceremony, death, and settling disputes and mediates amongst clans at the time of marriage to warrant that endogamy is not breached by the members of the clan (Dutta, 2016).

As such matriliny in Meghalaya is a patriarchal matriliny, not only because the woman is subjected in some respects, to the control of her brother and maternal uncle but also by virtue of her responsibilities as a woman. Patricia Mukhim (2000) argues that matriliny in Meghalaya that gives women the right of lineage also subjects her to the heavy burden of her family. As only a few clans have large properties, for most Khasis, the privileges derived from the right to lineage are actually of little significance (Mukhim, 2000). Nongbri (2000) has also argued that the daughters of matriliny need not necessarily be the benefiting parties of its privileges. For example, the youngest daughter who has to abide by the advice of her maternal uncle could be deprived of her inheritance rights if she fails to fulfil her responsibilities. She is expected to be of high moral standards and be the bearer of tradition and is not free to change her religion, any defiance of which rules could also curtail her inheritance rights. Many women, in the past, were deprived of their rights due to conversion to Christianity (Nongbri, 2000, p. 372). For the eldest daughter, who is relatively freer from the control of her maternal uncle since she does not inherit ancestral property, is on the other hand, more dependent on her husband because of her lack of inheritance rights. Matriliny does not protect the woman or her children from the consequences of a divorce. Because of the lack of concern that divorced men show towards their children (as children are considered to belong to the mother), most of the divorced women or single mothers have to take care of their children without any maintenance or support from their husbands or partners. Since the sole responsibility of meeting the needs (social and economic) of the family falls on the woman, Khasi/Jaintia women are continually engaged in working and raising resources because in the event of the dissolution of their marriage or failure of the brother to extend support, it is they who have to provide for the family (Nongbri, 2000). Khasi/Jaintia Women continue to be excluded from politics and administration of the state as well as from the village and state durbars because politics has always been traditionally held to be the men's domain. The Legislative Assembly and the Autonomous District Councils of Meghalaya has a negligible presence of women. Since the year of Meghalaya's state formation in 1972 until today, only five women have made it into the State Legislature. In the religious sphere too, women play a subordinate role. Even though the women make all the necessary preparations for religious rituals, the actual execution of the rites is done by men (Nongbri, 2000, pp. 372–375).

The situation of women's status in matrilineal Meghalaya is not very different from many other matrilineal societies of the world. For example, the matrilineal society in Minangkabau in Sumatra, which is the largest matrilineal community in the world, echoes the Meghalayan matrilineal experience on different levels. The lack of support for single mothers in Meghalaya is comparable to the age-long pattern of pattern of male migration in Minangkabau in the wake of urbanisation in the 1970s, meaning that men rarely returned to take up their roles in the family and society. This had left a considerable number of women, children, and old people alone as the main producers and income generators. This migration had also increased the already high frequency of divorce and polygyny. The gendered segregation of girls and boys in Minangkabau matrilineal starts at the age of 7, when the girls are subjected to more family control than the boys. In the past, girls were trained to become mothers and housekeepers, to be able to cook and sow. A modern Minangkabau girl is the one who is probably trained as a teacher yet knows her traditional duties of being a woman. Although her brother or son may be a wastrel and her husband may turn to another wife, an ideal Minangkabau woman is expected to maintain her own place in the house to be cared for during old age. Important though she is as a person in the house and the family, she must not raise her voice in public (Schrijvers and Postel-Coster, 1977, pp. 79–85). The status of Minangkabau women continues to suffer, as Abdul Mutolib et al. (2016) argues, since clan leadership in the society continues to be male dominated, common land administration continues to be under patriarchal control of the men, so also the forest management, as are the sales and transaction of common land and forest in the recent times (Mutolib et al., 2016). For the Chewa matrilineal society in Central Malawi too, the locus of control of the productive as well as reproductive capabilities of the Chewa nuclear family lie in the hands of the men of the maternal family on whom the women depend for social support, and without whom the women are considered as slave and extremely unfortunate (Phiri, 1983, p. 259).

Since the proliferation of the coal economy in Meghalaya since the 1970s, the demand for a patrilineal society has seen a rise among the men in Meghalaya. A powerful example of this is reflected in the range of debates that swayed the state when the Government of Meghalaya attempted to codify the Khasi Custom of Lineage Bill in 1997.[9] The debates ranged from one extreme to another where one section vehemently protesting the need to replace the matrilineal system of Meghalaya with a patrilineal system, while another sought to redefine, in extreme gendered ways, the entire identification basis of who could be a legitimate Khasi. Proposed by the Khasi Hills Autonomous District Council (KHADC), the Khasi Custom of Lineage Bill sought to preserve the Khasi matrilineal system by making it a law. Faced with a threat of the erosion of the Khasi Matrilineal system, the bill proposed to codify the matrilineal custom of the Khasis, in order to resist social change and economic development by giving a legal definition to the word 'Khasi.' The inspiration for this also came from the argument that social and economic change have not only exposed the Khasi to the values of individualism and personal autonomy which are opposed to their communitarian and cooperative ethos, but have also resulted in a large influx of outsiders who manipulate the matrilineal system to compete with the local population for their resources (Nongbri, 2000). The bill was also passed twice by the District Council in 1980 and later in 1992 but failed to receive the governor's assent due to a number of protests staged by various interest groups and associations. It was only in February 2005 that the Governor finally gave his assent to the bill and it became an Act. Yet again in 2018, the Act has been amended by the addition of two clauses on marriage of a Khasi woman to a non-Khasi man which nullifies the rights of a Khasi woman and her children if she marries a non-Khasi man. If these amendments are passed, many women who are married to non-Khasi men, along with their children, will be socially ostracised.[10] The third amendment of Section 3 of the Principal Act states that any Khasi who takes the clan and title of his father for himself or his children shall no longer be a "Khasi" and he and his children shall be disqualified from all the privileges, status and benefits as a Khasi."[11] The Syngkhong Rympei Thymmai (SRT) meaning "a new hearth" which was founded in 1990 in the capital of Meghalaya, Shillong, and works towards overthrowing the matrilineal system of Meghalaya in order to "liberate" men from female "dominance."[12] This organisation has termed the Khasi Lineage Bill discriminatory by arguing that the 3rd amendment is absolutely discriminatory for Khasi men, especially for those Khasis who want to take, or be given their father's title or clan.[13] In the past too, the SRT had also not only rejected the bill but also demanded the reform of the Khasi kinship system and even strongly called for a switch over to the patrilineal system (Nongbri, 2000, p. 376). The SRT believes that their organisation is central to the survival of the Khasis. For the 22 years of SRT has existed, the group has worked towards securing men's rights in Meghalaya and organises awareness session on the importance of increasing men's rights. It also explains its ideology to the general public by putting up loudspeakers and distributing pamphlets in the central market areas of Meghalaya. SRT aims at a gradual overthrow of the matrilineal system and also intervenes in the support and assistance of men who, in their view are *victimised* for asserting their rights.[14]

The Khasi Students Union[15] and the Central Riwar Youth Foundation who have promoted the idea that Khasi-women who marry outsiders and have children with them tarnishes not only the Khasi identity but also exposes the Khasi land to economic risks (Nongbri, 2000, p. 380). Needless to say, the majority of these voices consist of Khasi/Jaintia men who lead the course of this debate. Equating matriliny with primitive, unscientific and barbaric societies, they attempt to abolish matriliny for what they believe is a patrilineal modern industrious society in order to achieve greater progress. Even eminent scholars such as the Late Vice Chancellor of North Eastern Hill University in Shillong, Professor Pakem observed that Meghalaya has come a long way from the state of nature into that of a modern economic, if not industrialised, society. According to Pakem, matriliny is well suited for a society of hunters, food gatherers, and shifting cultivators, but as the people of Meghalaya are gradually leaving behind these occupations and preparing to attain the status of a post-industrial society this system is no longer suitable (Syiemlieh P. B, undated quoted in Nongbri, 2000, p. 377).

These debates are indicative of a constant structuring and restructuring of competing masculinities that are trying to adapt, negotiate or even alter the matrilineal system of Meghalaya in lines of broader economic and cultural currents around the world. They became much stronger after the impact of mining was felt, even though in many ways the mining development weakened the matrilineal structure and privileged men.

Coal mining in Meghalaya

My core field research areas in Jaintia hills are Lad Rymbai, Khleriat, Sutnga, Lumshong, and Jowai. The distribution of coal in Meghalaya is found on the belt which extends from Jaintia hills in the east to the East Garo hills district in the west. The state is a rich storehouse of different minerals such as coal, limestone, uranium, granite, kaolin clay, and glass sand. Coal found in Meghalaya is of high quality in terms of calorific value and ash content, as well as in sulphur content. Despite its large reserves of coal, domestic consumption is low due to the absence of industrial activity. Therefore, most of the coal produced in Meghalaya is exported illegally to other states in India and to Bangladesh.[16] According to the Department of Mining and Geology, of the Government of Meghalaya, the total coal reserves are 576.48 million metric tonnes, of which 133.13 are proved and 443.35 are inferred.[17] But the "Vision Document for the State of Meghalaya 2030" has estimated coal reserves of 558 million tonnes spread over different districts (see Table 3.2). Due to the unorganised nature of mining in Meghalaya, there is no reliable information about the quantity of coal produced. As such Official records are based on the coal that is officially transported through the checkpoints.

The estimated reserves of coal in Jaintia hills are only 39 million tonnes, constituting a mere 6.99% of the total estimated reserves in Meghalaya. On the other hand, the estimated reserves in Garo hills are 390 million tonnes, constituting 69.89% of the total. But coal production is much higher in the Jaintia hills than in the Garo hills which also implies that the coal reserves in the Jaintia hills will be exhausted within few years.

Small-scale coal mining in Meghalaya dates to the colonial era. But, coal mining began in its modern form in Jaintia hills in the mid-seventies and

Table 3.2 Estimated Coal Reserves in Meghalaya

District	*Estimated Reserves of Coal (in million tonnes)*
Garo hills	390 (69.89%)
West Khasi hills	98 (17.56%)
East Khasi hills	31 (5.56%)
Jaintia hills	39 (6.99%)
Total	558 (100.00%)

Source: Vision Document for the State of Meghalaya 2030 (January 2011), pp. 104–105.

from this time Jaintia hills were recognised as a potential rich coal belt. Coals began to be marketed to southern Assam (present Silchar) to the tea estates and brick kiln industries. From the 1980s onwards, large-scale commercialisation of coal mining developed and coal transportation extended to different parts in India. Presently, coal mining activities constitute the major occupation of the people in Meghalaya including the migrant workers. Local farmers have changed their livelihood to mining from farming. Small-scale cultivators have leased their agricultural land to private investors for extracting coal. Farmlands that are unsuitable for coal extraction or have been rendered uncultivable because of the coal extraction have been disposed-off by the farmers (Nongtdu and Sahu, 2013, p. 7).

Legalities of coal mining in Meghalaya

There are two discourses on the ownership of the coalmines and other minerals in India. The first one based on customary laws claims the minerals as the property of the community, whereas the dominant view maintains that minerals are the properties of the state. The fifth and sixth schedule of the Constitution of India aims not only to stop land alienation among the tribals but also to ensure that the "tribals remain in possession and enjoyment of the land in the scheduled areas."[18] The Samatha Judgement of the Supreme Court had nullified mining leases issued by the Andhra Pradesh Government of India to private mining companies in scheduled areas.[19] This judgment of the Supreme Court did not entirely prohibit non-tribal mining but also maintained that this should not be done at the expense of the tribal people. However, the contrary side of this protective section of the constitution is that in Meghalaya, none of the local governing bodies, traditional institutions, district councils, or the state government have made any attempt to regulate the extraction of minerals (Karlsson, 2011, pp. 196–197), until the National Green Tribunal bans on illegal coal mining in Meghalaya in 2014. This has raised serious questions relating to the issues of social justice, that is, the profits of the mining activities that remain confined to select individuals as well as concerns on environmental justice of pollution and the environmental degradation that mining has caused (Karlsson, 2011, p. 197). After much agitation, the Government of Meghalaya prepared a Draft Mining Policy in 2010 but took a long time to finalise it. *The Meghalaya Mines and Minerals Policy 2012* was officially notified on 5 November 2012. However, the policy had various loopholes primarily because it maintained that "Small and traditional system of mining by local people in their own land shall not be unnecessarily disturbed." This implied that practices based on traditional or customary law would continue, which also meant the dangerous "rat role" extractive system would continue.

In Meghalaya, the "Malik" is the owner of the coal mine and is the primary person who conducts the coal extraction. However, a Malik may or may not be the owner of the land with the coal deposit. This happens when the owner of a particular plot of land with coal deposits does not have the means to extract or mine the coal and someone from outside, that is, the Malik buys the coal deposit or takes over the land in order to extract coal. When the coal is completely extracted and the mine is exhausted, the land returns to the original owner. The Malik who "buys" the coal deposit employs a Manager to organise the extraction of coal, its transportation to the depot, and other activities till the coal is loaded and taken out of Meghalaya (Alphonsus D'Souza, 2013). The Manager employs *Sordars* (Supervisors) who bring the labour required, organise their work, and make the payment of wages. The Sordar is in direct contact with the labourers. The miners extract the coal and bring it out of the "rat-holes" in wheelbarrows and load it into a box. Miners are paid according to the number of *telas* (wheelbarrows) of coal they extract. Other workers are usually paid daily wages (Alphonsus D'Souza, 2013).

The two key figures are Malik and Manager. The Malik does not usually come in contact with the Sordars and the miners. The original owner of the land is nowhere in the picture (Alphonsus D'Souza, 2013). As Karlsson (2011, pp. 226–235) describes, the entire coal industry in Meghalaya operates in "a kind of legal vacuum" beginning with the ambiguous legal position of coal mining as a private enterprise and as a cottage industry. Then there is the practice of overloading and underreporting, as noted by the Audit Reports of the Comptroller and Auditor General of India. Thus, coal mining and coal trade in Meghalaya is a complex and shadowy affair.

Following a petition filed by the Assam based All Dimasa Student's Union and Dima Hasao district committee, the National Green Tribunal (NGT) ordered an interim ban on "rat-hole" coal mining in Jaintia hills of Meghalaya on 17 April 2014 which was later extended for later years.[20] The petition raised concerns about pollution of downstream rivers such as the Kopili due to acidic discharge from coal mines in the Jaintia hills.[21] Although the case began with concerns with environmental pollution, the matter got complicated as the investigation continued and The Mines and Minerals Development and Regulation Act, 1957 came into the picture. Concerns over safety of the miners and ownership of mineral were raised. The investigation by NGT investigated these different aspects of the unsafe mining conditions which incude how the mine ratholes becomes flooded during the rainy seasons due to rainfalls, as well as the general unsafe conditions in which miners work in the ratholes. The NGT also investigated the presence of coal mafia in the mining scenario. According to calculations done by Impulse Social Enterprises, a non-profit organisation based in Shillong, 10,000 to 15,000 people were estimated to have died in "rat-holes" between 2007 and 2014 in Meghalaya.[22] Along with environmental degradation, the loss of traditional cultural values was also a key factor for the ban (report by OP Singh and Sumarlin Swer).[23]

Majority of the coal miners' associations in the state expressed their stiff opposition to the order and protested that their means of livelihoods were stopped overnight after the ban. The NGT bench had allowed for transportation of the extracted coal for certain periods but refused to lift the ban. However, in January 2019, the Supreme Court had banned the transport of extracted coal till February 2019. The court questioned the continued practice of illegal mining despite the ban by the National Green Tribunal and asked the government of Meghalaya to file an affidavit (India Today, 15th January 2019). In May 2019, the Supreme Court had allowed a last 15 days to transport the extracted coal beginning from 17 May and strictly ordered that no other category of coal should be transported or mined in the under the guise of this permission.[24] But in July 2019, the Supreme Court revoked the ban by upholding individual and community rights over minerals in the state[25] subject to compliance with provisions of Mines and Minerals (Development and Regulation) Act 1957 and Mineral Concession Rules 1960 and permission granted by the landowners, making the 2014 NGT ban on mining irrelevant. The judgment of the Supreme Court was hailed by the present Conrad Sangma Government of Meghalaya.

Coal politics has been one of the main pillars of the General elections in Meghalaya since 2015.[26] In 2019, the ruling party Congress failed to return to power due to its inability to lift the coal ban, although the former chief minister Mukul Sangma had been lobbying New Delhi to lift the ban and constituted a group of ministers to mobilise against the ban in March 2018. The political blame game around the failure to lift the coal mining ban continued; the Conrad Sangma government shortly after its election in 2019 had blamed the previous government for its inability to keep its promises on lifting the coal mining ban.[27]

The petitions by the government as well as the coal associations only mention the already mined coal; they ignore the presence of a "coal mafia" and of illegal mining which is an open secret in the state. For example, 15 miners died after being trapped inside a "rat-hole" passage of an illegal coal mining site at Saiphung district of East Jaintia hills in December 2018.[28] The mining site collapsed in December 2019 and was flooded by the adjacent Lytein river. The rescue operations tried to pump out the water from the rat-holes but this did not prove to be effective and was halted. Divers from the Indian navy were recruited but could not go down to the depth of the shaft where the miners were trapped. Nothing was rescued except for three helmets of the workers. A month after the incident, one body of a worker was recovered from a depth of around 200 feet of the 370 feet deep mine[29] (this incident happened violating the National Green Tribunal ban 2017 on "rat-hole" mining in Meghalaya). The region was also enraged over the minimal coverage of the dreadful incident in national media.[30] Just two years after this incident, on 21 January 2021, another six mineworkers were killed when an underground mining pit again collapsed in the East Jaintia district in Meghalaya, bringing back the focus to allegations of rampant illegal coal mining.[31]

Although such cases of trapped miners caught attention as a violation of the NGT orders, according to online police records of the Meghalaya state police, there were already 477 reported cases of violation of the ban.[32] Just after the incident of miners being trapped inside the "rat-holes" of the coal reserves, the NGT imposed a fine of 100 crore on the State Government of Meghalaya for its inability to check illegal coal mining in the state[33] (which the Supreme Court also directed the Government of Meghalaya to pay in its landmark judgement that on the contrary lifted the mining ban in July 2019, just seven months after the tragic death of the mineworkers in December 2018). A Citizens report stated the alleged involvement of the government of Meghalaya in the extract and transportation of coal.[34] This is not surprising since the coal mining industry was among the biggest revenue earners for the state, generating about Rs. 700 crore annually (which is around 85 million euros), prior to its ban in 2014, according to Government reports.[35]

In this context, those protesting conditions in the mining industry and the illegal coal mining actions are subject to abuse and threats. Just a month before the 15 miners were killed, a social activist and President of the Civil Society Women's organisation Agnes Kharshiing was attacked by men suspected of having links with the "coal mafia."[36] Kharshining is well known for her fight against degrading environmental pollution in Meghalaya.[37] She was attacked just a day after the police seized trucks carrying illegal coal at a village called Mawiong Rim following Kharsiling's complaint on the issue. Kharsiling was taking pictures of coal dumping on the national highway in East Jaintia hills when unidentified people attacked her. On the same day of the attack, another activist Marshall Biam, chairman of the North East Indigenous People's Federation filed a police report stating seven people had attacked him, demanding the withdrawal of cases by him and members of the Federation against coal dealers, and hinting at police-coal mafia nexus.[38]

It means that the social reality of Meghalaya has been shaped by the intersection or coming together of several factors like (i) its history of cross-border migration and its impact on the ethnic fabric of Meghalaya, (ii) the unique matrilineal system of the state on which the soci-cultural structure of the state primarily rests, and (iii) the impact of the profiferation of christianisation on the local/traditional system of the people. The following chapters deal with the empirical gendered realities of Meghalaya that are also shaped by this intersectional and multi-layered reality of the state. The next chapter discusses the issue of flux of the matrilineal system in Meghalaya in greater detail, as it unfolds in people's opinion and perceptions of matriliny.

Notes

1 See, Economy, Ethnicity and Migration in Meghalaya. Available at http://amanpanchayat.org/wp-content/uploads/2018/01/PEI_meghalaya.pdf

2 Sanjib Kr. Baruah. February 2019. Where RSS men Love Their Pork. Available in https://www.firstpost.com/india/where-rss-men-love-their-pork-6053551.html (accessed on 7th October 2019).

Viva Eiben. 2018. Hindutva's Double Game in the Northeast. Available at https://www.newsclick.in/hindutvas-double-game-northeast (accessed on 7th October 2019).

3 Centre for Policy Studies. "The Christianisation of the Northeast: It all began on the eve of Independence." See here http://www.cpsindia.org/dl/Blogs/Blog%20 28-Northeast%20Web.pdf (accessed on 15th September 2019).

4 Ibid.

5 Ibid.

6 Madhumita Das. Changing Family System in a Matrilineal Group in India. Available at https://iussp.org/sites/default/files/Brazil2001/s10/S12_04_Das.pdf (accessed on August 2019).

7 Ibid.

8 Mary Kay Gilliland, Family and Marriage. Available at https://courses.lumenlearning.com/suny-culturalanthropology/chapter/family_and_marriage/ (accessed on August 2019).

9 See, The Khasi Hills Autonomous District (Khasi Social Custom of Lineage) Act. 1997. Available at http://khadc.nic.in/acts_rules_regulations_bills/Acts_Rules_arranged/Khasi_Lineage_Act_1997.pdf (accessed on 4th June 2019).

10 The Shillong Times. 2018. KHADC Khasi Lineage Bill. Available at https://theshillongtimes.com/2018/07/28/khadc-khasi-lineage-bill/ (accessed on 4th June 2019).

11 Shillong Today. 2018. SRT urged the governer not to assent the Khasi Social Custom of Lineage(First Ammendment) Bill passed by the KHADC. Available at, https://shillongtoday.com/syngkhong-rympei-thymmai-urged-the-governor-not-to-assent-the-khasi-social-custom-of-lineage-first-amendment-bill-2018-passed-by-the-khasi-hills-autonomous-district-council/ (accessed on 4th June 2019).

12 See, Simantik Dowerah. 2016. Married in Meghalaya: Feminist dream or the iron fist of matriarchy? Available in https://www.firstpost.com/specials/married-in-meghalaya-feminist-dream-or-the-iron-fist-of-matriarchy-2368472.html (accessed on 29th May 2019).

13 Ibid.

14 Lhendup G Bhutia. 2013. Men's right in Meghalaya. Available at https://openthemagazine.com/art-culture/mens-rights-in-meghalaya/ (accessed on 5th August 2019).

Mohua Das. 2017. Meet the men's libbers of Meghalaya. Available on https://timesofindia.indiatimes.com/home/sunday-times/meet-the-mens-libbers-of-meghalaya/articleshow/60237760.cms (accessed on 5th August 2019).

15 Check the Kahsi Student's Union's website here http:and and www.khasistudentsunion.organd (accessed on 4th June 2019).

16 The Shillong Times. 2019. 33 Bhutanese Coal Trucks stopped at Dawki from heading to Bangladesh. Available at https://theshillongtimes.com/2019/01/18/33-bhutanese-coal-trucks-stopped-at-dawki-from-heading-to-bangladesh/ (accessed on 27th May 2019).

Amlan Home Choudhury. 2019. Down The Rat Hole in Meghalaya Again. The Citizen, March 2019. Available at https://www.thecitizen.in/index.php/en/NewsDetail/index/3/16571/Down-the-Rat-Hole-in-Meghalaya-Again (accessed on 27th May 2019).

Northeast Today. 2017. Meghalaya: Illegal transportation of Coal on the rise, MCTOOA blames Govt. available at https://thenortheasttoday.com/archive/meghalaya-illegal-transportation-of-coal-on-the-rise-mctooa-blames-govt/ (accessed on 27th May 2019).

17 Directorate of Mineral Resources, Government of Meghalaya, Department of Mining and Geology. Available at http://megdmg.gov.in/minerals.html (accessed on 19th September 2021).

18 Samatha Versus State of Andhra Pradesh, a Supreme Court Judmeny, 11 July 1997, para 111.
19 Samatha Versus State of Andhra Pradesh, a Supreme Court Judmeny, 11 July 1997.
20 Down ro Earth. 2015. NGT Ban on rat hole mining in Meghalaya to continue. Available at https://www.downtoearth.org.in/news/ngt-ban-on-rathole-mining-in-meghalaya-to-continue-44701 (accessed on 27th May 2019).
21 Ban on rat hole mining across Meghalaya. Available at https://ejatlas.org/print/ban-of-rat-hole-mining-in-jaintia-hills-meghalaya (accessed on 27th May 2019).
22 Ban on rat hole mining across Meghalaya. Available at https://ejatlas.org/print/ban-of-rat-hole-mining-in-jaintia-hills-meghalaya (accessed on 27th May 2019).
23 Ibid.
24 Andrew W. Lyngdoh. 2019. Supreme Court grants 15 days for coal transport from Meghalaya. The Telegraph. Available at https://www.telegraphindia.com/states/north-east/supreme-court-grants-15-days-for-coal-transport-from-meghalaya/cid/1690306 (accessed on May 2019).
25 Indian Express. July 2019. Victory for Conrad Sangma Government, SC allows Coal Mining Operation in Meghalaya. Available at https://www.newindianexpress.com/nation/2019/jul/03/victory-for-conrad-sangma-government-sc-allows-coal-mining-operation-in-meghalaya-1998887.html (accessed on August 2019).
26 Reuters. 2015. Meghalaya CM pushes for Coal mining; critics say he is helping wife. Available at https://in.reuters.com/article/india-coal-meghalaya-mines-idINKCN0SM0N220151028 (accessed on 27th May 2019).
27 The Shillong Times. 2019. Blame Game on Coal Mining Ban Continues: CM slams Mukul, Cong hits back at BJP and NPP. Available at http://www.theshillongtimes.com/2019/03/28/blame-game-on-coal-mining-ban-continues/ (accessed on 27th May 2019).
28 Zarir Hussain. 2019. Indian Miners trapped in illegal 'rathole pit' for more than three weeks. Available at https://www.independent.co.uk/news/world/asia/india-miners-trapped-rescue-coal-mine-pit-latest-meghalaya-a8711701.html (accessed on 26th May 2019).
29 India Today. 2019. Meghalaya Mine Resucue: 1 of 15 trapped miners found. Available at https://www.indiatoday.in/india/story/meghalaya-mine-rescue-body-recovered-indian-navy-1432653-2019-01-17 (accessed on 27th May 2019).
30 Rinchen Norbu Wangchuk. 2019. Meghalaya's trapped miners deserved better from Us. Available at https://www.thebetterindia.com/169424/opinion-meghalayas-trapped-miners-deserved-better-from-us-all/ (accessed on 26th May 2019).
31 Ayaskant Das. 2021. Meghalaya: Scourge of Illegal Coal Mining Persists Despite Ban. Newsclick, 6th February 2021.
Available at https://www.newsclick.in/Meghalaya-Scourge-Illegal-Coal-Mining-Persists-Despite-Ban (accessed on 28th February 2021).
32 The Telegraph. 2018. Hundreds of illegal Coal trucks skirt ban in Meghalaya. Available on https://www.telegraphindia.com/states/north-east/400-ngt-violations-reported/cid/1674867 (accessed on 27th May 2019).
33 Scroll in 2019. National Green Tribunal imposes Rs. 100 crore fine on Meghalaya Government for illegal coal mining. Available at https://scroll.in/latest/908275/national-green-tribunal-imposes-rs-100-crore-fine-on-meghalaya-government-for-illegal-coal-mining (accessed on 27th May 2019).
34 Hemanta Kumar Nath. 2019. Congress rule abetted illegal mining in Meghalaya, reveals report. My nation, 15th January 2019. Available at https://www.mynation.com/news/congress-rule-abetted-illegal-mining-in-meghalaya-reveals-report-plcw1p (accessed on 27th May 2019).

35 Economic Times. 2018. Rat hole mining rampant in Meghalaya despite NGT Ban. Available at https://economictimes.indiatimes.com/news/politics-and-nation/rat-hole-mining-rampant-in-meghalaya-despite-ngt-ban/articleshow/67242097.cms?from=mdr (accessed on 27th May 2019).
36 Rajeev Bhattacharya. 2018. In Photos: As Activist recovers from attack, Illegal Coal Mining continues in Meghalaya. Available at https://thewire.in/rights/meghalaya-illegal-coal-mining-agnes-kharshiing (accessed on 26 May 2019).
37 Arunabh Saikia. 2018. Assaulted Meghalaya Activist has a long record of speaking up against illegal coal mining. Available at https://scroll.in/article/901520/assaulted-meghalaya-activist-has-a-long-track-record-of-speaking-up-against-illegal-coal-mining (accessed on 26th May 2019).
38 The Hindu. 2018. Meghalaya activist claim coal mafia-police nexus. Available at https://www.thehindu.com/news/national/other-states/meghalaya-activist-claims-coal-mafia-police-nexus/article25458887.ece

4

GENDER, MINING, AND MATRILINY IN THE JAINTIA HILLS

Scholars like Morgan (1885), Engels (1972), Murdock (1949), Aberlie (1972), Gough (1972), Schneider (1972), etc., argued that matriliny has to inevitably go extinct in the face of modernisation, urbanisation, and colonialism, whereas work of Elizabeth Colson (1980), Karla Powewe (1981) and Leela Dube (1996) provides sharp critique to the disintegration perspective by arguing that matrilineal groups have a high degree of resilience and capability to adapt to changing times. Since matriliny (which is often quoted as marker of a relatively gender equal society) is a central criterion on which Meghalaya was chosen as a case study for this research, how people view matriliny is important. This chapter records men's and women's perceptions on matriliny and later compares their perceptions to develop an understanding on the points of contention (or cooperation) between men and women on how they view their lives in the matrilineal culture that they have been born and raised. The larger questions that this chapter engages with concerns if matriliny in Meghalaya disintegrating with the intrusion of mining or has matriliny been resilient despite the changing forces accompanying mining. What do men and women's narrative reveals about this wind of change on matriliny, if there are any? What are the grounds on which men resist or support matriliny and what is their imagination of an ideal matrilineal structure? Are women's reasons and conditions of supporting or resisting matriliny the same as men? By exploring these questions, this chapter aims to have a peek into the future of matriliny and what that means for the future of women's status in Meghalaya while taking into account the background of mining that is getting increasingly integrated into the gendered fabric of the region.

Men's negative perception on matriliny

The narratives of Pnar and War men in the Jaintia hills with regard to matriliny are not homogenous. Age, economic status and negotiation, and decision-making power play a vital role in men's response to the matrilineal system in Meghalaya. This section analyses men's negative perception of matriliny through the interviews with the married men of the Jaintia

DOI: 10.4324/9781003149460-5

hills, both from the middle-aged generation and the younger generation. As has already been discussed, the age categorisation for the purpose of this research has been done with reference to the nature of people's exposure to coal boom period of Meghalaya.

Robert (name changed) is a 38-year-old man from Urium village in the Jaintia hills who expressed deep disappointment with the matrilineal system. Robert was born into a family located far away from Urium village but moved to Urium to his wife's house after marriage. Because of financial constraints, Robert had to drop out of school to help his parents at work. The long distance from his maternal home makes him feel lonely. Robert shared that he has lived with this sense of rootlessness of not belonging anywhere since the time he was living with his mother because, he knew that he had to eventually move out of the house after marriage. He feels a sense of alienation from his own children because his wife and her family have all the power over his children and not him.

Robert said, "... I roam around here and there, work wherever I get work – it feels like I was a person who belonged nowhere so can roam around like a nomad; it does not feel good. it is a daily struggle."[1]

Robert's wife is the youngest daughter of her family. Because Robert cannot inherit anything from his mother, he must move in with his wife in order to access the property that his wife inherits in order to live with a sense of economic security. If it was a man's lineage, which Robert earnestly wishes it was, he would have relocated his wife to his mother's house to make his life simpler.[2] Robert is the headman of Urium village and works as a farmer and a wage labourer. The office of the headman and village chief in the Jaintia hills is an unpaid voluntary work. Most of the village-chiefs that I had met had given up on a lot of their income-generating work as they cannot take enough time out of their busy schedule of a headman's responsibility. Many of these village chiefs, including Robert, had expressed dissatisfaction with the unpaid work that they have to do and complained about the chain of alienation that they suffer with their family customs and also with the customary laws of self-governance under the sixth schedule.

Traditionally, an unmarried Khasi man was expected to contribute all his income to his mother's home. Phiri (1983) argues that Uxorilocality has several implications for both wife and husband, in ways that it leaves the wife conflicted between loyalty to her own kinsmen and loyalty to her husband, whereas for the husband, it meant isolation from the base of his authority in his own matrilineal village. The movement against matriliny in Meghalaya argues against the customary isolation of Khasi men from the resources by emphasising that it is not only inappropriate for the men but also a hindrance for the region's economic productivity (Dutta, 2016).

A similar narrative like that of Robert's was consistent through most of the low-income middle-aged male population of the Jaintia hills who complained about the matrilineal norms that do not allow them access or ownership and control over their wife's property which is why they wished to dismantle the matrilineal system. This lack of control, they feel, stopped them from being "respectable men" or "proud fathers." Many felt their lives are put at stake by giving many rights to women and that even though men put in a lot of effort to their marriage, are often abandoned at their old age without any support.

What is most distinguishing about most of the men's narrative is that they did not challenge the rights of their mothers even though they challenged the rights of their wives. Even so, the rights of the wives were not challenged in the women's own right but for the woman's brothers' and maternal uncle's control over their wives' life and property. This is strongly reflected in the narrative of the men from Mutong village in the East Jaintia district.

> You can imagine a situation where if the maternal uncle is cruel and the daughter listens to her maternal uncle more than her father, it could be a dangerous situation for the father. There should be a major change in this system, even if not radical.[3]

The men, who I interviewed, themselves were maternal uncles in their own maternal home. But the power that they enjoy in that role was not frequently quoted primarily because the role of the maternal uncle has diminished in contemporary times as compared to the past. While the traditionally venerated role of the maternal uncle has begun to lose its significance, the role of a man as a father is being increasingly recognised and upheld, which, too, has further overshadowed the man's role as a maternal uncle like never before (Dutta, 2016). It is also important to note here that, while the fear of being abandoned by his daughter attributed to a sense of alienation among the men, it did not necessarily mean that they saw the women as equally powerful as her brother and maternal uncle. The fear was not if the youngest daughter listened to the mother more than she listened to the father; the threat was rather about the youngest daughter owing allegiance to the maternal uncle over her father. In most of the narratives, the woman is non-existent and no threat. She is more of a vulnerable object for possession via which her male relatives could exercise their authority. The men complained of powerlessness because their wives are not under their direct protection and control but that of their brothers. Hence, the woman is not powerful herself, or for being a woman; it is rather masculinities competing with each other and trying to derive a sense of power through the women. This perceived powerless position of the tribal women in matrilineal societies presents a counter-narrative to the supposed powerlessness of men in matrilineal societies. Robert and many of his fellow villagers and villagers from neighbouring villagers placed emphasis on patrilocality or bargained for greater powers of the father. This reveals the acute gendered nature of this bargain that goes beyond mere ownership of resources, especially when many men expressed their comfort with the woman or the wife still being the inheritor as long as the man, as the husband and father, is in direct control of his wife and daughter. This attitude to gender relations echoes one of the arguments of the moderates of the anti-matriliny movement in Meghalaya, who believe that the tradition of matriliny could persist, as long as men's identity is no longer derivative of his wife's relatives, whereas they do not talk about ending the derivative status of the woman. This means, the woman who was at the mercy of her brother then, will be at the mercy of her husband in their ideal matrilineal world.

Robert also shared a folk story to validate his disappointment with matriliny. According to this folklore, matriliny was an interim intervention by an ancient king of the Pnar kingdom to protect the women from the exploitation and violence of the Pnar men in the past. The Pnar King changed the social system and gave women the lineage and inheritance right so that no matter how bad anyone treated her, she would always have the property and the clan's support with her. In Robert's opinion, since matriliny was an interim intervention only for the protection of the vulnerable women, it needs to be revoked now because it has ended up putting men in the same position as women were in the past.

Robert expressed his disappointment,

> no one follows this system anymore…nowhere that I have been to follows matriliny… it is only in Meghalaya that we have this strange system.. God knows why we are so backward when the whole world has progressed…[4]

While the middle-aged Khasi men strategically talked about abolition of the matrilineal system by emphasising on the misery of men, the language of control and possession is stronger among the young married Khasi men from the low-income group.

Willy (name changed), a 27-year-old married forest worker, noted,

> I would like her to settle with me in my family. I don't like the present system… there are lots of problems. If my wife would move in with me to my family, I could have more control over her. She would not be able to roam here and there. She would be scared to talk shit. It would be an easier life… when the girl lives with her parents she can just be reckless and her parents won't control her. I cannot yell at her because her parents defend her… not that I have a problem with them yelling at me. They are like my own parents.[5]

Willy is the father of two daughters. He wants to have two more sons because he believes sons are more powerful and can protect him in his old age. Willy fears if his daughters marry dis-compassionate and drunkard husbands, they might violate him and his daughters would not be able to protect him or even get beaten up themselves. But sons, according to Willy, will hit back. Willy does not believe that his sons-in-law cannot take the place of sons as they are not going to be his own *khoon* (blood). Into drinking himself, Willy shared that he does not beat up his in-laws when drunk, but he is worried about his own future because time and people are changing.[6]

The trust in sons for protection frequently featured in the middle and younger generation of men's narrative from the low-income group of the Jaintia hills. Willy is vehemently against his wife going out of the house or women drinking. For him the ideal woman takes care of the children, does not roam around un-necessarily, and sits at home. He is fine with his wife going into the forest for working, because that is tradition. But any mobility other than what work demands is dis-modest of a woman. That his wife does the same work as he does in the forest or on the farms does not challenge his masculinity. This is because traditional occupations that require both male and female labour outside the household has remained relatively de-gendered. But his wife claiming similar kind of freedom, outside of the "labour space" that she shares with him or alone, challenges his masculinity. Willy's narrative is particularly interesting because his strong patriarchal ideas do not reflect the gender friendliness of traditional matriliny that granted women enough mobility and access to public spaces. Willy had also expressed his desire to travel and shared how he has travelled with his male friends and has extensively visited many places in India. On asking if his wife accompanied him, Willy replied that he prefers traveling with the boys than his wife because without the girls, they can be freer and do all *boys talk* and *boys things*. It could be so that Willy's exposure to other contemporary patrilineal cultures might have played a role in forming his strong sexist notions on women.

Unmarried young men did not comment on the matrilineal system and they neither expressed support for it nor thought that matriliny should be reformed. The reason for this is probably that masculinities are not challenged until the men are married. But masculinities are challenged once the men get married and change their residence to live in their wife's and mother-in-law's house. The dynamics of a married life and how men experience their marriage determines their support for or resistance to matriliny. This sexist polarisation was relatively absent in the older generation.

Elite male support for matriliny

There is an observable difference in the support given by affluent men to matriliny compared to the low-income group of men. Men, who hold elite position and who have access to personal wealth also control the property of their wives, are not threatened by matriliny. In fact, adherence to the matrilineal tradition is tied up with their personal sense of status.

"A real man makes his own road and doesn't feel insecure because he has no property inheritance rights. He builds up his own road" said Michael (name changed, 43 years old). Michael is the headman of another interior village of the East Jaintia hills, and is a rich man who also owned a blooming coal business. He has built a stunning house with fine woodwork, silk curtains, and carved designs. What distinguished him from other headmen of the region was his affluence. On requesting more women's presence for the interview, Michael invited his wife and another elder woman from the village, both of who sat coyly in a corner of the living room.

Michael has a very different view on matriliny from that of Robert. He believes that the matrilineal system in Meghalaya should be protected because it is matriliny that makes their culture unique. The men who feel challenged by matriliny are not men enough and want to benefit from their sister's property in order to be affluent. However, Michael believes that unlike the recent past, where the maternal uncle played an important role in the family, the father should play a more important role in present times. That is because the father is always physically present whereas the maternal uncle moves out after marriage. Michael believes that the identity of a man is not limited to only being a husband but also as a father and it is desirable that he plays a bigger role in the lives of his children. However, an incompetent man, according to Michael is a shame to his children. A good wife, he emphasised, should take care of the housework, be warm and welcoming to guests, and caring to the family members.

Michael runs the family, manages the family property that was inherited by his wife, and is the major decision maker in the household. The way Michael runs his family is what is sought by the moderates of the anti-matriliny movement in Meghalaya who seek to align matriliny with Christian and western ideas of a conventional nuclear family consisting of the caretaker mother and the breadwinner father with their children. Michael's life is what Robert and other men having similar opinions like Robert desire. Michael is a proud father who feels that he has the correct degree of control and rights over his daughter and his wife, whom he protects. He sees himself as the honourable breadwinner and voice of an ideal household that he believes is good to women, while Michael's wife hesitantly intervened into the conversation to say, "Early marriages are bad. Women are just left with no time for their own lives. That should stop completely. Atleast I don't want my daughter to have an early marriage." Michael immediately resumed control over the conversation to emphasise that he too wants to marry off his daughter late and if his daughter's husband would not let her pursue her dreams, they will have to sit down as a family and make him understand. Michael continued to speak about his ideal woman Mary Kom[7] who is not only a mother but also an athlete and how he would like to see his daughter become someone like Mary Kom. Michael's wife, after a few attempts to eagerly intervene in the conversation without success, resumed sitting in silence, while her few yet powerful words unveiled an entirely different universe of what women from such modern affluent households might have to say but are denied that space to speak up.

The idea of "a respectable man" as held by Robert and the idea of "Man of honour" as held by Michael, in essence, are similar. Robert's ideal matriliny is probably the one enjoyed by Michael, whereas for Michael the disappointment that Robert has expressed with matriliny is dishonourable. The irony here is that Robert's expectation from matriliny ends with a demand of the privileges of Michael. This observation unravels how men's response to matriliny is premised on their intersectional position and privileges in their own communities in Meghalaya. The rich and elite Khasi men who have access to their wife's property find it easier to support matriliny as it does not impact their quality of lives or their sense of control and authority. Elite' households are also more likely to have imbibed patrilineal values of a modern western and Christian family structure. However, the relatively poorer households have not yet adopted a strictly western nuclear family structure, have a stronger matrilineal structure, and have greater adherence to customary laws. In these families too, men favour a more patriarchal matriliny along the same lines as the way in which elite households, like that of Michael, operate. Men from these low-income households are more dependent on their wife's family for their livelihood, and their demands for a reform in the matrilineal system of Meghalaya are reinforced and drawn from a comparison of the male authority of the elite households.

Michael has benefitted from mining-related developments, which allowed him to build up his personal wealth. The opportunity for this nature of wealth creation is open to men rather than to women. Because the amount of this wealth is far greater than what was available in the community prior to the arrival of mining, it has altered the power dynamics between men and women, especially in elite households. These households also have greater access and exposure, by virtue of their affluence, to external influences, and patrilineal cultures unlike their own, that could reinforce male dominance in the family and a supportive role of the wives. Deepening of patriarchy in family gender relations at this level also impacts the wider community.

Conservative masculinity and the problem of external threats

The idea that men's direct control of their wives should prevail in a matrilineal system takes a slightly different form when it comes to preserving the pure blood of the Khasi/Jaintia people. Because of a high rate of alcoholism prevalent amongst the men in the Khasi/Jaintia communities, women are increasingly choosing to marry non-Khasi men. Marriage between a Khasi woman and a man from the plains is often frowned upon since it is believed that the outsider husbands do not support and adhere to the Khasi/Jaintia culture and therefore will not protect the Khasi land from external and internal threats. Children born out of such intercultural marriages are considered of mixed blood and are incapable of developing a close connection with the Khasi culture. It is feared that, over time, the practice of women marrying non-Khashi men from outside the region will weaken the local culture to the point where it can be overwhelmed by external influences.

Echoing the ideology of the traditional male role as the warrior and defender of one's land and culture, Andrew (name changed, 35 years old), from village Lumshong in the East Jaintia hills expressed,

> ..we are Khasi blood. If someone tries to occupy our land, we will give our sweat and blood and fight to protect our land. You cannot expect that commitment from an outsider or a mix blood. He will just accept defeat and this place goes under the control of those who want to exploit

Andrew's narrative is also in line with the views of the anti-matriliny movement spearheaded by organisations like The Syngkhong Rympei Thymmai (SRT) who believe in controlling Khasi women's sexuality and transitioning Meghalaya to a patrilineal culture for a better future of the tribal land. Andrew stated that giving his children his surname and lineage would make the Khasi/Jaintia land safer. The increasing alcoholism among today's Khasi men, according to him, is because of the present matrilineal system under which men own nothing and therefore are conditioned to be irresponsible. Change to a patrilineal system, in his opinion, will evoke more responsibility and encourage Khasi/Jaintia men to make the society a better place. While alcoholic women are seen as a disgrace and threat for family values, it is believed that the large number of alcoholic Khasi can be reformed if they are given the right to represent their descent and granted a clearer economic and family role with increased status and control over the family sphere.[8] Andrew's wife expressed her desire to hand over all property possession rights to their husband because she thought it expressed her utmost love for her husband. She could continue loving him even though she inherited the property, but that would not make him the head of the household, which, she thinks, is a hole in her love for her *brave* husband – her husband who is a man of honour and who wants the lineage not for himself but for his country. The recent amendment introduced to the Social Custom and Lineage Act 1997 that attempts to control marital choices of women has reinforced his view of transferring the lineage name to the men. However, several tribal women of Meghalaya, especially the educated women, have come out and strongly resisted such patriarchal control over their bodies and asserted that their marital status, either with a Khasi tribal or a non-tribal, is not an indicative of their loyalty to the clan and therefore neither the state and community, nor their spouse can take away their rights to continue be a Khasi woman irrespective of whom they choose to marry.[9] Many tribal women of Meghalaya have been highly critical of this patriarchal disposition of the state of Meghalaya that holds the women of Meghalaya responsible for the dilution of the tribe.[10] The male voices like that of Andrew illuminates not only a war by men against men where the "sons of the soil"[11] would protect the land from the land grabs of outside mining industrialists but also from the smaller scale incursions of men who marry in. This political position indicates a deepening patriarchy of indigenous men who want to use increased control over the women of Meghalaya to resist external male incursions.

This is a strong political division within a subaltern group. Men like Andrew may draw on their life experience to oppose matriliny but they are also a part of a more widespread rise of political ideology passed on an assumption of patriarchal masculinity. That Andrew's wife fully endorses his position confirms that attitudes to gender relations do not necessarily divide men and women into two opposing camps. Here the hyper masculinisation of the mining culture, its undermining of traditional society (resulting in increased social problems including alcoholism), and the way in which it has opened up the region to external exploitation have produced this conservative patriarchal response. This response seeks to remove the distinctive cultural norm of matriliny and has focussed primarily on the question of who owns the land, further undermining traditional practices as this is also a shift from the communal to an individual structure.

Women's voices of resistance

This section looks at women's voices of resistance and actions to defend their rights to equality and claim over the public sphere, and their strong advocacy for the need of matriliny's sustenance.

A section of men who support matriliny in Meghalaya is inspired by the ideals of a progressive masculinity. A few educated young men of Chamcham and Muttong village[12] in East Jaintia hills expressed their support for matriliny and for equal leadership of women in the political life of the villages. However, this support from this group of men could also be attributed to the fact that village Chamcham has seen a vibrant women's movement and leadership in the last five years through the Women Self Help Group(SHG) established by the District Commissioners Office in Jowai, the headquarters of the Jaintia hills. Muttong village, which is adjacent to Chamcham, has also been significantly influenced by the women's movement in Chamcham. Most of the members of the SHG are married women, since the younger unmarried women are busy studying or are working outside the village. Many married women who choose not to join the SHG do so because they find it difficult to manage both household work and SHG work together. In the view of the members of the SHG, the women outside of the SHG circle in Chamcham continue to remain confined to their homes and lack the agency to shape their lives.[13] That the women in the SHG have established a claim to is evident in the support that some men of Chamcham and Mutong give to the idea of women's leadership.

Expressing the challenges that women in Meghalaya face in general, the President of the self-help group also echoed Michael's wife narrative that late marriages gave women a period of freedom before taking on the burdens of a married life that a Khasi/Jaintia woman has to bear. However, she also expressed about the transformative power of joining the all-women's SHG group, irrespective of her immense domestic responsibilities.

> As a woman, I feel if I was not married, I could have done so much more with my life. It is extremely difficult to manage the household and SHG work together. But it is also true that if I had no responsibilities, I would be under no pressure to do something meaningful in my life or feel the compulsion to step out of my comfort zone. So both sides are there. Women who have not yet joined the SHG are not confident yet. I was also the same until I joined the SHG. But I like as the present me more.

The women from Chamcham indicate the resilience of matriliny that has the capacity to thrive with formal institutional and organisational support structures which aims at building women's leadership. The women of Chamcham village, through the empowerment process that they accessed through the SHG, have been able to resolve, to some extent, the internal contradictions that the men opposing matriliny complain about. The women have done so by establishing themselves as independent and empowered individuals, capable of leadership like that of men and also by establishing their status independent of their brothers and matri-kins. The SHG women members proudly shared how they are no longer intimidated by the paper and bureaucratic processes in government offices and how they can confidently speak up for their rights. In their view, this transformation has made their husbands respect them more than they did before, even though the husbands were initially not very supportive of the women moving into the public domain. Hence, by demonstrating their capability in the public domain, in addition to their already established expertise in managing the household, the women in Chamcham village have contributed to the resilience of the matrilineal system by reinforcing their leadership in their community.

The assertion of rights and challenging male privileges is also seen among the younger generation of women in Jaintia hills. This category of women includes the western curriculum educated section who bargain in a feminist language of equality and independence.

For example, Si, a 22-year-old undergraduate student, expressed her extreme disagreement with one of the older women of her village who regarded the men as the head of the family even though the inheritance should reside the woman. Si shared that when she gets married, she will not tolerate her husband being regarded as the head of the household, would be regarded as the head after she gets married, because she believes that the tradition of regarding the man as the superior is archaic.

"Sometimes I feel pity for the guy who might end up with me, I might be too much for him to handle. Also, I like our matrilineal system. It should not change. Men already have everything, why give them more?" Si said with a giggle on her face.[14]

Similar views were expressed by Tracy (25 years old), who had recently completed her Master's in Social work. Tracy emphasised her desire to keep working in the future, even after marriage and away from home if that would be necessary, irrespective of the fact that, ideally, she should be living with her mother as the youngest daughter of the family. This reflects the way that the position of the youngest daughter is changing. Nowadays, if the youngest daughter moves out of the house for better education and career prospects and the sister next in line or any sister who is ready to take charge is assigned her duties (Dutta, 2016). Changes like these, according to Tracy, are desirable but she also believes that matriliny should also be maintained as without matriliny women would not be protected.[15] Tracy also discussed the incessant pressure on girls to be performing their responsibilities to the household and the disgrace meted out to households who do not have a girl-child to take the lineage. How Tracy is aware and critical of the nuances of wider analysis of this gendered cycle of matriliny that is detrimental to women because of the tremendous pressure that traditional matriliny puts on women in terms of household responsibilities and their reproductive choices, is indicative of how the matrilineal discourse in the Jaintia hills is shaping up with the voices of these young women. Strong voices like that of Si and Tracy points to the possibility of a sharp conflict that the women of the Jaintia hills are going to have with the pro-changers in the near future. The voices like that of Si and Tracy are easy to relate to by a non-indigenous audience because they exactly represent the ethos of western feminism – educated women with a strong vision for a career, assertive of her individual identity, and capable of intellectual negotiations with the gendered diaspora that they are born in. Their social capital of being educated and contemporary gives them the choice, status, and confidence to be able to negotiate with and listened to by the community. Having a job outside the home, or a university to attend, releases them from a range of conventional gendered family responsibilities that their mothers (the middle-aged generation of women) are socially bound to perform, while at the same time helps them to establish themselves as the capable carriers of the future matrilineal system in Meghalaya, perhaps in an even more independent fashion than their mothers and grandmothers.

Hence, external ideas are also influencing arguments in favour of maintaining matriliny among the women. Young educated women, although use the language of western feminism, see the maintenance of traditional practices as a way of defending themselves from conservation forces in the region. But this support for tradition also comes with their negotiations to loosen the rules of traditional matriliny that binds the actions of these youngest educated daughters and restrict their need for greater mobility. The actions and opinions of older women in the women's organisation and the young educated women indicate a resistance to the trend towards increasing patriarchy.

Support for maintenance of the matrilineal system is also widely prevalent among the middle-aged women. However, their reasons for it are very different from the younger generation of women. Unlike a man who believes sons would support him in old age, the middle-aged mother believes the opposite. She believes daughters are more likely to be emotional and selfless who would support their mother even if the daughters married an unsupportive and aggressive husband. A daughter with the clan members will always look after her mother and, if necessary, protect her from the cruelty of her son-in-law. A family unit including herself and her daughter backed up by her clan provides a woman with a safety net, which will not exist in a patrilineal system.[16] The women's narrative in supporting matriliny originates in the same gendered terrains as their male counterparts who oppose matriliny and believe that a patrilineal system will provide them greater protection from their sons. Unlike the men who fear cruelty from son-in-laws or their wife's brother, for the women the outsider is the daughter-in-law who could manipulate the son against his mother,[17] echoing the typical misogynist interpretation of how some women are viewed as dangerous manipulators. A study by Valentine Pakyntein (1999) in the Khasi hills of Meghalaya had shown that strong preferences for a female child exist in the Khasi hills in both men's and women's preferences, the primary reason for which is, however, security in old age and not continuation of lineage nor inheritance of property (Pakyntein, 1999, pp. 171–182). This tendency to look for care from women and protection in men is a widely held view by both men and women in Meghalaya. Linked to this the faith in "own blood" – i.e. sons for men and daughters for women which is a consistent element in both men's and women's narrative. A duality also exists in women's view of themselves and how men view them. Women view themselves as important subjects who are powerful, whereas their male counterparts, who are obsessed with the influence of the wife's brother and the daughter's maternal uncle's influence, hardly see the women as holding any power. Even if from different positions, support for matriliny is strong amongst women across the generations. From these perspectives, matriliny is maintained by women as a bulkward to maintain their rights and welfare in an increasingly patriarchal social and public sphere.

Displacement, mining, and matriliny

The sense of insecurity that the middle-aged and younger married men experience from a matrilineal system, or the sense of insecurity that the middle-aged generation of women fear from the disintegration of the matrilineal system is absent from the older generations of both men and women in the Jaintia hills. Matriliny gave the older generation of women the space to have their own identities and be inter-dependent with men. Men and women worked on the land together that has been now polluted and rendered unfit for agriculture because of the mines. These experiences give this generation of men and women reasons to support matriliny.[18] In the experience of this generation, it was customary for the older men to control the public and political life of the community while women controlled all spheres of the family sphere. Remembering the time when she was young, 76-year-old Rynkhelm (name changed) discussed how men of her generation would work all day and the women would prepare meals, but women were not expected to compulsorily feed or serve men. For example, Rynkhlem shared, if the husband returned home late from the field and their wives were already half asleep, the husband would serve himself and the wife was not forced to get out of her bed to be serving him food. Moderate drinking was a part of tradition and it was not forbidden for women to drink or smoke occasionally even along with the men. It was nothing like the present time, Ryngkhlem emphasised, where men are drunkards who dominate and even beat up their wives if their wives refuse to serve them food or ask them to serve themselves.

Rynkhelm blames these changes on the spread of the mining industry, bringing with it both social dislocation and a cash economy.

Rynkhelm explains,

> since the time they started mining, some ghost has just emerged from those rat holes and possessed these guys, they don't see anything else other than money! they are hypnotised, they don't know what they are doing... they don't know how to love their wives, they don't know how to behave and respect each other... it all started from the coal I believe.

A central narrative in the Jaintia hills is that money has changed the men, but there is much less awareness of the way in which the cash economy is changing gender relations more generally. The spread of the coal economy is not yet seen as a major factor in the process of cultural and structural change by the majority of people, outside of the educated elites. While the women interviewed think of the land and the related household, as having a gendered character, and also that change in the rights over the household and land would negatively impact on their welfare and status, they see money as essentially genderless. Even though it is primarily men who have access to money, most of the women who were interviewed, see the flow of money into the family as positive without qualification, as it is viewed as a good thing for the family as a whole. This is a factor in maintaining the belief that matriliny as the status quo will remain strong even in the face of the anti-matriliny movement.

Support for mining that comes from the poor is not only because they believe that income from mining has the potential to pull them out of poverty and fulfil their new aspirations, but also because there is, now, nothing else that they have left to do to generate income other than mining. A number of newly emerging rich households went bankrupt after the mining ban because the families had no idea on putting the huge amount of wealth earned to sustainable use and spent all the money that they earned from mining on consumerist goods. This further indicates that money being a very new addition to the agricultural economy of the past, the people are yet to comprehend the basic functioning of a monetised economy, let alone the gendered aspect of it.

Although men still dominate mining employment, women are getting greater access to mine work. In February 2019, the Union Labour Ministry of the Government of Meghalaya decided to allow women to work in the undergrounds in coalmines during the daytime shifts and any time during the day or night in open cast mines. This move, according to the ministry, is to promote gender equality and generate job opportunities for women. Until this reform, women were not allowed to work in underground coal mines and those who work in open cast mines could only do so for a fixed amount of time or for minor purposes and in supportive roles like working in workshops and drilling holes for blasting, etc.[19]

While the Government of Meghalaya has decided on inclusion of women in the mining labour force, the question, however, remains whether or not this inclusion of women will change the dominantly masculinist nature of mining in Meghalaya and assist the development of gender equality and in what ways will it impact the negative dynamic between mining and matriliny. In Meghalaya, many of the (de-jure) coalmine owners are non-tribals and non-residents, even though under the sixth schedule, non-tribal are not allowed to buy and own land in the state. The Maliks (owners) of the coal miles belong to patrilineal cultures and the mine sites operate on patriarchal principles. Therefore, it is important to note here that the coal economy not only operates as a masculine occupation due to its nature, but also there is a close and direct exposure of the matrilineal culture of Meghalaya to the patrilineal ideology of the non-tribal mine owners. This combines with the impact of the several decades-long Christianisation in Meghalaya that already has had promoted western nuclear family values vested with patriarchal ideologies on the matrilineal communities.[20] The matrilineal tradition of Meghalaya is also based on a strong tradition of Common Property Resources[21] (CPR), which provides the basis of autonomy in lives of women through their role in CPRs, which is also under threat of the cash economy. Matriliny has also been threatened by the increasing sale of the CPR land that has not only destroyed the basis of the Khasi/Jaintia women's autonomy but has also shifted occupational interest of the people from traditional agriculture to mining. This carries significant implications for women since women have been excluded from core mining employment work in the recent past (Fernandes 2009). Even with the inclusion of women in mining work, mining will continue to require the destruction of farmland, which is the primary basis of the matrilineal society of Meghalaya. With the recent Supreme Court of India's verdict in August 2019 that has permanently lifted the mining ban from Meghalaya, it is expected that mining operations in the state will accelerate. In such circumstances, it is important to ask if the inclusion of women in the mining work occurs in conjunction with the weakening of women's rights under matriliny. Hence, although matriliny is still seen as the status quo and most women still defend it, there is a strong force of structural change weakening traditional matriliny and seeking to replace it with patriliny. As matriliny is seen as a status quo, this has meant that no organised movement has emerged to defend matriliny. However, the younger and educated women are developing a strong resilient narrative in defence of matriliny and indigenous women are taking on positions of leadership through their involvement in certain government schemes which is adding to this resilient narrative.

This is a complex transition and is characterised by a gendered tug of war where; while on one hand, the matriliny in Meghalaya has been showing remarkable resilience, on the other hand, the forces of urbanisation and a mining-induced market economy, and the deepening patriarchal values are gaining roots in the Meghalayan society which has directly threatened the existence of its matrilineal culture. Even in the absence of mining, the matrilineal system in Meghalaya would be under threat from external and internal influences. Meghalaya is no longer the comparatively isolated region that it was decades ago and would have to always come under pressure of the knowledge of the patriarchal systems outside the region and especially in the rest of India. Internally the system has already been weakened by the influence of social values that accompanied Christianity. The advent of mining has, on one hand, accelerated and deepened the pressure for change, while on the other hand, the many negative social outcomes that result from mining may have also deepened the detachment to the cultural aspects of a matrilineal system.

It is also clear that attitudes to matriliny and mining have a strong class and gender dimension. Women unsurprisingly have a higher level of support for matriliny across classes and across generations, even if the basis for that support is diverse, whereas men are more divided. Many men wish to see matriliny replaced with a patrilineal system as one which would reflect their interests as opposed to women, and more firmly entrench their dominance over women. Other men who are on support for matriliny support it either for their personal wealth or for social position in the family. They do want to enhance the role of the fathers rather than uncles, which would fit their idea of a nuclear family model within the framework of a matrilineal structure.

The next chapter discusses the gendered implications of the socio-cultural displacement that mining has introduced.

Notes

1 Interview with Robert (name changed), Urium Village, East Jaintia Hills.
2 Interview with Robert (name changed), Urium Village, East Jaintia Hills.

3 Focus Group Discussion with Men, Mutong Village, East Jaintia District.
4 Interview with Robert (name changed), 38 years old, Urium Village, East Jaintia Hills.
5 Interview with Willy (name changed), 27 years old, Lumshong Village, East Jaintia District.
6 Interview with Willy (name changed), 27 years old, Lumshong Village, East Jaintia District.
7 Mary Kom, full name Chungneijang Mary Kom Hmangte, is an Indian Olympic boxer from Manipur in North East India who has won championship in the World Amateur Boxing champion for a record six times. Mary Kom is a married woman and has often expressed her role as a mother. When Robert expressed about his love for Mary Kom, he expressed his admiration for her devotion towards her family and children at the same time not giving up on her career.
8 Interview with Andrew and his friend Anil (name changed 38 years), Lumshong, East Jaintia district.
9 Emarine Kharbi. I am a Khasi Owman and No bill can take my identity. Available at https://www.youthkiawaaz.com/2018/07/i-am-a-khasi-no-bill-can-take-my-identity-by-emarine-kharbhih/ (accessed on 4th June 2019).
10 Linda Chakachuk. 2018. Why are Khasi Women Being Held Responsible for the 'Dilution' of the Tribe? Available at https://thewire.in/women/why-are-khasi-women-being-held-responsible-for-the-dilution-of-the-tribe (accessed on 4th June 2019).
11 The Sons of Soil idea underlies the belief that a particular land and territory and its culture exclusively belong to the original inhabitations of that land and not to any outsiders who have come and settled in their 'homeland'.
12 Chamcham and Muttong village in the East Jaintia district have also been affected by mining activities.
13 Focus Group Discussion at Chamcham village.
14 Interview with 22 year old Si from Ladrymbai village, East Jaintia Hills.
15 This issue has been discussed in detail in Chapter 7 on the section of changing marriage system in Meghalaya.
16 Interview with a 50 year woman from Wapung village who works with a lifes-tock business of her own.
17 Interview with Cherry, 45 years old, Wapung village, East Jaintia district.
18 Interview with Ryngkhlem (name changed, 76years) Lumshong village, East Jaintia district.
19 Notheast Now. 2019. Be Aware Meghalaya, now women to go down underground coal mines. Available at https://nenow.in/north-east-news/be-aware-meghalaya-now-women-to-go-down-underground-coal-mines.html (accessed on 6th June 2019).
20 As disussed in Chapter 1.
21 Deigracia Nongkynrih. 2014. "Land Relations in the Tribal Societies of Meghalaya: Changing patterns of land use and ownership." http://www.okd.in/downloads/jr_14_july/Deigracia.pdf (accessed on 1 and 05 and 2016).

5

"GROWING UP IN A MINING AREA"

Gendering labour, leisure, and mobility

What could it mean to have witnessed a complete transformation from abundance to poverty in just few decades? What happens to women when an economy that they controlled completely collapsed to modern ideas of development? Against a backdrop of this layered history of the Jaintia hills in Meghalaya, this chapter discusses the major and contemporary gendered transition of Meghalaya from a women-centred economy to a masculinised occupational culture dominated by mining, and how this transition has reduced the status of the indigenous tribal women in Meghalaya. In doing so, it maps these gendered socio-economic, cultural, and political transitions that women in this matrilineal society have witnessed across generations and how their experiences of changing ideas of labour, leisure, and mobility reveals the changing content of their status and worldview throughout their lives in a broader sense. I have combined the discussion on labour, leisure and mobility of women in the Jaintia hills in a single chapter because these three issues are intimately linked to one other, with changes in one aspect directly impacting and producing changes in another. For example, the nature of labour that women performed in the Jaintia hills in the past was integrated with the leisure activities that they enjoyed. The nature of labour that women performed also determined the amount of their mobility. I argue that because of the various socio-economic and political changes that have unfurled in Meghalaya in the last 30–40 years primarily as a result of mining, the ancient connections between labour, leisure, and mobility for women became increasingly separated and distorted. This has resulted in major changes in the overall quality of women's life through a multiplier effect. Analysing this complex relationship is the main aim of this chapter. This broader aim of the chapter requires it to address different issues that have been instrumental in changing the ideas of labour, leisure, and mobility for women in Meghalaya. A key issue is changing land relations in Meghalaya brought in by the move from a collective and communal landholding system to individual land holdings, which has not only changed women's relationship with land but has undermined the basis of their autonomy granted by tradition. The second issue is that of changing land relations that have their genesis in the appropriation of the mining

DOI: 10.4324/9781003149460-6

economy in the state, which has resulted in an abrogation of the traditional bond that the indigenous people of Meghalaya shared with nature and land. The shift in occupational aspirations and patterns from traditional occupations, primarily agriculture, or small-scale subsistence-based economic activities to monetised and cash-based occupations have been unplanned and are characterised by a violent transition. After briefly discussing the issue of changing land relations in Meghalaya, this chapter goes back on a retrospective journey that traces the history of changing materiality of the Jaintia hills of Meghalaya from the past until present times. It then begins the discussion on the occupational shifts in the Jaintia hills across generations of women, which then is integrated into the discussion of how these occupational shifts have changed the idea of leisure and mobility for women. The chapter ends with a reflection on how these complex processes of change over 30–40 years have implications on the changing idea of agency, empowerment, and disempowerment of the women of Meghalaya. All analysis of this chapter is primarily based on the experiences of the Jaintia hills which is the primary research area of this study.

The changing land relations and mining in Meghalaya

As I have already discussed, a rapid alienation of common land in Meghalaya accompanied by the mining proliferation in the state in the last two decades has been startling. Despite the strict safeguards of customary laws that prohibit any common land to be individually owned, Meghalaya has been witnessing a massive chunk of collective land being illegally registered as individual land while most of the legitimate individually owned private land in the state had already been sold or leased out for mining purposes for its higher returns in profit. Traditionally, the clan used to play a strong role in common land management. In most regions of the Jaintia hills, families were allotted some homestead and agricultural land by the clan in the past. If any family stopped cultivating, the allotted land reverted to the clan as a default practice. Hence, landlessness was not a common problem, for, almost everyone had a plot of land to live and cultivate on. As custodians of common land, the clan did the administration of the land collectively.[1] That is what marked it apart from the exploitative zamindari system[2] of feudal India, where big landowners singlehandedly owned land and employed poor and landless Dalit and low caste people as agricultural labourers that trapped the labourers in an unending cycle of debt and poverty whereas their landlords benefitted from this exploitation of labour.

However, in the last few decades, Meghalaya too has started witnessing a steep rise in landlessness with more and more common land being illegally sold to the mine owners by influential clan leaders, who are men. The clan leaders have done so by misusing their traditional status of being (common) land custodians. Consequently, huge tracts of land that used to be common land for collective use have now become individual land that are exclusively used for mining. One such example of common land alienation is the court case registered over the "selling" of common land in village Mynthning in the Jaintia hills that went on until the NGT ban[3] on mining in 2014.[4] The appellant counsels contended that the transaction of the common land happened without any approval and discussion with the clan members and villagers, which is a breach of the customary laws of Meghalaya. In another case that was fought on grounds of security breach that caused a serious accident of a mine worker, the counsel for the defence of the mine owner argued that the mining was carried out with the order and permission from the village chief and since there were no formal protection and regulatory mechanism adopted by Meghalaya in carrying out mining activity yet, any accusation on breach of security measures by the mine owner was unfounded. Equally interesting is the fact that no charge sheet was filed for this case for two years after the incident, despite that it concerned matters under the Indian Penal Code.[5] Needless to state that, such illegal accumulation of private wealth out of collective property which operates with impunity through a strong political and elite and bureaucratic nexus, stands in sharp contradiction to the traditional ethos of the communal and collective solidarity of the Khasi and Jaintia society.

However, the reaction of the people of Meghalaya to mining has not always been that of acceptance. In fact, Meghalaya had seen an outburst of unified protests against mining corporations and cement factories, like Lafarge that attempted to acquire tribal land in 2010–2011.[6] The protests defended indigenous people's right to their own land and culture that would be destroyed if Lafarge acquired land and established its factory in Meghalaya.[7] In parallel to this reality, on the other hand, mining activities are also conducted by the indigenous people themselves. But unlike the protests against Lafarge, protest against mining that are conducted by the indigenous people are not tolerated. This opposition to anti-mining protests comes from not only the mine owners but also the mine labourers, who have seen a drastic increase in their income from working in the mines, compared to the income earned from their traditional agricultural practices. For example, in one of the protests against mining, the activist and organiser H. H. Mohrmen published an advertisement seeking support and solidarity for the protest from the people. Instead of mobilising support for the protest, this attempt backfired on the activist as there was a counter-protest organised by a group of mineworkers by forming a human chain against the protest by Mohrmen on the same day. The counter-protest was organised on the same day by the mineworkers against the protest organised by H. H. Mohrmen. This complex situation is a cause of confusion for activists resisting mining.

> ...they were claiming that mining is their livelihood. When I asked them 'what were you doing for a living before mining came in? Did you starve to death?' They had no answer. This protest was

> much more difficult compared to the protest that we organised against Lafarge because Lafarge was an outsider. But how does one fight against one's own people? ...we are tribal people... we are supposed to love nature and live with it. But destroying our own nature ...this was never us... but what have we become?[8]

This divided response to mining in Meghalaya can be treated as yet another example of the complicated history between capitalism, indigenous societies, and neoliberal ideas of development. As such, even though the indigenous people in Meghalaya might have a story to tell on how mining has led to the destruction of the foundations of their homeland that was once self-sufficient, that story might have different perspectives to it, each of which needs not necessarily be in perfect coherence with the traditional philosophy of oneness with nature.

Changing materiality and land ownership

The changing land ownership system in Meghalaya also reflects a massive lifestyle change in the matrilineal society, mirrored in its changing materiality. To understand the magnitude of this material transition, it is important to discuss the history of the villages located in the present-day coal belts of the Jaintia hills in contrast to how they appear today, before delving deeper into the socio-political and gendered aspects of this transition.

Lumshong and Sutnga are two small villages in the East Jaintia hills with a dominant Pnar population and a vibrant history of mining activities. However, what marks both the villages different from each other is that, in Lumshong, it is the cement and mining companies that hold control over the mining activities unlike in Sutnga where the villagers who hold ownership on the mining process. The men of Lumshong that I interviewed, expressed disappointment on the land acquisition and destruction of the environment in their village but they also regarded Sutnga as an ideal village because unlike Lumshong, it is Sutnga's own people who are enjoying the fruits of their own land unlike the outsiders in Lumshong.

Lumshong used to be a thick forest with a number of wild elephants, which had kept it unsuitable for any human habitation for a long time until the government offered an award of Rs. 1,000 to people from a neighbouring area called Narpuh if they agreed to migrate and start a village in Lumshong. The huge sum of money motivated the first settlers of Lumshong to begin a life in the village in few years before India's independence. The Narpuh region from where one of the earliest settlers of Lumshong migrated from holds importance to the Jaintia hills for a variety of reasons. Narpuh used to be a thick and vast tropical forest, often referred to as the dark forest in the past because of its thick vegetation that prevented sunlight from entering into the forest floor.[9] Shifting cultivation was the common form of cultivation where farming happened in cycles and more importantly, was collectively farmed. The major rivers of the Jaintia hills, which had clear water then, originated from the forest cover of the Narpuh. The rich vegetation of Narpuh forest, its wildlife, and beauty offered a unique character to the Jaintia hills and everything around the forest derived its name from the Narpuh. The first families migrated to Lumshong in and around 1944, which is before India's independence. A small forest lane running through huge trees connected the villagers with the outside world. Hired jeeps were common vehicles of that time since the road was too rough for cars. The jeeps commuted people from Jowai, the present district headquarter of the Jaintia hills, to Badarpur, a small town on India–Bangladesh border. Badarpur was a small commercial place then, with a very thin population. Much before motor vehicles made it to the inroads of Lumshong, horses were used for transportation, especially by the British, to commute from Jowai to Lumshong. A solo journey from Jowai to Lumshong was considered a long and dangerous journey in those days. The highway came to be built only in the 1980s by the General Reserve Engineering Forces.[10]

After migrating to Lumshong from Narpuh, the settlers continued with their practice of shifting cultivation based on a common land system. What hold great significance to the people in Lumshong were its famous orange plantations, which were controlled by women and were the primary livelihood for the indigenous people of the village as well as the neighbouring areas. A large-scale limestone mining and massive land grab by cement factories that penetrated into the village from 2005 onwards has altered the geographic and social history of the area. Today, there are eight cement factories in the Narpuh area, each located at a radius of less than 5 kilometres from each other.[11] This is irrespective of the fact that large tract of the cement factory land, falls under the "unclassed forest" of the Autonomous District Council of the Jaintia hills that is legally prohibited from any kind of acquisition. Cement companies like Topcem and Star cement have occupied more than five hundred to one thousand hectares of land in the area, which has left no land under the ownership of the local indigenous people.

The same is also true for village Lumshong that looks less like a village and like a semi-urban neighbourhood in present times. A small concrete lane runs right from the National Highway and goes into the village, connecting the village households. Another grid of houses stands right next to the National Highway. After getting off the vehicle at the National Highway, one could walk straight on the concrete lane to the heart of the village, or take a right or left to make their way to the houses that stand parallel to the highway. What is striking about the village are its colourful concrete houses. With the proliferation of the cement factories in Lumshong, the cement companies started buying huge plots of land from the local people. As the cement companies started buying the village land, people started claiming parts of the common land as their own and sold them to the factories. In the past, individuals could claim common land simply by placing a marker by stones, building a fence, or planning a tree on the boundaries of the land claimed. The money earned from selling the land to the companies was invested in building concrete houses to replace the traditional mud huts. This process went on until the indigenous people were left only with their homestead land with the newly built modern houses while all other lands were lost to the factories. Meanwhile, Lumshong's famous caves, like the "Krem Kotsati Umlawan" which is the second longest (21, 530 metres) and third deepest cave in India (215 metre as on February 2006), started attracting tourist, and scientists from across the world and created more and more money-making opportunities. This process facilitated an international exposure for the villages and introduced a monetised life completely alien to its traditional mode of living. Lumshong gradually took on a different path from its traditional agriculture-based life. The traditional elites and other powerful village leaders continue to secretly register the common land as their own individual land in the district registration offices despite the prohibition of the customary laws. The few protesting voices from the general public spoke out against these illegal registrations, but this was overshadowed by the inflow of money into the area. After the highway was built, mining and trade further flourished leading to an increase in business and population. From being one big village with no locality divide in the past, Lumshong today has grown into four big Neighbourhoods. Meanwhile, four heritage caves, including Krem Kotsati Umlawan, along with Krem Malo, Krem Umkseh, Krem Umkhang-Kharasniang have been completely destroyed due to limestone mining.[12]

The village Sutnga is located just an hour away from Lumshong. From being a poor village in the past, today Sutnga has large houses with fine furnishings that stand in black coalfields. The road to Sutnga passes through a number of mining sites and layers of black soil that has carpeted the areas neighbouring the mines. The small road that runs through a relatively forested valley takes a steep up-turn and suddenly opens up to a very high-income Neighbourhood with mansions having marble flooring and several storied buildings. Most of the families that live in those buildings were poor farmers just few years ago. Many of the families have their own coal mines which are not controlled by outsiders but by individual indigenous people themselves, something which is considered ideal by many Khasi-Jaintia people in terms of how they wish to grow the mining business. This is one of the primary reasons, as discussed above, for the language of protest to have seen a marked shift from when it was only aimed at companies coming in from outside. As anybody could mine the land and therefore had the opportunity to grow rich, many local miners critiqued the need to have mining licenses from the government as being the same as seeking permission from the state to dig one's own backyard.

"*Nobody resisted. Everyone wanted money. That greed only destroyed Lumshlong.*" shared Agnes (name changed, 86 years) who refused to share anything personal about her life other than a brief history of how she has seen the village change from its lush green history to the present state of acute poverty and environmental degradation. Agnes expressed strong contentment against politicians and the cement companies who made promises to the people of her village only to betray them later. She remained firmed on her decision not to talk about her life while criticising the younger generation for their blind belief in the government policies like the ones of the aadhar card (unique identification card for Indians) that asks for all information of one's possessions and history.

"......these young guys don't listen to the older people but only later will they realise how the government ripped off their asses in the name of Aadhar. Aadhar, Sarkar sob Saitan! (Adhar, government all are demons!)" said Agnes with a wide grin as she served me tea.

As I walked out of Agnes's house, a group of young children, not more than 7 years old, were playing with a cart. Some sat on the cart while the others steered the wheels. On asking if we could have a photo with them, the smallest one sitting on the cart immediately covered his face, and the ones at the wheels screamed at the top of their voice and ran away in a flip second. The spontaneity of this resistance to be photographed by such young children was startling and very unusual compared to what I experienced in any other parts of Meghalaya where children were always enthusiastic about having their photos taken – and once again alerted me of the steady penetration of the mining industry into Lumshong that took away people's traditional way of life and their self-sufficiency and established a deep fear and mistrust of outsiders.

Limestone mining came to be heavily regulated in June 2015 after a series of court interventions. Pre 2015, limestone mining in the Jaintia hills amounted for above 15,000 million metric tons and transported to Bangladesh through various export points by every miner in lieu of a small transportation tax on the extracted limestone after producing a clearance certificate which was easily obtainable from the local forest authorities. However, on 30 June 2015, the High court of Meghalaya ordered all mining activities to be immediately stopped (except for those that have mining licences) on grounds of environment protection. The court declared that new licences would be granted after consultation with the Central Empowerment committee constituted by the Supreme Court of India. In June 2016, traditional mining, largely as non-mechanised mining, was brought back by another high court order in response to a petition filed by a miner from the East Jaintia district, which drew on a judgment of 2012 where the Supreme Court had stated, "Indigenous people are conscious of their rights and obligations towards clean environment and economic development." In July 2017, the High Court again ruled out the relief given to traditional miners stating that it violated the mining regulating rules passed by the Government of Meghalaya in 2016. The state's interference in traditional limestone mining evoked controversial responses.[13] While few welcomed the move, many others saw it as interference on the sixth schedule status of Meghalaya. The youths whom I interviewed, even though expressed deep disappointment with the environmental degradation caused by mining, also reiterated how they feel that the ones advocating for the ban are unable to accept the fact that the poor are getting out of poverty through mining. They argued that if those opposing mining were concerned only about environmental protection, they would have advocated for the ban long time earlier and not waited until all the villagers had become dependent on mining. Many of these voices also represented a number of young people who had to drop out of their studies because of the sudden lack of income that affected families after the mining ban. In latest news, Lafarge Hoichim has resumed limestone mining in the East Khasi hills of Meghalaya after receiving clearance for the same.[14]

Occupational shifts

Farming and orange

Lahun (name changed, 72 years old) and her family have lived in Lumshong since her childhood. Lahun's house is one of those houses that stand parallel to the National highway and her veranda faces the road that is regularly used by trucks, a thick blanket of dust, and lots of noise. Lahun had to lean towards me and raise her voice to make herself audible above the noises of trucks and vehicles as we conversed. Although I moved closer to Lahun to hear her clearly, the noise was eclipsing Lahun's voice in my recorder even with the noise cancellation switched on. Lahun's family members sat calm amidst the noise in a state of reluctant acceptance. After trying for a while to battle her voice against the noise of the trucks, Lahun offered to continue the interview inside her house. The noise level was lower inside the house; nevertheless, it continued to interrupt the interview. What was unsettling was to realise that this huge transformation induced by the mining industry from the past to the present had taken only a few decades.

The soil of Narpuh and Lumshong was famous for its fertility. After migrating to the Narpuh area, Lahun and their fellow villagers settled in a valley called Tshinongring before finally moving to Lumshong. They cleared a chunk of the forest and started cultivation after cleaning up the area with vegetables and paddy. The older generation of women who worked in the field used to live in the field and come back home only once a week to spend some time in the village. Hence, the field had a lot of meaning to their lives, since it was not only the workplace but also the space where women built lasting friendship, fell in love, and created a sense of community with their peers. Because of the fertile soil that returned huge yields in the new settlement, many sold off their farmland in the original places where they migrated from, including Lahun's family who belonged to the War tribe area of a locality called Amlarem. Other than rice and vegetable cultivation, Orange farming became a key crop I the region.

"...Even I remember, until 1991–1992, this whole area used to look orange because of the orange trees, with big sized oranges...they were very sweet and tasty...the orange skin used to be very fine and thin. And they were very juicy. Oranges from this village used to be considered number one...." Lahun's 35 years old son said.

Lumshong and its neighbouring villagers used to supply oranges to Bangladesh and other parts of Meghalaya. It was a blooming business and the primary livelihood for the people. Apart from orange production, the orange business too was primarily controlled by women, which made them the major entrepreneur in the orange business dealings that happened with the buyers from the outside world. The oranges used to ripe in the month of December, but they were pre-booked by the buyers way ahead in June. The oranges were sold for rates as high as 15 to 20k INR and depending on demand, some buyers were supplied around 10 to 20 trucks oranges.[15] The buyers hailed from different places. Some were from Bangladesh while some were from other states of the North East India like Tripura. The buyers from Tripura primarily exported the oranges they bought in Lumshong to Bangladesh. The income earned from oranges amounted to around Rs. 35–45 per month, with a daily income of Rs. 1.50. It was a lot of money for that time when nothing cost more than 25–50 paisa and expensive items like clothes cost only Rs. 1–2.

The work that each generation did was similar to the previous generation from whom they had learned the skills of farming. But what marked both the generations different was their involvement in trade. While Lahun's grandmothers' generation did not trade oranges and used it only for consumption, Lahuns' generation started trading oranges. Difficulties in accessing the market prevented most women from Lahun's previous generation, except for few, from selling not only the oranges but other items that they made like bamboo baskets, furniture, food, pickles, etc. Nonetheless, each family was able to farm one to two hectares of land at the minimum that fed the family for a year. Introduction of orange trade was a significant change between Lahun's grandmother's generation to her own, but it did not change the root ethos of environmental and developmental sustainability of the tribes.

This trade was disrupted by a massive hailstorm in the year 1986, which damaged the oranges. The oranges caught some strange illness after the hailstorm which damaged the oranges to such an extent that the trees did not really recover. Then the pollution caused by limestone mining further destroyed the orange plantations to such levels that, in the last five years, oranges have completely disappeared from Lumshong.[16]

Fishing and smoked fish

Fishing is another important occupation that has now completely disappeared from Meghalaya. Previously fishing had been an important part of diet and income generation for the people, especially for fishermen villages like Lumpanyang of the West Jaintia hills. Until the beginning of 1990s, the river water was clean and one and half kilos of fish could be caught just after an hour of fishing. The coming in of mining deeply polluted the river water causing the fishes to become extinct. So sharp this transition for Lumpanyang that, with the exception of the older generations, the community has no memory or knowledge of the fish richness of the village's past.

> ..I thought probably he was exaggerating when he talked about boat full of fishes in the past..it was only when he showed me a picture which had quintals of fishes in the boat with the fishermen literally sitting over the fishes is when I realised the magnitude of this loss.

Mr H. H. Mohrmen said, as he shared about a fellow elderly fisherman from Lumpanyang, who now does wage labour work after the destruction of the fishing business.

The elimination of the fishing as an occupation has in turn affected another women-dominated occupation – the Smoking of fish. Smoked fish used to be a dominant village economy in the Amlarem area located in the West Jayantia hills (the Amlarem area is also the region where Lahun and her family migrated to Lumshong from). Amlarem today is a small commercial centre of West Jaintia hills. Umladkhur village, near Amlarem is a village famous for its smoked fishes. Unlike Lumshong, Umlaldkhur is a well-maintained traditional village that has resisted allowing its land from being used for coal mining, even though there are reserves of coal underneath the village. Umladkhur village is pollution free and its village council ensures that the whole village is cleaned every month. Cattle and other livestock are not allowed to be grazed or sheltered until 100 meters of the household areas of the village. Nonetheless, the whole village saw a major occupational shift from traditional agriculture and the smoked fish business with the onset of coal mining in Meghalaya. Smoked fish was not only an important economic activity but also held cultural significance for the Jaintia hills. With the coming in of mining, many households that were involved in traditional smoked fish business had given up smoking fish for mining. It was only after mining was banned that some older women started going back to smoking fish again.

Simi (name changed, 75 years), a villager of Umaldkhur whose family occupation was smoked fish, left it for mining and has again gone back to fish-smoking since 2017, i.e. after the mining ban. Smoked fish had been the primary occupation for Simi and her family for the three generations preceding hers. The only change that was introduced in the last three generations was in terms of different equipment, even though a few still prefer to use the traditional style of equipment which makes the process more detailed and taxing than the contemporary easier method. In the traditional method, fishes are tied to a long bamboo stick with small bamboo stings in a line and put to fire on a long fireplace. The fire stove used in traditional style of smoking fish is around 7 feet long and around half feet tall. Whereas the contemporary style of doing smoked fish involves smoking the fish in a round fire stove made of mud which is around four feet tall and less than a feet in width. A smoking tray made of iron with lots of fishes on the tray is put to smoke on the fire. The stove has a small entrance at its base to put the logs into the fire. Before putting the fishes to smokes, their scales and intestines are taken off. Once smoked, the fishes can be stored for almost week in normal temperature making them a useful food source, which was also another reason for their popularity.[17]

Many women who have been practicing smoking fish as their primary occupation for more than 25 years are also single women, including Simi and another woman called Nanny (name changed, 65 years old). Nany's husband left her after 14 years of marriage when she was pregnant with her 9th child. Simi's husband left her with her three children after four years of marriage. Both Simi and Nany decided not to remarry. While Simi decided to work as a wage labourer in the mining site, Nany continued with her smoked fish business. Nany was not the youngest daughter of her parents which is why she did not inherit any land. The only land that she owns is her homestead land; hence she had no choice but to keep doing smoked fish as she never felt comfortable working in the mines. Unlike Nany, Simi did inherit some land from her parents as her parents' youngest daughter but eventually stopped farming because it did not give her enough money, although it did give her rice family consumption. One reason for this was that polished rice gaining more popularity over the years, nobody preferred to buy rice locally produced in the village. Consequently, traditional agriculture was increasingly abandoned by the people of Umladkhur because of its poor profit returns. Newer needs like accessing modern healthcare system, buying modern household items, accessing formal education and buying vegetables (as the vegetable yield too had gone down with increasing land pollution), etc., heightened the need to earn more cash. Another reason was also the popularity of the idea of accumulating savings in the bank which is drastically different from the traditional method of keeping limited saving, if any at all, underground in the soil or somewhere hidden in roof of the house. Also, on the face of declining profits over the years, most women with the exceptions of a very few like Nanny, gave up smoked fish as their livelihood. The disappearance of river water fishes due to contamination from mining made the smoked fish workers solely dependent on imported fish from other parts of India like Andhra Pradesh. The imported fishes were not only expensive, but also frozen which affected the quality of the smoked fish. The purchasing power of the women to buy raw fish from Andhra Pradesh depended on the profit they made by selling their smoked fish. The purchasing power of the customers of smoked fish, on the other hand, became dependent on mining. As such, mining engulfed the whole smoked fish business. From a monthly income of 12,000 INR that Nany made prior to the mining ban, her monthly income from her smoked fish business dropped down to 5000 INR which is less than a half from her earlier income.[18] In fact, this kind of steep drop in of income is not only true of the traditional occupations that women did but even for the modern retail shops that women run in the Jantia hills in contemporary times. Simi compares the contemporary need for cash compared to the needs of the earlier generations.

"....My parents' lives were different. They did not do savings, they did not plan to build houses in the town, they did not have high aspirations from life. They did not go to the modern doctors when they fell sick. So they did not need money. But now time is different. you need some money, build a house and live a more comfortable life. For that you need cash" Simi said.

Hence, for many like Simi, owning or not owning land did not imply a huge difference since local produce lost its former demand in the market, while subsistence farming did not provide the income to support the new emerging aspirations of the indigenous people. Except for Nany and Simi, nobody in their families smokes fish anymore, which makes them the last generation of their families engaging in this traditional activity. Nany's daughter has already migrated to South India in search of alternative employment.

Livestock

The Livestock business is another traditional woman-dominated occupation which has suffered a set-back because no suitable land is left for the cattle to graze. The vegetation dried down because of mining pollution and many animals starved to death. Women involved with livestock business tried sending their cattle to distant unpolluted fields, but unpolluted grazing land was very hard to find. Many had to depend on buying hay from others to feed their animals, but finding hay was not easy either.[19] Like smoked fish and the orange plantations, the present generation of animal herder women too had converted livestock to a business spirit rather than treating it as a subsistence level activity. Most of their children have taken up salaried jobs or other wage labouring opportunities. These women therefore are also the last generation of livestock-business-women of the Jaintia hills. Although traditionally it is the youngest daughter who takes the mother's legacy forward, none of the younger daughters of the women who practices the traditional women-based occupation that I interviewed are engaged in farming, livestock, or smoked fish production anymore. While the educated daughters of these women have migrated out of Meghalaya to gain access to higher education or to do service jobs in the major cities in India, few of the youngest generation of men who did not get formal education, helped their mothers with their livestock business but instead opted to join the mining workforce.

A significant part of the economy of the indigenous tribe consisted of orange plantations, livestock, and smoked fishes, which was controlled by women for generations using subsistence practices and then breaking into the cash economy has been disturbed by mining. Men who assisted women in the traditional occupations drifted into mining. This also implied that men who were socialised into respecting Khasi/Jaintia women for their social and economic value were brought into an alternative and contrary ideology of the mining business that thrives on a discriminatory and devalued extraction of female labour. This transition, in its content, is a shift from a past when it took 2 hectares of massive yield to feed a single family, with enough fishes in the river to ensure a luxurious meal on a daily basis and more than enough income that came from the oranges to today's experience of poverty and landlessness. The ending of collective land ownership and traditional women-controlled primary livelihoods like orange plantations also imply an extinction of other traditional trade and social support systems that did not depend on money. For example, in the past, poor families were helped by the extended families financially or even by being given land, so that the family could build a house.[20] Lack of money did not pose a problem because of the prevalence of the barter system, which too was primarily dominated by women. People could exchange vegetables for rice, salt, and other items and vice versa, a process controlled by women. This barter was not just limited to Lumshong and its Neighbouring villages but happened across international borders with people from Bangladesh and was on a significant scale. All of these traditional systems of reciprocity and trade have completely vanished today.

"There is hardly any work for women now a days. Some work in the factory. Some work as wage labourers. Some run small shops. But no matter what we do, there is not much work available for women. Some used to work in the mines. Some collect firewood from the jungle. But no beneficial work available now like it was in the past" shared 75 years old Anna (name changed) from Lumshong village.

In Lumshong, the cement factories employed mostly men, of which only a few were local indigenous people. Most of the women in the area are illiterate and hence got employment only in unskilled work as sweepers, gardeners, and cleaners with minimal wages. A few educated young women, presently around 100–150 in numbers, are absorbed into skilled labour in data management and other basic computer work. The few educated get a desk job, the uneducated ones get menial jobs. Low wages, lack of training, and lack of support systems that could help induct the tribal indigenous people into the working culture of the cement factories are frequent problems stated by the indigenous people. The men interviewed expressed that companies often fire the indigenous workers for their inability to follow the 8 hours work schedule, whereas it is impossible for the indigenous people to devote 8 hours of the day to the company work because the wages offered by the company is as low as Rs. 3,000–400 per month for unskilled work.[21] Since the low wages do not suffice the indigenous workers to sustain their families, they have to do other additional wage labour work in the village. This means that the indigenous workers are compelled to divide their time for the company as well as for other additional work that they do. There is a lack of support from the company officials for the indigenous people as they do not offer proper training to the locals so that the locals could be fired easily under the guise of low performance, is another grievance expressed by a majority of the narratives. A strong nexus of the people in power, including the company managerial and political influential Khasi/Jaintia people have successfully kept activist or general public out of decision-making board of the companies. This is also true for even the government executive committees where half of the members are from the factories, who even though are tribal people, are accused by the general public of Lumshong of holding loyalty to the factories for their vested interest and financial greed.[22] Although there are some low skilled employments in the mechanical and technical fields of the factories, where a few local people have been employed by the factories for an average salary of around Rs. 20,000 per month, it is only the regular and permanent workers who get a reasonable hike in salary. The wage for the irregular workers has declined over time. This means that, for local people, employment in the mines is not structured in such a way that it can raise the general standard of living. This is similar to the Australian experience, where despite the doubled economic development by mining, the employment growth in the region has negligible growth and the economy for the local people had structurally changed from a dependence on agriculture to mining, with no evidence of increasing regional specialisation required for mining as the ageing population is retiring from mining activities (McFarlane, et al., 2015).

The unguided assimilation of the tribal indigenous people of Lumshong into the cement factories and their lack of formal education also has to be understood in terms of the marked cultural difference placed on the value of labour between a mining company and a tribal society. The pressure for formal education was absent for the tribal people because they depended on agriculture and other related activities and did not have access to educational institutions. The dream to become modern doctors and engineers was limited to the elite tribal who had exposure to the nearby cities and could afford the cost to send their children to educational institutions outside the state. Although lack of money did not simply imply poverty in the past, it implied a considerable distance of the tribal people from a modern life that was regulated by a monetary economy. What formal education had to offer, in that sense, was not only expensive but also irrelevant to the worldview of the tribal people. This cycle of poverty meant a far steeper decline for women's status even though in general both indigenous women and men are hit hard in this process because unlike women, men were absorbed in unskilled jobs in the mining companies and had access to a wider range of jobs at a higher income than did women.

Leisure, labour, and mobility

The idea of mobility and access to public spaces was engrained in the nature of labour performed by the tribal women of Meghalaya in the past. The labour performed by the older generations was their sole responsibility and required extraordinary hard work. But the nature of their work ensured them a higher status and the right to mobility. The necessity of roaming around as a part of their work gave the older generation of tribal women a sense of ownership of the public space. With more technology and modern modes of transportation making their way into the Jaintia hills, the subsequent generation could avail the privilege of working less than their parents and grandparents, even though they did the same kind of work. However, with proliferation of mining and the ending of the traditional occupations also meant women withdrawing from the public spaces that once belonged to them and spending more time inside their homes doing household chores, while the men became the primary income earners. The youngest generation of women interviewed, now no longer do the work that their parents and grandparents did, but instead prefer to be western educated and do salaried jobs. This also means that the idea of mobility and freedom that their grandmothers enjoyed is something that they do not relate to or at worse have never seen operating in practice. This section discusses the changing nature of labour, mobility, and leisure for the women in Meghalaya across generations, against the growth of the coal industry in the state.

In Lumshong, the caves and the rivers used to be the leisure space for the older generation of women. This involved collecting water from the river in bamboo buckets, swimming in the depths of the caves, swinging by trees in the waterfalls, etc. These leisure hours also provided the women with an opportunity to chat, bond, and spend time with each other and to create a collective memory of a life shared together. For example, those who did smoke fish in the older generations of women in Umladkhur village used to walk a whole day to a distant village called Nongtalang to buy fish. Nongtalang village was famous for its fishes like the village Lumpanyang. After spending the night in Nongtalang they walked back to Umladkhur the next day, carrying the fishes on their heads providing an opportunity to socislise. A majority of the time, the women in Jaintia hills who worked in the forest was spent in the forest, with their children who played, collected fruits and vegetables to eat, and also learned about alternative traditional medicinal herbs.

However, except for the rich households, most of the women did not have the privilege of attending schools, and if they did, had to drop out of studies to contribute to the household income or following the death of the mother had to learn responsibilities for their younger siblings.

"...our time was different no? We were not encouraged to attend school... people would say 'what will do you do in school? you don't gain anything from there. Better start working so you can gain and earn something for yourself'. So I took work seriously, I wanted to do something...I wanted to give my children what I did not have..." shared Julie (name changed, 50 year old) who owns a large animal livestock business in village Wapung of the East Jaintia hills.

Juli's childhood was mostly spent in the company of her mother. Juli's mother used to pack food in a big leaf, lock the house and leave for the field while Julie accompanied her every day. She played throughout the day in the field and ate the food packed in the leaf when she felt hungry. The whole day until the evening was spent in the farms. On turning 8 years old, Julie started taking care of the cows under her father's guidance but left it for a short while when she was 14 years old because she felt shy to be around animals all the time and focused all her attention on household chores. However, after getting married, Julie got back to her livestock work with a vision of turning it around to a successful profit-making business. Most of the women did not only livestock work but also agriculture, handicraft, making furniture and broomsticks, shared stories of a similar childhood followed by a high level of work after adolescence, though they still managed some leisure time.

A 35-year-old women from Urium village shared

> As far as I can remember for myself, the elders in my family would only and all the time ask me to look after and hang out with the animals, our livestock. I was the livestock person (laughs) pigs and cows were my best friends..but we had to find out an escape from work to go and play my favorite marble game. Those games were a secret from our parents... but nonetheless we managed to play our favourite marble games!

Waking far off places in search of work took several hours each day, which was a common experience for the older generation of women who are over 75 years old at present. As hard was the toil, the income was equally low and mostly paid in kind than cash with rice and vegetables that sufficed for one meal or two. The culture in the past emphasised on sharing all the food gathered with every family member, irrespective of however little the quantity. Because there were no roads and one had to walk through dense jungles to the market in Jowai, only a few women from the remote villages like Urium could commute to sell their products in the Jowai market. The walk to Jowai took half a day and even if they started their journey early in the morning, it would be late night when the women made their way back home. Women from Urium village often had to stop at Wapung village for a while on their way back to get an earthen lamp, so that they could walk the remaining distance to Urium through the dark forest. Another popular marketplace other than Jowai used to be Kheleriat (which it continues to be), located few miles away from Jowai. The distance to Khleriat market from certain interior villages in the East Jaintia hills was as long as 12-hour walks without any rest and break in between. Women usually travelled in groups and ate some of the food and fruits that they carried with them to sell, a popular travel food of which was oranges. The groups of women usually arrived at the marketplace one day before the market day. After arriving at Khleriat, they rested at a friend's home for the night and left the day later after the market day. Throughout the whole walk, women carried everything that they took to sell, including heavy furniture like stools and cane baskets, on their backs. Despite the tremendous amount of hard work that this kind of labour entailed, income earned was extremely poor – which was only Rs. 5 earned for every stool sold. The concept of savings was absent primarily because the little money earned was spent on buying food like rice, betel nuts, and other household goods. Even for healthcare service providers like midwives, walking was the only way to commute between villages, no matter how close or distantly located they were. Most of the older women expressed the view that in spite of how tiring the walks to the markets were, they were also enjoyable as they chatted with each other about the progress of their business, earnings, and personal lives. Most of the older women complained of lack of a variety in the food that used to eat and the lack of leisure when compared to their children. The younger generation, according to them, although have enough to eat and have access to varieties of food, yet lack in strength and motivation to work like them. The middle aged and younger generation agreed and accepted that they could not match the strength and discipline levels of their parents, and that of their grandparents.

People's lives drastically changed after the construction of the National Highway followed by public transport making their way into the Jaintia hills, including the remote villages. This happened after coal deposits were discovered in many of these interior villages like Urium. At present time, a shared taxi ride takes only one and half hour from Jowai to Urium, while it takes a four-hour drive from the capital city of Assam, Guwahati, to Jowai in Meghalaya. Although this has helped women to access different markets and commute easily, it did not lead to any improvement in their increasingly degrading status since the traditional occupations that earned them that status, granted them mobility and a sense of ownership of the public spaces have already disappeared. This is especially true for the middle-aged women who spend most of their time indoors doing household work unlike their mothers who were highly mobile and spent most of their time outside the house working. For example, in the richer households in Sutnga village, the management of household business operate very much in patrilineal style where sons and husbands of the women take care of the family coal business without any interference from the women's matrikins, whereas the daughters have taken up salaried and professional jobs or have returned to the village to start their own ventures. A common narrative that came out in the interviews with the middle-aged women is how their mothers have been unable to adapt to this changing lifestyle of being indoors for the day and prefer to carry on with their work in the forest, even though it is not required nor beneficial in terms of earnings.

"...it is habit you know. My mother's generation spent most of the time outside the house. So they like to be freer. Oh you should see how my mother is always complaining about being house arrested; she gets really bored. She is old but she can't stay without working. She still goes to the distant forest to work. Even if you try to stop her, she won't listen! I don't stop her either, because that makes her happy..." Shylla (name changed), a 42-year-old woman from Sutnga village shared.

What is striking here is unlike the older generation who had been unhappy with the loss of mobility and the younger women who are seeking out modern occupations, the middle-aged women expressed relative comfort with their shrinking mobility, which makes them different from their mother's generation as well as their daughters. The middle generation of women, in the case of affluent household in Sutnga, have taken to work like gardening at their homes, or adopting children from poorer households as a token of giving back for their good. The women from the rich households shared how they understand the pain of abject poverty as they also have lived in poverty until coal mining changed their lives which is why they wish to help the poor people of the village. Shylla, for example, has adopted a few children from the poor families in Sutnga and has been supporting their education, something that she could not do for herself because of financial constraints when she was young. For her, this change implies a journey from living a life that in the past demanded hard work from her part, to today, where she has a number of domestic helps who does the housework under her supervision. Unlike her mother, she feels comfortable spending time at the house and no longer goes out to work, because that is no longer required.

Women from poorer households in Jaintia hills continue to run shops in the markets of coal towns like Ladrymbai and the market centre at Khleriat and Jowai, only today use public transport to travel to the marketplace. A brief description of the nature of travel in public transport that women take will give an idea of how most women travel in the Jaintia hills today. The public transport commute to Ladrymbai[23] from Jowai is a 45 min drive. During my travel experience, the small passenger cars that drove people from Jowai to Ladrymbai had a small note pasted on the top of the front windows saying, "maximum capacity five," where the fifth person is meant to share the middle space at the back seat for two. However, in reality, the cars carried eight passengers exceeding their normal capacity of four. The driver shared his seat with another person. Two more persons shared the seat next to the driver. The passenger who shared the seat with the driver put one of his legs on the right side of the gear handle and the other leg on the left and sat in a way so that the driver could conveniently use the gear handle. It was always a man who shared the seat with the driver; in some rare case if it was a woman, she sat cross-legged keeping both her legs on one side of the gear handle, mostly on the left, and diagonally leaned against the driver's seat on the right. The back seat was stuffed with four passengers who adjusted to the scarcity of space by hovering back and forth, trying to align and experiment with the sitting positions. Throughout the drive, the passengers sat in the same positions without any movement since any movement could disrupt that best sitting arrangement, as there was no more space left for any body movement. The car boot was stuffed with the women vendor's goods to be sold off in the markets of Ladrymbai – a town in the East Jaintia hills that is the nucleus of mining activities in the state. Whatever could not be fit in the car boot was carried on the laps or adjusted into the spaces that were left under the seats or between the passengers' limbs. Every day, hundreds of passenger cars packed in similar ways set out to Ladrymbai until dark. But what was striking to notice was the remnants of the community and cooperative spirit of the past echoing throughout the drive among the fellow passengers, especially in their support to the women vendors whose goods they carried to Ladrymbai. The drive would take almost an hour in busy days and the cars stopped to drop passengers and take new ones on the way. People spoke to each other with much familiarity and affection even though they might have met each other for the first time in the car. This is probably a feature a close-knit community, that a certain sense of affinity amongst its members by virtue of belonging to the same region or culture could hold everyone together, including strangers, in close solidarity, which is much deeper than everyday social or casual connections that characterise urban modern societies. It was apparent how people felt connected and comfortable with each other in their conversations, how their sense of the "personal" extended beyond one's own self and how the idea of a private body space did not create discomfort or anger between them. As the passenger cars moved through the heavy traffic of the highway, the drivers tried to overtake the big trucks to escape the thick blanket of smoke that the trucks threw onto the small cars. The windows in the passenger cars were mostly kept half-open. It cost extra money to close off the windows completely and turn the air-conditioner on. However, only a few passenger cars had an air conditioner in them, which were seldom or never used. Even with the air-condition turned on, the smoke found a way to slip inside the cars releasing a peculiar smell of sweat and smoke to which, as my co-passengers shared, the people got used to the black smoke and the sickness that it carried because they had no other choice.

Unlike the female-only travel and social space that women enjoyed when they travelled in groups, the public transport that women take to their market destinations, now lacks the social and cultural significance of the past. Women today commute to the market mostly alone or with a friend or co-worker. The space of public transport implies an integration of the women into it unlike the past where the travel itself was a women-centric space. The market space, however, continues to be dominated by women. Yet the value of the marketplace has become poorer and second to mining on which its survival is dependent.

Women in mining work

The involvement of women in the mining work started with the older generation around 25 years ago, when many women and men from the remote villages migrated to the coal belt villages like Ladrymbai to work in the mines. Most of the women who worked in the mines carried their babies with them as they did when they worked in the fields. Although they were aware of the danger posed by a constant exposure to the mining sites for their children's health, they were helpless as mining was all that they could do when the traditional occupations had shut down. Many women, in their later years in old age, had to quit mine work because of their inability to carry on with diminishing physical capacity and were compelled to stay indoors. These former female mineworkers, who are presently around 60 to 70 years old, complained about the loss of the social comraderies that they enjoyed while working in the fields or while doing smoked fish. Unlike the middle-aged women who were in their early 20s when the coal economy took over and hence were socialised into a domestic lifestyle at a young age unlike the older women who had already spent most of their lives doing traditional labour without experiencing the strict divide between the public and the private sphere, unlike their future daughters. This explains why the resistance to being indoors for most of the day is more common among the older generation of women than the middle-aged women.

However, as compared to the daily Rs. 500 per box that the women today make in the mines, the older generation were paid only 50 paisa per box in the beginning, which later increased to Rs. 100 per box few years later. Until the mining ban, women's work in the mines consisted of separating the slate from the coal for Rs. 500 to 600 per box. Men on the other hand earned Rs. 1,000 to Rs. 2,000 per box for carrying those boxes to the trucks for transport. Nonetheless, the huge increase in women's income in the mines, from a mere.50 paisa to Rs. 500. in as short a span as 35 years explains the reason for the sacrifices that women were ready to take on for a new life of modern consumerist goods, appliances, and technology, even though it meant working in the very masculine and male-dominated space of mining.

"My elder sister bought the first radio in our village. We were so excited that we used to listen to the radio the whole night... the whole Neighbourhood used to come to our house to listen to the radio .... it was an exciting experience. I saw electricity and TV in mining towns only... my childhood was spent with earthen lamps..." shared a shopkeeper woman at town Ladymbai.

Collective screening of films, television programmes, radio programmes bought from the increased income informed the first encounter of the people with technology. Presently, almost every household owns a Television set and has electricity. As such, the base for a gradual shift from a very traditional lifestyle to a modern one had already laid its foundation.

Labour, mobility, and vision of the younger generations

The changes in terms of exposure to a modernised life that began 35 years ago have now reached a very advanced stage in Meghalaya. The younger people under the age of 35, as has been discussed above, prefer modern occupations to the traditional ones that their parents did, with the exception of mining. Most of the young people have not been trained in the work of their parents and grandparents, including agriculture, especially young people who go to schools and colleges. Most of the younger people also expressed a lack of interest in learning or practising any of the traditional occupations not only because they are less profitable, but also because they find the idea of modern professions more appealing as it can give them an enhanced status and lifestyle, that traditional occupations cannot. Unlike their previous generation who spent a lot of time in the forest during their leisure hours, the younger generations no longer spend time in the forest in their free time. The reason for this is the availability of a marketplace that sells everything that one needs and the preference of the younger generation for some money to spend on modern means of entertainment. As such, they would rather work in the mines to make money than roaming around in the jungle.[24]

Many young people moved out of the Jaintia hills to the capital city of Meghalaya, i.e. Shillong, and to other cities in India for higher education and job opportunities. Some have returned to start their own ventures in their hometowns while others visit their homes only in holidays. The idea of mobility and leisure among the younger generation is based on an urban-styled life. Most of the younger people interviewed expressed an interest in travelling around India and abroad. Watching television, movies, and spending time on the internet are the major leisure hours that almost all the younger people spoke about. Apart from the aspirations of being doctors, engineers, few girls and boys also expressed interest about alternative career goals like stand-up comedy and even being a DJ, the idea of which kind of work (especially DJ) were strongly moral-policed in the past because they were regarded disgraceful activities performed by "immoral" people. One of the young interviewees from Urium village expressed his frustration that despite the support of his parents, he has been in two minds about becoming a DJ, primarily because he does not want to be labelled an improper man by his loved ones; however, he is hopeful to have seen things changed and that people are becoming more open.

Unlike the older generations who grew up in close affinity with the clan members in a time when clan as a group used to play a decisive role in the people's lives, the younger have grown up in nuclear families and in a clan affinity that has transformed into online platforms rather than the old-styled face-to-face interaction. The clan no longer plays decisive roles in people's lives as it did in the past, other than functioning as an exogamous unit for marriage.[25] Nonetheless, the international and geographic spread of the clans as a unit, whose members continue to remain connected virtually, has directly or indirectly heralded newer ideas and imaginations of space, living, and worldviews transmitted through the clan members who live in different parts of the world.

Many young women also expressed a sense of responsibility and a spirit of globlalism in their vision of bettering their homeland. Learning through international exposure from different countries and applying that knowledge to better their own place is a general aspiration that came out in a lot of young women's narrative, especially the ones who are highly educated. Apart from social media exposures, the different international exchange programmes facilitated by the church-based educational institutions along with different scholarship opportunities facilitated by government and non-governmental training courses could be a reason for the growth of this ideology and awareness among the younger generation.

22 years old Si talked about one of her friend who went on an exchange programme to the USA.

> My friend got so obsessed with America that when he came back, he would not miss a chance to despise Ladrymbai and say, 'Oh man, it is so dirty here; I can't live here anymore man, I will go back to America.' He thinks he is being cool but he isn't. He learnt nothing by going there. I tell him, 'If you saw how clean America is, you should be trying to make your village clean no? But you are only complaining about your own place, as if you were a born foreigner.' I don't want to become like him. I clean the trash in my Neighbourhood very often. People come and convince me that there is no point in cleaning it because it will get dirty again. I reply by saying that I would keep cleaning irrespective, may be someone else also join me in cleaning, or be inspired to keep the Neighbourhood clean.

In order to combat the gradual extinction of the traditional socio-economic fabric of the Jaintia hills, the Deputy Commissioners office at Jowai has started an intervention that attempts to bring back a balance of modernity and tradition by re-introducing the traditional occupations, especially agriculture in the Jaintia hills and it also attempts to include younger people in the initiative and promote women's leadership in the process. Certain other government programmes have also introduced interventions like planting trees across the Jaintia hills to fight environmental degradation. The women SHG of Chamcham village[26] provide the tree sapling for these tree plantation programmes. It is interesting to note here that while on one hand, the environmental and climate crisis has reinforced a movement for climate sustainability in the state, speedy modernisation, and urbanisation continues to deplete the traditional Khasi/Jaintia identity, to combat which, there have been major initiatives taken to revive and protect the traditional indigenous culture of Meghalaya. For instance, the Meghalaya Government had conducted a massive tree plantation programme[27] to battle climate crisis, and recently, a news about Meghalaya assembly replacing plastic water bottles with glass jar went viral in social media;[28] likewise an IAS officer in Meghalaya was hailed in social media for walking 10 kilometres to buy organic vegetables and support local vendors and sensitise people on climate sustainability and waste management.[29] Whereas, simultaneously, the Chief Minister of Meghalaya "Conrad Sangma" hailed the final verdict of the Supreme Court of India that lifted the National Green Tribunal ban on Coal Mining in August 2019. Mr. Sangma stated the verdict as a victory of the indigenous people,[30] ignoring multiple reports over the years on how the indigenous culture of Meghalaya has suffered under mining.[31] Conrad Sangma, at the same time, also hailed the Sen Kut Snem, a traditional festival in Meghalaya that aims to preserve the Khasi identity.[32]

This speed of change is startling because it happened in a matter of 30–40 years. The various programmes and projects, and voluntary efforts that attempt a modern revival of the past indicate how the indigenous people have been trying to process and adapt to the impacts of modernisation and mining that it has witnessed since the early 1990s. The idea of the gendered nature of labour, mobility, and empowerment greatly differ for each of the generation of women across the 40 years. Some of the recent development initiatives by the Deputy Commissioner's office require the lead project person to be a woman to promote gender equality in public leadership, which is an important shift from the invisibility of women's leadership compared to public positions in the past. However, this idea of empowerment of women has changed across time. The older generation of women had spaces for dissent and even though the households were gendered spaces, they had a choice to take off from those prescribed duties without being violated. Women were not actively prohibited from taking part in the village governance[33] but the heavy workload at the family pushed them to take up the full responsibility of the domestic sphere, which remained under their control.[34] The nature of their lifestyle in the past gave them mobility and access to the community's resources that were collectively owned and hence were comparatively less male dominated. The sexual division of labour in this sense was real but not as sharply polarised (as it had become later) which accounted for a relatively cooperative relationship between men and women. This probably explains why a majority of the older generation of women who learnt and exercised empowerment through their life and the daily-ness of their living itself, were vociferous throughout the interviews. This level of confidence and vociferousness was also exhibited by the educated younger generation of women, whereas the younger girls who have not been able to access education exhibited lesser confidence and opinions and hence were less willing to express opinions than their educated counterparts. The younger girls today have the ideas of freedom and confidence of their grandmothers more so than their mothers, although their idea of empowerment has been learned more in the classrooms unlike their grandmothers who learned through the nature of their daily life and culture that they grew up in. The middle generation of women, on the other hand, stood somewhere in between their parents' idea of empowerment and their educated daughters'. Analysing these transitions in life of the indigenous society reveals a complicated gendered process of transition in Meghalaya.

Notes

1 The idea of common land in the North East India can be understood in the context of the Common Property resources. Conventional definition of CPRs encompasses only natural resources like land, forests and water resources. Whereas the CPRs have much deeper meaning in the lives of tribal people than how formal economists define them. Land, water and forest are not only a site but also the prime means of production, and the basis of the communal social identity of the tribal people (Fernandes, 2009, pp. 107–108) (Guha and Gadgil, 1996, pp. 37–38). In most tribes the village council of the tribes controls all land and allots it to individuals for a season. It also determines the allotment of land depending upon the mouths to be fed and decides which family with excess adults will assist a family with deficit of adult workers. However the operations of CPRs differ from tribe to tribe. For example among the Angami of Nagaland and Dimasa of Assam, combine individual ownership with clan. But in each case it is recognized by the community and is under its control. Some such as the Aka tribe in Arunachal Pradesh of NORTH EAST INDIA lack the very concept of individual ownership and only have usufruct rights. Each family cultivates as much land as it requires during Jhum (shifting cultivation) and at the close of which reverts to the community (Fernandes and Khatso, 2007, pp. 31–32). The same goes for forest and water resources which are communally owned and governed and are used by the tribal indigenous people for their livelihood.

2 See, Zamindari System. Available at https://www.utsavpedia.com/cultural-connections/zamindari-system-recalling-royal-roads/ (accessed on 14th June 2019).

3 For details on NGT ban, see Chapter 2.

4 Interview with H. H. Mohrmen.

Also mentioned in this article, 'Semasi: A village which rediscover itself after the mining ban. Available at http://hhmohrmen.blogspot.com/2017/02/semasi-village-which-rediscover-itself.html (accessed on June 2019).

Copy of the judgment by the Gauhati High Court available at https://www.legitquest.com/case/dorbar-shnong-mynthning-others-v-jaintia-hills-autonomous-district-council-others/8B0D2 (accessed on June 2019).

5 Huggo Stokke. 2017. Legal Limits to Tribal Governance: coal mining in Meghalaya India. Available at https://www.cmi.no/publications/6185-legal-limits-to-tribal-governance (accessed on 14th June 2019).

6 In the midst of the Covid 19 pandemic, Lafarge Holcim has recently been given clearance to resume limestone mining in the East Khasi hills district, attracting strong criticisms from environmentalists.

Shillong Times 2020. Environmentalists question Lafarge mining clearance. Available at https://theshillongtimes.com/2020/05/15/environmentalists-question-lafarge-mining-clearance/ (accessed on 6th March 2021).

Business Standard. 2020. LafargeHolcim resumes operations in limestone mine in Meghalaya. Available at https://www.business-standard.com/article/pti-stories/lafargeholcim-resumes-operations-in-limestone-mine-in-meghalaya-120051300886_1.html (accessed on 6th March 2021).

7 Thomas Crawley. 2011. The battle for indigenous land: Protesting mining in Northeast India. Available at http://base.d-p-h.info/en/fiches/dph/fiche-dph-8889.html (accessed on 14th June 2019).

8 Interview with writer and activist H. H. Mohrmen.

9 H. H. Mohrmen. 2017. Who will save Narpuh from Imminent Destruction? Available at http://www.theshillongtimes.com/2017/06/26/who-will-save-narpuh-from-imminent-destruction/ (accessed on June 24, 2019).

10 General Reserve Engineering Force is maintained under the authority of the Central Government.

11 H. H. Mohrmen. 2017. Who will save Narpuh from Imminent Destruction? Available at http://www.theshillongtimes.com/2017/06/26/who-will-save-narpuh-from-imminent-destruction/ (accessed on 24th June 2019).

12 Raymond Kharmujai. 2021. Destructive mining by cement companies demolish 4 majestic caves in Meghalaya. Northest Now, 3rd February. Available in https://nenow.in/north-east-news/meghalaya/destructive-mining-by-cement-companies-demolish-4-majestic-caves-in-meghalaya.html (accessed on 6th March 2021).

13 Arunabh Saikia. 2018. As Limestone piles up on Bangladesh border, anger against Congress brews in Meghalaya. Available at https://scroll.in/article/867669/as-limestone-piles-up-on-bangladesh-border-anger-against-congress-brews-in-meghalaya (accessed on 24th June 2019).

14 Lafarge Holcim resumes operations in limestone mining in Meghalaya. Available in https://www.business-standard.com/article/pti-stories/lafargeholcim-resumes-operations-in-limestone-mine-in-meghalaya-120051300886_1.html

15 Interview with Lahun's son, 35 years, Lumshong, East Jaintia district.

16 Interview with Damsur, 50 years, Jowai, West Jaintia district.

17 Interview with Simi, 75 years, Ulladkhur Village, Eas Jaintia district.

18 Interview with Nanny (name changed), 65 years, Umladkhur Village, West Jaintia Hills.

19 Interview with Cherry, 45 years old, Wapung Village, East Jaintia Hills.

20 Interview with Lahun, 70 years, Lumshong Village.

21 Family Focus Group Discussion, Lumshong Village, East Jaintia district.

22 Interview with a 45 year old man from Lumshong. The interviewee refused to be named.

23 Ladrymbai is another town and the nucleus of coal mining activities in the East Jaintia hills, the details of which is discussed in Chapter 6.

24 Interview with Michael(name changed), a 25 year old man from Jowai.

25 Interview with H. Mohrmen, Jowai.

26 As discussed in the previous chapter.

27 Meghalaya Times. June 2019. Meghalaya plants 1.5 million trees to mitigate dangers of Climate Change. Available on https://meghalayatimes.info/meghalaya-plants-1-5-million-trees-to-mitigate-dangers-of-climate-change/ (accessed on 5th October 2019).

United News of India. June 2019. 1.5 million tree samplings planted in Meghalaya. Available on http://www.uniindia.com/1-5-million-tree-saplings-planted-in-meghalaya/east/news/1622449.html (accessed on 5th October 2019).

28 Shillong Times. September 2019. Glass Jars replace Water Bottles in Meghalaya Assemble. Available on http://theshillongtimes.com/2019/09/06/glass-jars-replace-plastic-water-bottles-in-meghalaya-assembly/?fbclid=IwAR1S6Rh0SjsBbUhJpnqbA-n13wdwYnbqgpe5WCpOWH_Yn5REw9XCWT_4zrM (accessed on 25th October 2019).

29 The Logical Indian. September 2019. This Meghalaya IAS officer walks 10 kilometres to support local farmers, earns praise. Available in https://thelogicalindian.com/news/meghalaya-ram-singh-walks/ (accessed on 5th October 2019).

Rimi Chakraborty. 25th September 2019. Meghalaya IAS officer Walking 10 kilometres to Buy Fruits and Vegetables Is The Real Hero of Fit India. Available on https://www.mensxp.com/social-hits/news/57111-meghalaya-ias-officer-walks-10-km-to-buy-fruits-vegetables.html (accessed on 5th October 2019).

Microsoft News. September 2019. This IAS officer in Meghalaya Walking 10 kilometres to Buy groceries Is the Inspiration We need. Available on https://www.msn.com/en-in/news/good-news/this-ias-officer-in-meghalaya-walking-10km-to-buy-groceries-is-the-inspiration-we-need/ar-AAHVOhH?li=AAggbRN&%2525252525252525253Bocid=iehp (accessed on 5th October 2019).

NDTV. September 2019. Why This Meghalaya IAS officers Weekly Veggie Shopping Is Getting a Slow Clap. Available on https://www.ndtv.com/offbeat/meghalaya-ias-officer-walks-10-kms-to-buy-organic-inspires-internet-2106789 (accessed on 5th October 2019).

30 NDTV. August 2019. Meghalaya Chief Minister Praises Supreme Court Verdict on Coal Mining. Available on https://www.ndtv.com/india-news/conrad-sangma-meghalaya-chief-minister-praises-supreme-court-verdict-on-coal-mining-2085597 (accessed on 5th October 2019).

31 Sarma, Kiranmay and Yadav, Pramod. 2013. Relentless Mining in Meghalaya, India. Conservation Science. Available at https://www.nepjol.info/index.php/CS/article/view/8578 (accessed on 30th October 2019).

32 The Times of India. November 2018. Meghalaya Governor greets people on Seng Kut Snem. Available on https://timesofindia.indiatimes.com/city/shillong/meghalaya-governor-greets-people-on-seng-kut-snem/articleshow/66781490.cms (accessed on 6th October 2019).

33 Manoram Sharma (2004) in her working paper "Critically assessing Traditions" the case of Meghalaya has discussed a very interesting point in this regard. In his examination of the account of British captain R. B. Pemberton called "Report on the Eastern Frontier of British India, Gauhati: DHAS, 1966" of the 1835 Jaintia era, Pemberton writes, " The Rajahs of Jynteeah [Jaintia] are under the necessity of consulting on all important occasions the queen mother, and the chief of districts, and officers of state; and although the appointment and removal of both the latter descriptions of persons rests with the Rajah himself, they are nevertheless enabled to exercise a considerable degree of control over him, as he is obliged, in confirming such appointments, to consult the wishes of the chief people in the interior, who seem to be of a very independent and rather turbulent character". In analysing this narrative, Sharma (2004) observes that the Jaintia women in 1835 women who were referred to as queen mother were considered capable of taking decisions. As such, Sharma (2004) argues that the marginalisation of women from political decision making could have been a clear result of patriarchy inherent in the Christianisation of Meghalaya, that era being a time when women in the west were still fighting for their voting rights.

34 FGD, Mutong Village, East Jaintia Hills. An older man who participated in the FGD shared about this voluntary withdrawal of women from public affairs. This can be analysed with the information shared in footnote 20 to understand the possibility of a gradual disappearance of women from public and political affairs of Meghalaya, a reinvention of which history could be a significant discovery in further understanding the traditional status of women in Meghalaya.

6

INTIMACIES AND VIOLENCE IN THE MINES

This chapter examines the intersection between domestic violence against women and a growing sex work industry in Meghalaya against a backdrop of the mining boom. Although investigating the growth of sex work industry was not envisaged as a part of this research, the frequent occurrence of the intersection between domestic violence, destruction of traditional structures, and an emerging sex work industry that I witnessed during my fieldwork was too propelling to ignore. Women's experiences of desertion, violence, and the use of the sex industry are the antithesis of the security of status and the support that is expected of a matrilineal structure. It is these aspects of the shift in gender relations that demonstrates the devastating impact of mining in the region on social structures and on the status and welfare of women. This chapter engages with this topic at two levels. First, it is an issue-based investigation, that is, how women in Meghalaya have been battling with domestic violence and desertion by their spouses,[1] which has left them with no support or assistance and forced them to take up sex work to support themselves and their children. The second aspect is the complex moralities that characterise this discourse of domestic violence and sex work in the region. It examines how the narratives of domestic violence are differently coloured by a moral undertone depending on the ethnic origin of the violator husbands, that is, if they are "outsider" migrant mineworkers or the "insider" tribal Khasi and Jaintia men. The chapter then builds on this to examine how the growing sex industry absorbed a large number of deserted women looking out for a means of financial support, which process, in turn, has constructed different notions of romantic and sexual partnerships with a complex moral undertone to it. Though these two issues of domestic violence and sex work appear distinct otherwise (apart from the apparent connection of violated women being absorbed into the sex work industry), they are closely tied together by a common popular morality discourse shaped by the socio-cultural as well as the politico-economic history of Meghalaya, meaning the lenses of morality through which the migrant man is judged, the sex worker is judged, or an ideal romantic relationship is judged or the lens of morality that the sex worker uses to judge herself and others, including the migrant men. All of these morality judgments appear

DOI: 10.4324/9781003149460-7

separate from each other on the surface, but, in essence, these moral lenses are actually shaped by the same socio-cultural, political, and economic discourse in Meghalaya. Approaching this investigation from this perspective also uncovers the elusive nature of boundaries of the gendered categories such as who is a good man or good woman, versus who is not, or, what kind of a man or a woman can be classed as immoral, etc. These boundaries are constantly shifting in accordance with the socio-economic and political context that they are located in, even though they might appear as dominant moral discourses with clear boundaries. The aim of this chapter is to understand this play of morality.

The regular growth of a sex industry in mining towns has been widely discussed by academics and activists; the reason for which has been attributed to the masculine culture promoted by mining. However, only a limited research has looked at this issue from the sex workers' point of view (Mahy, 2011). Mahy (2011) has argued against the compulsively negative portrayal of women in the sex industry in a mining settlement that reduces women's experiences into a victimhood narrative that fails to capture women's diverse relationship to the sex industry as sex workers, miner's wives, or just as women living in a mining community holding agency to protest and act (Mahy, 2011). Mahy (2011) also raises objection on the two moralistic categories of women constructed in this polarised discourse – the first category being of sex workers who are often excluded from the larger category of "mining women community" and assumed as equal victims of "mining and commercial sex," regardless of their choice or agency. The second category being divided into two sub-categories of the "bad, opportunistic migrant sex worker women who take advantage of 'good' women's husbands' vis a vis the 'chaste indigenous community women who are the powerless victims of their husband's sexuality and spend-riff habits on spending money for the service of the prostitutes'" (Mahy, 2011). An indigenous woman who becomes a sex worker, according to this second category, is seen as being compelled by social and economic circumstances to take up a demeaning occupation (Mahy, 2011). Mahy (2011) also critiques the tendency of the general "women and mining" literature to attribute a similar background and interest of sex workers (particularly for indigenous women) which had existed before and after the start of large-scale mining. Mahy (2011) also discusses another dualistic category of female sex workers who are either portrayed as the "victims" but also the "heroines" who despite being taken off from their traditional status and being subjected to male oppression, alcoholism, violence, and sexual urges continue to bravely struggle. For Mahy (2011), although this categorisation might help in policy formulation and initiate action, it fails to reflect complex gendered realities. Acknowledging the fact that every mine is located in its unique temporal, social, and economic context, Mahy (2011) argues that it is important to re-examine the gender and sex work discourse since this kind of straightjacketed categories of women that the "women and mining" literature has so far established as relatively essential, fails to accommodate more complex experiences of the gendered realities of women.

Mahy's (2011) emphasis on resisting essential categorisation and the need to establish the diverse gendered realities of sex work in mining is reasonable, and also informs my analysis of the "issue based" as well as "the morality based" discussion around domestic violence and sex work in this chapter. However, even though I agree with Mahy's (2011) argument of the need to avoid essential categorisation, I will still use the categories of "men" and "women" that came up during my interviews to map a clear understanding of how these categories interact with each other, and finally to show how this interaction itself comes back to deconstruct any essential categorisation. It could also be argued that all of these categories simultaneously co-exist without any essential boundaries and are constantly interacting with each other. This makes the nature of the interaction of primary importance than the nature of category itself – but at the same time it does not deny the inherent quality of that category that has to play a role in this interaction. As such, while acknowledging the danger of essential categorisations, I would still maintain the benefits of using categories for convenience in analysis to understand women's response to domestic violence and sex work in Meghalaya.

This chapter begins with a typical dualistic category of the violent husband – the migrant versus the tribal, that often came up in the interview narratives; although it is not necessary to believe this duality (because there is no reason that experiences beyond this dualities might not exist as this chapter later goes on to argue while deconstructing this duality), the fact that this duality exists in the minds of the people interviewed, speaks of the power of popular opinion that shapes a hegemonic collective consciousness, irrespective of how complex the reality might have been and is. Unlike the bad migrant sex worker versus good indigenous sex worker dualistic divide that Mahy (2011) has been critical of, this chapter is exclusively based on the experiences of indigenous sex workers who joined sex work under different circumstances of their lives.

The context

Ladrymbai is a famous coal mining site and the most multicultural town in the East Jaintia hills of Meghalaya, located by the National Highway number 44. Like Lumshong, the construction of the National Highway in the 1980s also transformed Ladrymbai from a small village to the present busy town, incessantly spading its own soil to unearth the huge reserve of coal that lay beneath.[2] Ladrymbai today is a transit point for fast transports traveling between important cities such as Guwahati, Silchar, Manipur, and Mizoram in North East India. The highway made it convenient for exploitation and transportation of coal leading to the exponential rise of an unregulated mining industry in the town (Chinai, 2006). Ladrymbai has been famous for its busy streets, robust retail businesses, multi-cultural spirit, and huge amount of migrant coal mine workers, until the mining ban had brought about a major shutdown to its economy. My first visit to Ladrymbai was in 2017, three years post the mining ban. The whole place looked like an abandoned town and different from the period before the mining ban. The shopkeepers shared their worry on their declining profits over the years while they desperately waited for the customers; the huge piles of goods in the stores were waiting for months to be sold off; the roads that used to be filled with hundreds of trucks transporting coals from the site to its destinations lay empty; the busy traffic that used to take two hours to cross by a 500 meters distance had vanished. The once green fields on the side of the roads have turned into an empty black plateau with small stacks of un-cleared coal lying here and there. The people spoke in a state of constant reminiscence of what it used to be before the ban. The air was trying to recover from the smell of carbon and ashes. The mining ban was temporarily lifted in 2018 just before the elections in March, and Ladrymbai went back to its busy past with thousands of trucks on the roads, un-ending street markets and vegetable vendors, shops filled with people. It was frequently reiterated in my interaction with people that it was not as busy as it used to be before the ban. My experiences in Ladrymbai were similar to the fear and mistrust that I had witnessed in Lumshong. My id was checked multiple times before I was escorted to people I was to interview. "A girl who studies in London" was how I was introduced to most people I interviewed. On trying to correct that I was studying in Ireland, a frequent question followed "How far is it from London?" The fact that Ireland was "just one hour from Ireland by air" always ended up making me the Assamese who lives near London. I was an insider and outsider at the same time, and was often received with, at worst, a sense of mistrust and suspicion or, at best and most of the time, with hope and excitement that a London girl from Assam was going to write their stories which will be read by "foreigners."

This section looks at the pattern of domestic violence that women in the Jaintia hills encounter with their husbands – both migrant and tribal. However, when it comes to condemning the violence, the migrant man is blamed for his inherent immorality as compared to the Khasi and Jaintia man whose violent behaviour is blamed on the arrogance that coal has brought him. This is irrespective of the fact that both tribal and migrant men have been equally horrible in terms of violating their spouses.

Domestic violence

The migrant versus the tribal husband

The coal belts of the Jaintia hills have witnessed hundreds of cross-cultural relationships between migrant labours and indigenous Khasi and Jaintia women and also a large number of deserted women whose husbands decided to go back to their homelands without their wives.

The mining industry pulled a huge number of migrants from places such as Assam, Nepal, Bangladesh, Bihar, Rajasthan, etc., to Meghalaya. A rough estimate of the growth of migrant workers ranges from 35,000 to 150,000 (Madhavan, 2005). The mines in the Jaintia hills have more than 90% of migrant workers working as quarry workers, loaders, unloaders, truck drivers, and helpers.[3] Many of the migrant workers settled in Ladrymbai and formed their own community ghettos in the town. Ladymbai also became a place of co-existence of different cultures with people mingling with each other, where the female population is largely local, but a large number of the migrant population are male. There was an increase in cross-cultural marriages between migrant male workers and tribal women. But a number of these marriages were short lived since these men came to Ladrymbai for purely economic reasons with no intention of settling there, and eventually returned to their homelands with all the money they made in the mines, leaving their Khasi and Jaintia wives behind, and frequently remarrying women from their own community. Many women also refused to move out of their homeland with their non-tribal husbands. However, there are also few marriages which lasted especially when the migrant workers permanently settled in Ladrymbai or when some Khasi and Jaintia women migrated with their husbands when their husbands decided to return to their homelands. This pattern of behaviour has resulted in a negative perception of the male migrant workers.

"These Nepalese are the worst. They will always leave their Khasi wives and marry among their kind. Betrayers! I am not saying this only because it happened to me. But most of the women who have been deserted by their husbands in Ladrymbai had Nepali husbands. These boys even sleep with their own niece. Have you ever heard of anything such as this in other communities? What we consider sin, they find enjoyment in that. Sister-in-law sleeps with their brother in-laws and what not! They are seriously the worst" said Sunu (name changed, aged 30).

Sunu had grown up in Ladrymbai. When Sunu was a child, her family migrated to Ladrymbai from an interior village of the Jaintia hills for better economic opportunities. Sunu speaks five languages and understands English because her childhood was shared in the company of people who migrated to Ladrymbai from across India to work in the mines. Sunu's husband was one of the many who had gone back to their homelands after the coal ban was implemented which partly explains the anger and disillusionment against the migrant Nepali men that comes through Sunu's words. Her daughter was abducted by her husband and kept hidden and separated from her for nine months. Her in-laws refused to give her any information about her daughter. Sunu filed a police complaint and had to undergo a lengthy court case to get her daughter back. After getting her daughter back, Sunu's husband disappeared from Ladrymbai as he married a Nepali woman leaving no trace behind. There are many women with a similar story.

Such as Sunu, Rita (name changed, 60 years old) had also met her second husband, who was a Nepali in the mine site. Rita had migrated to Ladrymbai in 1985 along with her first husband for better economic opportunities. After the death of her first husband due to chronic illness from working in the mines, Rita continued with her work of carrying baskets in the mines to support her family and fell in love with her second husband who was a driver at the mines. However, Rita's second marriage did not last long especially after her second husband became a drunkard and started abusing Rita. Later, he left Rita and married a Nepali woman. In Rita's view, "That's what these Nepalese do, they always leave us and marry a Nepali sooner or later."

It is interesting to note that desertion of women by the non-tribal migrant husband is more frowned upon in the region than desertion by the tribal men. This is despite the fact that the abandonment of wives and children by tribal husbands has been a problem in the matrilineal community of the Jaintia hills for decades.[4] This strong tribal vs. non-tribal divide that exists in the state can be attributed to the history of migration and immigration in Meghalaya and the associated conflicts beginning with the first ethnic riot in 1979 against the migrant workers (Singha and Nayak, 2016) followed by more tribal versus migrant clashes in 1987 and 1992. During the early years of boom in the mining industry in Meghalaya, migrant labours were tolerated. But as the numbers of migrant labour increased, local opposition grew. However, the Nepali migrant workers became the focus of this growing opposition by the locals owing to the history of Nepalese immigration to Meghalaya and the fear that the overnumbered migrant workers were a threat to the livelihoods, territory, and culture of tribal communities (McDuie-Ra and Kikon, 2016). The politicisation of ethnicity for vested political gains which has been a factor in Meghalaya since 1979 has carefully maintained this fear that non-tribals will take away the region's jobs, land, and women (Mukhim, 2013).[5] This anti-migrant fear resulted in women being seen walking with non-tribals being shamed and their accompanying men beaten up (Mukhim, 2013). In Meghalaya, the insider–outsider conflict has now extended to internal conflict among the indigenous tribes themselves primarily due to perceived economic competition with each other (Singha and Nayak, 2016).

Hence, even though intercultural marriages are prevalent in Ladrymbai and other parts of the Jaintia hills, there is fear attached to it. Mr Daniel (name changed, 50 year old) whom I met in one of the colleges in Meghalaya, folded his hands on his forehead and sighed looking into the sky, "I can't tell you how our women have suffered in the hands of the migrant labourers who leave them alone to die! We are a matrilineal society, we keep our women high up, you know? And these guys are doing this to our women!." On asking Daniel about his opinion on the desertion of tribal women by tribal husbands, he expressed his belief that unlike tribal husbands who could still be traced back and taught a lesson for his ill-treatment of his wife, the migrant labourers just disappear with no trace which leaves no room to access any justice by the woman.

Cherry (name changed, 45 years old) shared

> ....the men from outside could already have family in their home state or they could be just using the women, you never know. But without clearly checking their backgrounds, the tribal women marry these men and are deserted by the men later. After those husbands have made enough money and are done working in the mines, they would suddenly get ready to leave. He would take everything that he has earned with him and just leave. I have so many friends who have gone through this nightmare... But not all are such as that. There are honest people also who stick by their wives till their death. So, it depends from case to case.[6]

The narratives of violence experienced by the women in the hands of migrant labourers were coloured by this fear and hate for the foreigner, irrespective of the fact that domestic violence against women by Khasi men has also been prevalent. The mistreatment of Khasi and Jaintia women includes women who were married off early, leaving all their aspirations behind, and women who ran away to escape from their abusive husbands and also abusive family members. A few cases discussed below bring out the different situations of domestic violence against women in the Jaintia hills in the hands of their Khasi and Jaintia husbands or family members.

Amie, a 28-year-old woman from Jowai was abducted by her first Khasi husband in broad daylight from the market in Jowai in 2010 when she was 20 years old. She never knew him before nor was ever approached by her husband to propose marriage. After abducting, he took Amie to his house at Nartiang village and introduced her as his wife to his mother without seeking any approval from Amie. Amie had no choice but to give in because Nartiang was far away from her home and her mobile phone had been confiscated by him. This left Amie with no way to contact her parents. After a month of the abduction, her husband called her parents and introduced himself as Amie's husband. Amie's family members, who were searching for her, came immediately to see her. They disapproved of her husband, who, they considered, was irresponsible and reluctant to support Amie. Amie was not taken back by her parents. In order to support the family, Amie had to take up the responsibility of running the house while her husband confiscated all the money that she earned along with physically abusing Amie on a regular basis. Amie had her first child in 2011. When she was pregnant, her husband was arrested and jailed on a rape charge. Amie finally ran away from her husband's house in 2014. She came back to her parents and started living with them even though she did not receive much financial support as her parents were also battling poverty. Amie is now married to her second husband who is a Nepali and works as a driver in the mines and is happy with her marriage.

Unlike Amie, Rihun (27 years old, East Jaintia hills) was married off by her parents without her consent when she was 15 years old to a rich man triple her age. She had an interest in continuing her studies but was prohibited from going to school after marriage. Rihun continued to go to school secretly after her husband left for work even when she was pregnant. But eventually, she had to give up her studies after her baby was born. She did not have access to any money earned by her husband nor was she allowed to work. After her husband died, she was left alone to support herself, without any help from her parents with whom she continued to live but was not supported financially to raise her child. Meghalaya is one of the top ten states of India with the highest rate of early marriages. Other states from the North East such as Arunachal Pradesh, Sikkim, Nagaland, Assam, and Tripura from the North have also featured in this list.[7]

Julie's story (name changed, 35 years old, Ladrymbai) speaks of violence by close kins and family members. Julie had lost her parents when she was a child. She was adopted by her aunt who subjected her to regular torture and physical abuse at home. To escape the violence, Julie fled to Kohima (located in the state of Nagaland in Northeast India) to seek a livelihood for herself and be independent but was eventually found out by her aunt and brought back home. After enduring torture and house arrest for a few more years, Julie fled to Shillong. In Shillong, Julie was rescued from a bad situation in a hotel by a man (she did not really explain the situation she was caught up in). After the incident in the hotel at Shillong, Julie fled to Kohima where she again met the man who rescued her in Shillong. They fell in love and got married. Fearing torture if she returned to her aunt with her husband, Julie moved in with her husband and his mother. Julie's aunt, nonetheless, found out about Julie's marriage and re-appeared to take her back, against which Julie and her mother-in-law protested. Finally, Julie was left alone by her aunt after this incident. However, soon after, Julie found out that her husband was into drugs. He was sick from the drug addiction and was hospitalised for 9 months after which he died. Julie had no idea of how addicts looked or behaved except that she always wondered about the unusually red eyes of her husband when he returned home at night, tired, and went straight to bed without much conversation. During the nine months of his hospitalisation, Julie never got to see her husband. After her husband's death, Julie's aunt appeared and took her back again. However, Julie did not live with her Aunt for long. The mining in Ladrymbai was blooming and Julie fled to Ladrymbai in search of a livelihood in the mines of Ladrymbai. She met her second husband in the mines. The marriage with her second husband was short-lived as he was physically and emotionally abusive. Julie now is single and wishes to remain so.

It is interesting to note that happy marriages with the migrant man are considered an exception, or attributed to the personal honesty of the migrant man, while the popular discourse remains of that of the fear of the foreigner. The violence and desertion faced by Khasi and Jaintia women however is subsumed in a generic discourse of violence against women as an unfortunate event and is seen as less stark in comparison with that of the abusive migrant husband. The migrant worker is either an honest person who assimilated and became a devoted husband or just another immoral migrant worker who betrayed his wife; this polarity in the judgment meted out to the migrant husband vis. a vis. the abusive tribal husband was very prevalent. The issue of Khasi men who deserted their wives was mostly seen as a result of the affluence that the Khasi men have accumulated by working in the mines. The popular narrative remains that the money has changed the Khasi men and they are no longer like their ancestors who respected women (as discussed in Chapter 5). The desertion of their wives by the Khasi men is even justified in the light of powerlessness experienced by these men as they do not have inheritance rights which make them violent, alcoholic, and irresponsible. It is considered that these men could be reformed if they were given some privileges. Khasi men did not lose their pure Khasi status as a result of leaving their wives. As such, the categorisation of the violent migrant worker as generally untrustworthy vis-à-vis the abusive Khasi man who is not necessarily subjected to a similar generalised judgement remains a reality in the popular discourse of domestic violence, even though in reality the presumed boundaries of these categories are not essential.

A similar polar narrative as it exists for the migrant husband, also exists for Khasi and Jaintia women who are deserted by their husbands but who chose not to remarry (even though divorce is not a taboo in the matrilineal society and the women were free to remarry if they wanted) primarily because they put their children's interests before their own lives.[8] The more women desexualised themselves, the purer they became in public imagination, which is a contradiction for a matrilineal society that granted enough sexual freedom to women. But if women associated themselves with migrant workers, they could be persecuted. For example, few months ago, a Khasi woman was shamed for protesting against an attack on a non-tribal.[9] She had requested the attackers to let the police deal with the case and determine if the non-tribal person was at fault. Strict dress-code against non-tribal dressing by women was imposed by the Khasi Students Union in the 1980s and 1990s, so that Khasi culture would be upheld by women's dressing. This restriction on clothing had ironically excluded the tribal men from being the bearer of culture. Women who did not comply to this restriction were also physically attacked on grounds that these women did not uphold the Khasi culture to stop and resist infiltration of other non-tribal cultures.[10] As such, the tribal society of Meghalaya operated on a double standard with regard to the behaviour of tribal men and women in terms of marriage and also in terms of how they behaved in public.

Sex work, sexual moralities, and mining in Meghalaya

This section analyses the complex gendered realities for the indigenous female sex workers in the Jaintia hills. The attempt here is not to dissociate the exploitative conditions of the sex industry in mining or otherwise across the world that have affected the lives of female sex workers in adverse ways. Existing literature has well established the exploitation inherent in the sex trade industry. Meghalaya has been one of the states in India with the highest rate of HIV among pregnant women and female sex workers, migrant labourers, and truckers being the high-risk population.[11] Similarly the sex work industry in other parts of the world is also not short of such stories – for example – the sex-work industry in Sub Saharan Africa which is full of innumerable stories of female sex workers battling regularly with physical abuse, increasing HIV infections and a high rate of criminalisation, stigmatisation, and poverty.[12] Yet, these exploitative and extremely horrifying demographics of the sex industry does not nullify the complex experiences of sex-workers of feeling empowered as well as disempowered, who are influenced by and also are directly influencing the wider reality of the sex work industry. Different organisations have also been doing extensive work on the health of female sex workers, which has gone a long way to mitigate certain infrastructural problems of the sex-work industry. However, the moral compass of viewing sex workers continues to exist – and this moral compass is what I argue is complex – especially when viewed from the sex workers own point of view on sex work and in terms of their perspectives of how they have experienced the society as sex workers – especially in the kind of responses they receive from their clients, meaning – how the clients, who otherwise consist of "regular" members of the society, view sexual morality for themselves and also for the sex workers of whom they are clients. This understanding subverts the typical societal perspective of sex workers as being immoral.

The sex workers that I interviewed were compelled to join sex work because of the dire situations in their lives. Sunu, Amie, Rihun, and Julie all took to sex work finding no other viable alternative to support themselves, especially after their divorce. However, it is important to understand that the whole process of their engagement in sex work, which starts with sad and unfavourable circumstances that provide the reason for joining sex work, is not characterised by either a linear depressing sad story or an extraordinary story of victory. Although the start of their engagement with sex work could be unfortunate as these women were compelled to do something that they did not want to do, the whole story need not be one of defeat, irrespective of whether the women continued to be sex workers or not. Also, there are women who took to sex work as a choice without being compelled by circumstances to do so and rather joined sex work for the huge sum of money and the luxurious lifestyle that being a sex worker during the mining boom provided them with. The experience as a sex worker for these women, as such, has been a complex one. This complexity consists in the happiness of being financially independent and being able to access a modern lifestyle and cultural freedom from the pressure of being an ideal Khasi and Jaintia woman. These positive aspects were accompanied by a desire for respect and recognition that they are denied because of their occupation as well as some amount of shame and guilt that they have to cope-up with as what they do is not acceptable to the society (or even to themselves) in terms of what they think through their primary socialisation of being a good woman is. These contradictory feelings are often revealed in terms of the negotiations that women make with themselves and also their families and wider society and in their inter-personal relationships. These negotiations involve hiding their work from their parents and children, doing occasional sex work in times of need, looking for a more deeper and more permanent relationship with their clients beyond just having sex, or even looking for alternative occupations to enable them to leave sex work for good.

For Sunu, when her divorce happened, mining ban had shut down all the businesses. The household income that used to come from Sunu's mother's small vegetable shop had suddenly gone down from the previous 5,000rs per month to less than a thousand rupees. Survival was becoming difficult and Sunu was compelled to take up sex work. Amie too joined the sex industry with the help of her friends, as did Rihun, after her husband died and she was left with no other option to be able to raise her baby. Julie had first started a small restaurant in Ladrymbai, but when the income from the restaurant went down after the ban, she opened a massage parlour for men and offered sexual services. These women chose not to tell their family members about their involvement in the sex industry and devised different ways to negotiate with their children and parents regarding their work. Sunu decided to tell her mother and daughter that she does some office work in the mines. Her mother continues to get suspicious when Sunu returns home late and pesters her with questions such as what kind of an office she is engaged in that makes her work till 8 in the evening in a place like Meghalaya. However, the big money that the sex workers were earning enabled them to convince their family members, for, their contribution was making a difference to the household's quality of life. Petra Mahy (2011) speaks of a similar situation in Indonesia where a majority of the sex workers in the East Kalimantan mines were divorced or separated with children whom they support through their work. Their children tend to live with grandparents in their hometowns. Many of the sex workers did not tell their families about the kind of work they do; instead, they informed them that they work in shops, hotels, as domestic servants or run small businesses. Or in some cases, even when the families knew, no-one really talked about it.

The personal characteristics of the sex-worker determined the level of pay they received in the Jaintia hills. It ranged from 10,000 to 30,000 INR per night. The amount of pay that the sex worker received automatically categorised them into different classes. The sex workers were free to decide how regularly they wanted to take clients or what kind of clients. The profiles of customers were varied, starting from mine owners to mine workers. During the mining boom days, almost everyone had enough money to buy sex work and the higher they paid, the better chances they had in getting access to the high profile of sex workers.

> During the mining days, I used to earn a lot! Minimum 10 to 15k per night! You would not believe that a simple looking man who looks just as a guy next door, who does not look ric, h even used to give 10 k to 15 k! Girls such as us were high priced. I am not saying that I am very beautiful or hot, but I used to be paid very highly, such as say 20k per night, because the customers find me hot (laughs). Even now, if the girl is hot, the customers agree to pay 10k for a night. But if one is not smart, she will be paid only such as say around 2k. If the girl is not hot, the money is also not hot (laughs). However, it is true that during the mining days the demand for sex work was more because the numbers of customers were also high. There was a time when customers were different – you just touch them and they would load you with money, no need of sex! (laughs).
>
> Sunu said

Such as Sunu, Amie too earned around 15,000 to 30,000 INR per night.

> … We got customers through Dalals (brokers/pimps). The customers were mostly mine owners and were tribal. However, there were also a small number of non-tribal mine owners. Once, three of my friends and I got a very good deal. We were taken to the 5-star hotel in Guwahati and were paid 30k for the night. I used to dress in jeans and tee shirt when I met my customers. The hotter and more modern we looked, the smarter our behaviour was, the higher we were paid. Nobody would wear traditional clothes because that was considered a turn off. It was not just sex work but an entire luxurious lifestyle.

It is interesting to note here that the impression of a modern sex worker stands quite in contrast to the image of an ideal Khasi woman. A highly priced sex worker desired by the men, including the Khasi and Jaintia men, was the one who looked modern, wore jeans and shirts, high heels, and modern ornaments. This stands in stark contrast to the 1980s masculine policing of women that prohibited women from wear nothing other than traditional clothes. For the Khasi and Jaintia sex workers, this exposure to a new self-expression also provided them a sense of freedom and agency, in having access to a space that allowed them to be desirable beyond traditional dictates and enabled them to have financial abundance in the sex workspace.

> … That's why many did it just for fun and for that lavish lifestyle. Parties, alcohol, cigarettes, music, big ear-rings and what not! Girls got paid 2k just for drinking with customers with no sex. Dance bars, parties, colourful clothes, lipsticks, high heels – that kind lifestyle bloomed during those days.
>
> Amie shared

However, after the mining ban, the sex work industry became less functional with the purchasing power of the clients going down. At the time of conducting my interview, modern looking sex workers still got clients who were ready to pay them around 10k for a night, but for the less successful sex workers, employment became scarce.

The sex workers that I met have different opinions regarding their involvement with sex work and how they viewed the moral question. For example, Sunu did not look like a victim, with a wide laugh, boundless self -love and confidence, without tears in her eyes. She did not fit into the image of a vulnerable sex worker who could evoke an immediate paternalistic sympathy in people's heart. As Sunu was narrating her story, her unapologetic and audacious acceptance for her work pushed one of my translators into an uncomfortable zone. She looked at me with embarrassed eyes and instructed Sunu to share only as much was asked. I intervened asking Sunu to continue as she liked.

Sunu replied "Oh yes, I will. I am not saying anything that is not true, there is nothing to be so ashamed of."

At the same time, no matter however much she owned her identity as a sex worker, Sunu did not want her daughter to be hurt or her mother to know that she is a sex worker. She hoped to get out of sex work soon because she thought it would be disgraceful for her daughter to later find out that her mother was a sex worker. She disapproved of the betrayal that women such as her had suffered with their husbands and expects loyalty if she ever marries again. As such, Sunu's narrative indicates the complex overlap between different categories of morality and justice that she navigates between, as a sex worker, a woman, and a wife in the mining society that she is a part of.

Julie, who had herself approached me to share her story, shared with a smile how her business had given her the respect that she never felt belonged to her. Julie said,

> The men like me and want to come back again and again (laughs). I make enough money. I feel more independent since the time I moved to Ladrymbai. This is what I call a life! The rest was a misery. I am single now and I want to remain single. I don't want to be with any man any more. I like it the way it is now.

For many others, sex work remains a professional option that they can fall back to as and when required as a contingency plan. A few others, such as Amie, have used the money earned through sex work to open up their own alternative retail business, or are still working towards accumulating enough money for this purpose. However, a few other women that I met were extremely unhappy about having to do sex work but felt that there were no other options. Rihun, for example, expressed her utter despair at having been involved in sex work, which she no longer wants to do and hence is looking for alternative business opportunities but so far, in vain.

"I was not happy to do it, but I had to. I cried in front of my 1st client. He felt bad for me and did not touch me. He gave me 16,000rs and advised me to get out of this trade." Rihun shared. Rihun wishes to go to Shillong to buy goods for a small shoes retail store that she plans to start, but as she has never been to Shillong, she is scared to get lost on her way while traveling alone, and, there is no body that she knows and trusts who can take her to Shillong and bring her back to the Jaintia hills safe.

The different shades of these narratives uncover a gendered reality of the sex work industry in the mining diaspora where women are trying to negotiate their lives in a complex web of pride, honour, guilt, and survival.

Changing sexual moralities

While big sums of money, independence, modern clothes, freedom from abusive husbands did characterise the sex workspace that gave a sense of agency and control over the lives of women which made it a choice for many in the Jaintia hills, women also nurtured a desire to leave sex work as soon as she found a husband. Such a pattern of the rise of new sexual moralities or new modes of negotiating sexual relationships in a mining context has been discussed by various scholars. For example, Bryceson et.al (2013) has discussed different types of wife-styling prevalent in the goldmines of Tanzania which need not be based on the conventional idea of prostitution. These wife-styling processes took off at ad hoc setting such as the bush, or the girl's accommodation, at a friend's place. The term wife was very loosely used in the mining settlements in Tanzania, which also included temporary sexual partners, although the girls aspired to get a permanent husband through this process (Bryceson, Jønsson and Verbrugge, 2013). A hierarchy between bar girls and contract wives existed in the Tanjung Hijau mining settlement in Indonesia where the effort of the sex workers always aimed to elevate themselves from the status of a bar girl to a contract wife and then eventually to a permanent wife (Ramanie Kunanayagam, 2003).[13] Most of the female sex workers had common life histories of abusive husbands, broken families, early pregnancies, and other economic constraints which pushed them into sex work for survival. They call themselves *wanita bisnis* meaning business women, whereas, the community viewed them as *wanita nakal* meaning bad women. The effort to reach the status of a contract wife was to shed the tag of a bad woman to become a good woman. They also referred to themselves as *butterflies of the night* who borrowed husbands and fluttered from one attraction point to another like butterflies. The bar girls often referred to themselves as girlfriends and also as real wives when they were living with a man. The luxury and expensive lifestyle that they could afford from sex work and through the high-profile clients gave them a superior status to housewives, market vendors, or domestic helps. Many of the sex workers, especially contract wives, who live with their clients, employ villagers as domestic helps. The higher the profile of the company employee that the sex workers are related to, the higher is the status of the sex worker (Ramanie Kunanayagam, 2003).

In Meghalaya, sexual and intimate relationships that emerged during the mining boom were not monogamous and operated very differently from polygamy or polyamory. Despite the contextual difference, what remains common between the Jaintia hills of Meghalaya and other cases discussed in the international literature points to the similarity in the change in the definitions of sexual relationship and a new set of grey areas around sexual morality that people were trying to negotiate, especially with respect to the stories of friendship and wife-styling that happened between sex workers and their clients in the Jaintia hills which redefined the moral compass of intimate relationship.

> Everyone was sleeping with everyone. The wives knew that their husbands were sleeping around and were friends with prostitutes but they did not complain because the men were getting a lot of money for the house; women were happy with the money and men would throw money at their wives just to keep her mouth shut about his sleeping around. It was such an open secret, and nobody seemed to mind![14]

However, once the massive income inflow from the mines was abruptly broken with the mining ban, these wife-styling or unconventional sexual relationships came to be seen as outrageous by the wives who tried to restore monogamy into their relationships.

> The wives would go to the women's house where their husbands are having a good time with their girlfriends; they will kick his ass back saying –"There is no food to eat at the house, and here you are enjoying yourself with your slut, you f*****" Sunu shared with a big laughter.

Many female sex workers also looked for a boyfriend in the mines, and many men ended up marrying sex workers leaving their former wives, or in some other case, they preferred to have a different kind of a wife-style with them. Amie met her second husband, a driver in the mines, who also used to be her regular client. Rihun too married her second husband who used to be her client after a year of dating him. Rihun shared how her husband had multiple wives in multiple places and not all the wives knew of each other. She was aware that her second husband was already married to one woman, but she did not expect him to have multiple wives.

> …he has many wives and keeps each one separately and secretly. Some wives do not even know about the other wives. Even I don't know how many wives he has in total. After getting married to him, I left sex work. But he does not give me enough money. He is going to retire in the next 8 months, and then we will have even less money…. In the midnight his phone rings and he talks whispering on the phone. He lies to me that it is some theft case or some other case that someone was calling him about. But I know very well that it must be one of his other wives who called him.

Rihun shared how her relationship has not been satisfying: neither emotionally nor sexually nor financially, which is why she plans to leave her husband as soon as she finds an alternate source of income as she does not wish to go back to sex work.

Intimate relationships, including marriage, or other modes of wife-styling were judged on various grounds of loyalty, or financial support or sexual and emotional fulfilment, as expressed in Rihun and Sunu's narratives, which demanded fulfilment in either one or more of these factors. This also explains the long-term romantic relationships that were established between the sex worker and their clients which did not necessarily end in marriage. Rihun had a long-term relationship with her first client who had financially supported her to help her get out of sex work when she expressed her dissatisfaction of having to take up sex work against her will. Many of such relationships navigate between friendship, goodwill, and sexual relationship between sex workers and their clients, who invest in the relationships that they share with the sex worker with gifts and other romantic gestures, beyond the regular fee for sexual services.

> Some clients fall in love with me but they don't promise to marry (laughs), some gift expensive things such as rings, who would not enjoy that! (laughs) We become good friends and also go out together you know. This guy who is waiting for me outside now, he is also a very good guy who comes to me; we are very good friends

said Sunu pointing to the young man who was waiting for Sunu to go out on a date with her after her interview with me.

These experiences in the mining diaspora unveil the process in which a mining economy shapes sexualities and sexual-moralities. Embedded in complexities of love and violence, grief and empowerment, hope, and survival, the sex work business that grew exponentially with the mining industry of Meghalaya introduced a host of unsettling changes into sexual and romantic relationships, marking a significant departure from traditional matrilineal culture and gender relations in the state. It exposed women to a range of possibilities of negotiating their sexualities which were empowering and dehumanising at the same time, and how women navigated through these possibilities, shaped these possibilities in turn.

On bringing the analysis of this chapter together, something very interesting emerges. First, in the context of domestic violence against women, the category of the ideal migrant man is the one who sticks to his tribal wife permanently without being violent, the morality that drives this is attributed to his personal character. The immoral migrant violent husband who abandoned his wife, on the contrary, is blamed for his membership of his Nepali community which can also be attributed to the fact that Meghalaya's inter-ethnic and political history with Nepal's migration inflow to the state has not been pleasant. The immorality and violence of the Khasi men, in contrast, is blamed on the coal industry, in which the economic reason rather a cultural criterion defines this understanding of morality for the Khasi men. Second, the ideal Khasi and Jaintia women in a conventional relationship remain the traditional, selfless, hardworking, and de-sexualised women: they act as a woman who, if she loses her husband, chooses not to marry for the sake of her children, even though she is free to do so. There is a remarkable moral shift when it comes to the "ideal sex-worker" that men desire who need not reflect any of the characteristics of the traditionally ideal Khasi and Jaintia women- in fact she is considered boring and paid less if she is traditional-looking. Monogamous morality was disappearing, and loyalty came to be measured with a different parameter in the changing wife-styling processes that took place in the Jaintia hills during the mining boom. Money and the idea of urban luxury shaped the sex work and alternative wife-styling processes. These two different and contradictory universes existed in the same socio-cultural context of the Jaintia hills, where the same people took on different roles or behaved differently when placed in these entirely distinct realities – and operated in a complexity where worldviews of these different universes kept overlapping, colliding or even syncing into each other, with different permutations and combinations of the cultural, social, economic and the political. This shaped the discourse of morality in the gendered intersection of these narratives of intimacies and violence in the mines.

The following chapter deals with the other side of this gendered experience, that is, women's experience of love and marriage in the mainstream matrilineal society.

Notes

1 The Shillong Times. 2015. Mizoram Tops, Meghalaya stands second. 2011 Census reveals high divorce, separation cases among NE cases. Available at http://theshillongtimes.com/2012/03/23/teen-pregnancy-cause-of-high-fertility-rate-in-mlaya/ (accessed on 15th September 2019).
2 See Ladrymbai. Available on https://www.revolvy.com/page/Lad-Rymbai (accessed on 6th July 2019).
3 See, Economy ethnicity and Migration in Meghalaya http://amanpanchayat.org/wp-content/uploads/2018/01/PEI_meghalaya.pdf (accessed on 21st June 2018).
4 Interview with Rikil, aged 30, Jowai, West Jaintia Hills.
5 Patricia Mukhim. 2013. Non Tribals in Meghalaya: Non-Citizens or Half Citizens? Available at, http://www.theshillongtimes.com/2013/03/22/non-tribals-in-meghalaya-non-citizens-or-half-citizens/ (accessed on 20th June 2018).
6 Interview with Cherry (name changed) 45 years old from Wapung village, East Jaintia district.
7 'A Statistical Analysis of Child Marriage in India based on Census 2011'.
See, http://ncpcr.gov.in/showfile.php?lang=1&level=1&sublinkid=1214&lid=1463
This report was released by the National Commission for Protection of Child Rights in collaboration with a non-government organisation called Young lives (accessed on June 2019).
8 Interview with Merry (name changed, 45 years, East Jaintia District).
9 Interview with H. H. Mohrmen.
10 India: Violence against non-tribals in Meghalaya – Shame on you Shillong! and Patricia Mukhim on non tribals in Meghalaya – non citizens or half citizens? Available at http://www.sacw.net/article6272.html (accessed on 7th July 2019).
11 Shillong Times. December 2018. HIV High alert in Meghalaya Manipur.
See, http://www.theshillongtimes.com/2017/12/07/hiv-high-alert-in-meghalaya-manipur/ (accessed on March 2019).
Shillong Times. November 2013. Meghalaya worryingly susceptible to HIVand AIDS.
See, http://www.theshillongtimes.com/2013/11/30/mlaya-worryingly-susceptible-to-hiv-aids/ (accessed on 22nd June 2018).
12 See, Adele Baleta. 2014. Lives on the line: Sex work in Sub Saharan Africa. https://www.thelancet.com/journals/lancet/article/PIIS0140-6736(14)61049-7/fulltext (accessed on 22nd June 2018).
13 See, Ramanie Kunanayagam. 2003. Sex Workers: Their Impact On and Interaction with the Mining Industry. Available at, http://siteresources.worldbank.org/INTOGMC/Resources/336099-1163605893612/kumanayagamsexworkers.pdf (accessed on 23rd June 2018).
14 Interview with Sunu, 30 years old and Amie, 28 years old.

7

GENDERING LOVE, MARRIAGE, AND REPRODUCTIVE HEALTH

The question of continuity and change

The chapter discusses the love, marriage, and reproductive life of women in Meghalaya across generations. It begins with a discussion on the traditional dating styles, marriage, and divorce systems in the Jaintia hills of Meghalaya and then compares the contemporary dating style and marriage systems in Meghalaya with the traditional practices. The role of Christianity in introducing changes to the traditional practices of marriage is discussed in this context. The changes from a night-visiting marriage system in the past to the contemporary matrilocal and the neo-local residence system of the present are central to the discussion of changing marriage practices since residence pattern is an integral characteristic of the matrilineal marital arrangement in Meghalaya which marks it out from any other patrilineal-patrilocal marriage system in India. The chapter then discusses the reaction of men and women's reaction to the recent "Meghalaya Compulsory Registration of Marriage Act, 2012" that announced a radical departure from the customary sprit of Khasi/Jaintia marriage systems. The last two sections of the chapter discuss the reproductive life of the Khasi-Jaintia women and how despite so many changes that can be seen in marriage, divorce, and dating lifestyles in Meghalaya across time, what has remained unchanged is the socio-cultural and religious stigma on abortion and on the use of modern contraception. This discussion is integrated with the issue of teenage pregnancies and increasing HIV infections in Meghalaya which has markedly increased in recent times, especially after the coal boom and how this aspect has been a primary reason for the Khasi-Jaintia women's disempowerment.

Love, marriage, and divorce in the past

What is mostly common among traditional matrilineal groups across the world is the secondary position that conjugal bonds occupy in comparison to one's membership to their matrilineage. Attaching oneself to more to a marriage partner at the expense of one's matrilineage is frequently disapproved (Takyi and Gyimah, 2007). It is not a regular practice for a married couple to pool income together under traditional matriliny. A matrilineal marital arrangement, as such, while it gives woman some level of autonomy

 DOI: 10.4324/9781003149460-8

from her spouse, also weakens her conjugal bonds. Like many other matrilineal communities across the world, the traditional Khasi/Jaintia society too was based on a similar marital arrangement that places a superior status to matrilineal bonds compared to conjugal ties. However, Meghalaya has been witnessing a gradual change in its marriage system from a matrilocal residence system to a neo-local residence, urbanisation, and consumerism introduced by the coal boom. This section discusses the love, marriage, and dating lifestyle in the Jaintia hills among the older and middle-aged generation before delving into the contemporary changes in dating and marriage among the younger generation.

The term "Poikila" among the Jaintias means cohabitation and procreation (Joshi, 2004). Marriage was not compulsory among the Jaintia people. Traditionally, cohabitation was practised and marriage was not essential. Children born from premarital sex or outside formal marriages were accepted without discrimination in the Khasi/Jaintia society. Co-habitation and relationships outside of marriage continue to be a part of the culture of Meghalaya and continue to exist (Mukhim, 2009). As such, marriage as an institutionalised idea is a very new addition to the Khasi/Jaintia culture. However, if one wanted to marry, a marriage offer was usually made by a man. For love marriages, the matter was discussed by the parents and maternal uncles. The maternal uncle approached the parents of the girl with a marriage proposal and fixed the marriage after discussion with the woman's parents (Joshi, 2004).

The Jaintia marriage system is based on rigid clan exogamy. A traditional Jaintia marriage was characterised by a "night visit system" in which the husband visited his mother-in-law's house after dusk to spend the night with his wife and leave next day early morning to his mother's house. He would not eat or smoke in his in-laws house, for, it was considered bad behaviour as none of his earnings were invested in supporting his in-laws. The system of visiting husbands was practised more by the traditional Niamtre religious household than the Christian households (Gurdon, 1914 qtd. in Chakravarty, undated). The night visit marriage system is also based on the idea that a Jaintia household belongs to a woman and her husband will continue to visit her only at the night as long as the marriage bond existed; which also implied that if a husband stopped visiting his wife, it was taken as a proceeding sign of separation and divorce. In a night visit marriage system, the children hardly saw their father. The mother had total control of her children; so much so that her sons first belonged to her and stayed with her even after they got married (Basaiawmoit, 1987). Mitali Chakravarty has also discussed what is called a "relaxed night visit system" which continues to be practised among the Niamtres of Jowai of West Jaintia hills even though the traditional night visit system has almost vanished.[1] In a relaxed night visit system, the husbands take food in their wives' house and contribute some of their earnings to their in-laws' household.

The freedom that women enjoyed in choosing their spouses and partners is what marked the Khasi/Jaintia marriage system unique. Each woman that I had interviewed had a love marriage without any serious objection from their parents.

"More than 20 boys gave me letters, but I did not like any. I showed all the letters to my mother. I told the boys that if you like me, come and talk to my mother, otherwise no use" shared Mary (name changed, 75 years old). But she changed her mind when she met her to-be husband who came as a guest to their house. Unlike every other man who approached her and about whom she shared with her mother, she decided to keep her interest in her to be-husband a secret until her mother figured out that Mary was visibly pregnant. They were married for 18 years until Mary's husband died and Mary remarried her present husband who is a Nepali migrant mine worker. All of Mary's children, except her youngest child, were born to her first husband.

Although elders' approval was extremely significant in the past, it did not pose any obstacle because only in rare instances did elders object to their children's choice of partners. And even if in some instances parents and elders refused to acknowledge a couple's relationship, the couple would continue to live together anyway and sooner or later the elders accepted the couple's decision to be together. However, although the night visit system was a norm in the past, there were also exceptional situations where the husband permanently moved into the wife's house. For example, when Bliss (65 years old, Ladrymbai) expressed her desire to marry her boyfriend who was an orphan, her grandmother refused to accept the relationship. Irrespective, Bliss continued her relationship with her boyfriend who later moved in with her and Bliss and her partner continued their relationship without ever formally getting married. Bliss's grandmother eventually accepted Bliss's partner. It was a very common practice for couples falling in love without their parent's approval to settle together and be later accepted by their elders. However, it was also equally true that a woman had to give in to her parents' wishes even if she did not like the man her parents would like her to marry. In a situation like this, she could refuse to have sex with the man as an expression of her dismissal and the man would withdraw from marrying her. As such allowing a man of her parent's choice to have sex with her was considered as an approval for marriage by the woman.[2]

As simple was the system of marriage and cohabitation, was so the process of Divorce. Divorce has been fairly common in the Jaintia hills since. Traditionally, divorce was completed in a day through the village authority known as the Sangot. According to the Sangot tradition, the party seeking divorce offered a 50paisa coin and betel-nut to the Sangot and the news of the couple getting divorced was publicised by the Sangot the same evening. A Jaintia woman could also forcibly take a divorce from her unwilling husband by a custom called *dat-san-shyien* (dat-e throw, san=five and shyiea-spicces, thus meaning "to throw five pieces"). In this practice, all that the woman had to do was to simply throw five pieces of cowrie shells, called pasbe, on her husband to divorce him. Likewise, for a man who wanted to divorce his wife without her consent, he simply needed to tear off a betel leaf and make a proclamation for divorce. For divorces that lacked mutual consensus, the divorcing party had to offer a compensation amount to the party who was unwilling to divorce. The amount of compensation was assessed by the village elders and varied from village to village. Following a divorce, the husband had to leave the wife's home, including his children and the house that he built. The children stayed with their mother as members of her matrilineage. Should she die, her matrilineage would traditionally care for them (Kusum and Bakshi, 1982, pp. 85–90). However, in contemporary Jaintia hills, the traditional divorce practices like the Sangot and *dat-san-shyien* are no longer practised. Although remarriage for both men and women is common, Leonetti et al. (2007) argued that under matriliny, it is mostly men who leave their wives as compared to women who left their husbands. That's because, as opposed to men who are more mobile, women prefer stability in a marriage which requires help from men to keep the household going. This is also the reason why women remarry to keep help coming from men (Leonetti, et al., 2007, p. 863).

Role of religion across generations

Conversion to Christianity changed the socio-cultural practices including the marriage system in the whole of Meghalaya, Jaintia hills being no exception. What exactly changed, at which historical juncture, is a difficult task to recover, since the trajectory of these changes was not comprehensively documented and also because Christianisation had already started to influence the region at the beginning of the nineteenth century.[3] As such, these changes due to Christianisation have been happening for more than 100 years, no detailed documentation of which is available. Manorama Sharma (2004) has argued how early documentation by the British and the Welsh missionaries lack details about the exact indigenous terms of traditional Khasi institutions coupled with the inherent bias of the British officials in understanding the traditional governance system of the Khasi people. The lack of information on the gradual evolution of Khasi governance in these early writings is a problem (Sharma, 2004) which is also a problem when I try to understand the recent cultural evolution. Without much details on how religious restrictions operated in the couples lives in the past on a daily basis, what I recovered from the interviews that I conducted was that religious codes continue to be strictly followed as they have been since a long time, and inter-religious marriages are not still not encouraged. In the event of inter-religious marriage between a Christian and a traditional Niamtre believer, there is a pressure for conversion to Christianity after marriage.

Until the conversion of the non-Christian partner to Christianity has happened, the marriage is not solemnised or recognised by the church no matter however long the couple are married or living together, with or without children.[4] Instances of divorces over conflict on conversion have also been common.[5] Cohabitation became less acceptable with the advent of Christianity that prescribes marriage (Bamon, 2004; Glasier et al., 2006; Mukhim, 2009). Protestant churches also punish co-habiting couples by suspending them from church membership for half a year to allow them to "repent of their sins" (Vincent, 1978) and in the Catholic church such couples are not permitted to receive Communion until they have confessed their "sins" and agree to confirm their marriage in the Catholic church (Mukhim, 2007a).

Other than conversion to Christianity, urbanisation and other practical difficulties encountered when the spouses belonged to different villages have replaced the traditional night visit marriage system with a system where the husband permanently moves into his wife's house after marriage while maintaining frequent visits to his matrikins. Although this practice of moving permanently to the wives' house was more practised by the Christian households in Meghalaya, the Niamtre households have also come to practicing it in contemporary times. The influence of Christian ideals that prizes male authority in nuclear household and exposure to patrilineal cultures have led to change in opinions, especially among men, who now favour patrilocal marriage system to matrilocal ones which continue to be a subject of debate (see Chapter 5).

Love, marriage, and divorce in contemporary times

Love, marriage, and divorce in contemporary times have seen a marked difference from the past in Meghalaya. The idea of choice in romantic union for the younger generation today (those below 30 years old) operates very differently from the older generations (who are above 60 years old). Though the general narrative of the older generation expressed an element of choice that the women had in choosing their partners, it also emphasised the role of elders in their decision-making. None talked about multiple casual affairs. Most of the women expressed about their busy life that did not really leave time for them to think about love. However, that existed with the possibility that whenever a woman liked someone, she could choose to have a love life even though it was not the priority of her youth as compared to her responsibility to the household. For the middle-aged generation, the pattern of love story changed from "having no time to love" to "secretly dating their lovers in fear of being found out by their parents." The secrecy was also taken as a matter of respect and fear for the elders which was considered a healthy necessity irrespective of the fact that the freedom to love was characteristic of the Khasi/Jaintia culture. Today's love stories in the Jaintia hills on the contrary are characterised by a digital world where a considerable number of the present generation have met their partners through social media and show preference for multiple affairs until they will settle for "the one." The secrecy in dating is no longer a frequent occurrence. The change in dating lifestyle often gives rise to conflict between the younger generation and their parents.

> Today children are different... Don't know if their parents know or not, but they don't hide their love life like we used to do. They don't fear that someone might report to their parents. We used to be scared... it is very different. We used to hide and meet, secretly, scared that our parents might find out...

shared Zubi (name changed), 36years, Umladhkhur village.

Because of these differing perspective, the dating life of the younger generation remains a topic that is executed in silence and secrecy primarily because the younger generation think their parents would not understand their dating preference.

"I am close to my mother, but not that much you know? She does not have any idea of half of the things that I do (laughs)... I have not told her about my present boyfriend yet" shared Stacy (25 years old, East Jaintia District).

Stacy (name changed, 25 years old) was helping me translate the interviews. Every day after we wrapped up our fieldwork, Stacy's boyfriend came to pick her up in the evening and after spending few hours together he dropped her back home. Although Stacy wishes that she could keep her mother informed whenever she goes out with her boyfriend, she fears that her mother would not approve of it, which is why, she continues to spend her time with her boyfriend in secret because she is sure that her mother would not approve of it.

"My boyfriend drops me home at around 9pm everyday... if not for work, my mother would not allow me to be out until 9 pm regularly. So I do not tell her that I am with him... The other option is that I invite my boyfriend home. Which I do, but I can't do that frequently you know. There are a lot of cultural restrictions on women even though we are a matrilineal society" Stacy said. A lot of these inhibitions from Stacy's mother also come from the fact that Stacy broke up with her ex-boyfriend after 7 years of being together which was not taken well by either of their families who knew about their relationship all along.

Like Stacy, most of the youngsters that I interviewed preferred not to share about their dating preferences with their elders primarily because of differing ideologies. Like any modern-day dating style, the youngsters today would rather seek more stability after marriage. They treat dating more as an experiment in the relationship to take it to the level of marriage or date for the sake of dating without any future goals of marriage. As such the outcome of a dating relationship is no longer very predictable or clear as it was in the earlier times. This contemporary dating style marks an interesting departure from the older generation. The older generation dated for a shorter while before marriage. Although divorce and multiple marriages were not (and still are not) a taboo in the past, long-term casual dating was not a regular or normal. The idea of choice was more limited to picking one's partner to settle down and not to experiment in relationships before getting serious about settling down, even though marriage was a lesser important matter than one's membership to matrilineage.

Madhusmita Das (2001) conducted a study of matrilineal marriage practices in Meghalaya in the year 2001, about a shift to a preference to neonatal household among younger women (below 30 years old) in her study. The younger women in Das's study preferred a neo-local household after marriage as they believed that living with her mother restricted a deeper bond from developing between her and her husband as the husband did not feel too secure living with his in laws. Dependence on her mother who had the final word on the day-to-day conduct of the house was also another reason, why the women preferred to have her own independent space free of any interference after marriage. This view of the younger women is a sharp contrast to the women in above 30 year age group who preferred to stay with their mothers post marriage as they believed that living with their mothers offered them greater help and support in times of pregnancy as well as in fulfilling in day to day chores (Das, 2001). Das (2001) also noted that 21% of her female respondents who followed the traditional family system lived in rural areas, whereas almost half of the women living outside of a traditional matrilineal family pattern also lived in the rural areas. This makes the transition, according to Das (2001) more complex than just a mere outcome of urbanisation and modernisation process. Das (2001) also noted that the youngest daughters who are the carrier of the traditional matrilineal system of Meghalaya are also very likely to move out of traditional matriliny and that women with higher educational status were more likely move out of a traditional matrilineal family as opposed to women with a lower level of education who were more likely to follow traditional matriliny. On marriage with a man who is more educated than the woman, the tendency to move out of traditional matrilineal marriage and setting up one's own neo-local house also increased. Likewise, urban women holding professional and service sector jobs were also likely to move out of a traditional matrilineal marriage residence system in the same way how the husband's professional job status pulled both rural and urban women out of a traditional matrilineal marriage residence system. On the contrary, if husbands worked in the traditional agricultural sector, women were more likely to be following traditional matrilineal residence system. Das (2001) also found that age was a determining factor here. Women who were above 35 years of age were more likely to be following traditional matrilineal residence whereas women below 25 years of age were more likely to follow a neo-local residence pattern.

Das's fieldwork is nearly 20 years old from today, which means that the younger women who she interviewed were at least 40 years old when I conducted this study. As such they fit into the category of middle-aged women for this research. Hence, for this study they denote the generation between the older and the younger ones and also the generation who were in their adolescence in the 1990s, a period in which the whole world and India opened up to privatisation and liberalisation and Meghalaya in particular was being moulded into a capitalist patriarchal ideology introduced by the coal economy. Das's (2001) category of the "above 30 years age group" of women are now in their 60s, which means they represent the older generation of women above 55 years for this research. The contrasting views of the then younger (now middle aged) generation and the then middle-aged (now older) generation in their preferences for matrilineal residence patterns further establishes the argument of this book, on how the mining exposure had introduced new ideas of western and urban patriarchal values that were imbibed by the now middle-age generation who were born and brought up in the era of the mining boom, that stands in sharp contrast with the older generation who continued to hold onto traditional beliefs of matriliny.

Das's (2001) work on the preference of the younger generation for neolocal residence holds relevance for the younger generation interviewed for this study. With modern values of individualism battling with the traditional values in the contemporary Meghalayan society and more love marriages happening irrespective of religious restrictions, changes in residence pattern with marriage followed by changes in the management of family property have become very significant.

Rikil (35 years old, West Jaintia district) shared that his youngest sister who is also the Khadduh of his family had a love marriage and she moved out of the house to live with her husband in Shillong.[6] She was willing to give up on all her rights of being the custodian of the family property, if that was required for her to move in with her husband.

> Nobody can stop you if you want to move out… the tradition is not to force you to follow rules.. one can try to make the girl understand but if she wants to move out, it is her call…if the husband is not earning well, the women might still think before deciding….but if the husband has a good job and is capable of supporting her, she would not worry about moving out to live with him at all.[7]

Rikil shared that often the youngest daughter has to give up on her rights and move in with her husband if she enters an inter-religious marriage – especially if she marries a Christian person being a Hindu herself. However, there are also instances where the youngest daughter might want to live away from the ancestral household for her work or with her husband in a neo-local residence (with the exception of inter-religious marriages) and still carry on her duties as the Khadduh from a distance, if the family agrees to such an arrangement.

Stacy (25year old) explained,

> If I want to have my own house after marriage, I can, even if I am the youngest in the family. In that case my elder sister can stay with my mother…I would also like to know who my mother would feel more comfortable to live with, and accordingly she can decide, even if in favour of my elder sister over me…it is not hard and fast for me…

If the youngest daughter gives up on her responsibilities and moves out to live with her husband and allows her uncles and brother to take care of the family, she could take back her responsibility on the death of her parents provided the fact that her brothers, uncles or other sisters are incapable of taking care of the family property by themselves.[8] There also have been instances that maternal uncles and brothers of the Khadduh take care of the family property since the Khadduh stays away from the family for her studies, until her return.[9]

Another major shift in the family dynamics as a result of the mining boom are newer conflict surfacing among male and female kinsand siblings regarding distribution of income earned from ancestral land. A lot of family land has been leased out for mining, the whole process of which remains under the access and control of the men of the family, including the income earned from mining on the ancestral land. There have been accusations that there are conflicts between the male and female siblings over lack of equal distribution of the income earned from the coal. Rikil explained,

> There are cases filed in the court when women have complained that their brothers do not share equally the income that comes from the coal mining done from the ancestral family land…the men refuse to give equal share of the money because they believe it is them alone who does the work and brings the money home without any involvement of the women, even if she is a khadduh…but these are cases you will not read in reports as people don't like to talk about such family disputes in public… but when you hear them discuss, you know these kind of conflicts appearing in Meghalaya… these conflicts are destroying the traditional household values.

Marriage registration

While Meghalaya was already grappling with such fast force of changes in the family structure, the Government of Meghalaya introduced "The Meghalaya compulsory registration of Marriage Act 2012" that made registration of marriage a compulsory criterion for the whole of Meghalaya. Under this act a married couple has to mandatorily furnish a marriage certificate for all official purposes such as securing a government job to be able to avail benefits secured for married officials. The Compulsory Marriage Registration Act is an interesting development since it clashes with the traditional marriage arrangement of the Jaintia and Khasi people for whom marriage was not essential. Even though in recent years the traditional night visit marriage system has been transformed into a system where the husband joins his wife's family, what has remained common in both situations is the lack of a formal registration of the marriage in a government office. As such, this act introduced a major shift from the past.

The reaction to the Compulsory Marriage Registration Act 2012 has evoked different response from men and women in Meghalaya. What is interesting to note is that these narratives of opinions differ across age groups of men and women which is indicative of their location in the history of (before and after) the coal mining boom in the state.

The only point where both men and women's narrative went against marriage registration is on grounds of being criminalised for marrying under the legal age.

If people in our village get married in the court, half of them will go to jail. Most people are illiterate... they don't know well about legalities of getting married. So they get married early, before the legal age... registration is not a safe option for them' shared Zubi (name changed, 36 year old, Village Umladkhur).

Most of the middle-aged women preferred a marriage registration to stop their husbands from abandoning them, but they are also equally worried that registering the marriage might take away their customary rights. Loki (name changed, 35years, West Jaintia hills), who had recently joined as an Assistant Professor in a university outside of Meghalaya shared the resistance that he faced from his wife in registering their marriage. Loki lives at his workplace city while his wife who works as a school teacher in her village stays with her mother. After marriage Loki had moved into his wife's house. So, whenever he visits Meghalaya, he lives with his wife and frequently visits his own matrikins.

Loki explained,

> I took a lot of time to convince my wife to register our marriage. I needed a marriage certificate to show at my university so that I can avail all the privileges offered under a married employed professorship. But my wife would not just agree to register the marriage. She felt insecure that this might mean her giving up some of her customary rights. It is only after almost a year of negotiation that I convinced her to register our marriage. She is not even the Khadduh (youngest daughter), so imagine how insecure might a Khadduh feel. in many cases registration is the main reason of divorce between couples…they prefer to separate than to register their marriage.

However, most of the educated younger women below 25 years old supported the necessity of registering their marriages not only because they thought a marriage registration might stop men from abandoning their wives easily, but also because they believed a formal legal registration is a stronger and more valid form of recognition of the marriage, apart from its other functional privileges in accessing the benefits of government jobs. At the same time, these women also believe that matriliny as a structure should continue to operate in the Jaintia hills and also in the rest of Meghalaya. The aspiration for the younger women in this sense is to combine aspects of modern law into their lives in such a way that makes the life of women safer which they believe can co-exist with the need to sustain matriliny. As opposed to women who support or resist the idea of formal registration of marriage, the narrative of (primarily middle aged) men showed a unanimous support for the marriage registration, primarily because they feel it will give them more power as husbands and fathers which they lack under traditional matriliny. As such while for men marriage registration was a means to power, for women it is a means to marital security. This general argument of men in favour of marriage registration also has to be understood in the context of the contemporary debates ongoing in Meghalaya, with groups vehemently arguing for the replacement of the matrilineal system with a patrilineal one. As such although the argument by women only implies the need for change in a marriage in functional terms, the argument by men seeks a deeper structural change in matriliny in a way that curtails women's existing right. As such the consensus between men and women concerning marriage registration is not really a consensus at all.

The older generation, on the other hand, did not express any strong opinion on the Marriage Registration Act but believed that it is a decision that later generations have to make whom the marriage act directly concerns. This opinion also came from an understanding where they acknowledged that later generations have a different life situation that did not concern them in their time in the past. For every marriage legally registered now, divorce also has to be done in accordance with formal laws. However, because of the lack of awareness on the act as well as due to people's inhibitions, the marriage act continues to be poorly implemented.

Reproductive health across generations

The issue of the sexual and reproductive health of Khasi/Jaintia women has been a matter of grave concern in Meghalaya. This section discusses the stigma on abortion, stigma, and shame attached to the use of contraceptives embedded in moral, religious, and cultural taboos in Meghalaya which continue to be the major reasons for the indigenous women's lack of control over their bodies. Even after so many forces for change have shook

Meghalaya over the last few decades, what remains the same is the fact of Khasi/Jaintia women's lack of rights, the right to control reproduction, which has worsened over the years.

Meghalaya has one of the highest fertility rates (3.8) in India with a fertility rate of 4.1 among Christian women.[10] A major reason for the rise in fertility has been attributed to the increased high rate of teenage pregnancy.[11] Yet the state continues to significantly lag behind modern contraceptive use and is in need of a 75% increase by 2030 (New, et al., 2017, p. 350). According to the 2015–2016 report by the National Commission for Protection of Child Rights (NCPCR), Meghalaya is one of the states in India with the highest rate of teenage pregnancy (53%) along with Goa (64%) and Mizoram (61%).[12] Many attributes the rise in teenage pregnancy to the mining boom in Meghalaya. A District-Level Family Health Survey (DLHS-4) conducted in 2012–2013 under the Ministry of Health and Family Welfare 2014 found that the majority (55.5%) of women in Meghalaya had an unmet need for contraception which included those with unmet need for limiting (39.7%) and spacing (15.8%) births. Unmet need for spacing included fecund women who were not pregnant, not using any method of family planning and who wanted to wait two or more years for their next birth, or were unsure if they wanted another child, or who wanted another child but were unsure when to have the pregnancy. Unmet need for limiting family sizes included fecund women who were not pregnant, not using any method of family planning and who wanted no more children.[13]

Stigma on abortion and contraception

Roumi Deb (2010) in her study on the use of contraceptives in the Khasi hills of Meghalaya found out that although most of the women she interviewed were aware of the possibility of the use of contraceptives, only half of them used them. The contraceptive prevalence rate in the Khasi hills of Meghalaya is just 4.7 (2.8 for sterilisation and 1.9 for other temporary methods), which is the lowest in the whole of India (Santhya, 2003 qtd. in Deb 2010). The rate of use of modern contraceptives increased with the level of education of women, and the younger group of women between 25 and 35 years old recorded the highest percentage in the use of contraceptives (Deb, 2010). Compared to modern contraceptives, the use of traditional contraceptives was more common. Fear of using modern contraceptives was also expressed by 24.1% women who had never used any contraceptives in their lives also because they thought (among other reasons) that contraceptives might lead to deformities and harm future pregnancies (Deb, 2010). Marak and Bhatnagar (2015) in their work on sexual behaviour and condom use among young women in Meghalaya found out that while pre-marital sex was widely prevalent among young women (54% of the women interviewed in the study), only 38% reported using contraception, while the mean age at first sex of all the respondents was 18 years. 52% of the married women reported never using a condom. Those who did not use condom most of the times reported that they do not have knowledge where to get one. Others who did not use condom were having the opinion that condom was not necessary due to the fact that they or their partners did not like using condoms (Marak and Bhatnagar, 2015). As less as 2–4% could explain all the symptoms of STI or explain all the ways to prevent HIV, even though almost 76–81% had heard of STI and HIV (Marak and Bhatnagar, 2015). Although young women had a sexually active life, they were reluctant to discuss sexual matters due to social stigma on sex-related discussion, fear of parents, and social embarrassment. Only one-fifth of the total two-third of sexually active unmarried women reported a regular partner or boyfriend (Marak and Bhatnagar, 2015).

Even if women want to avoid unwanted pregnancy, they prefer to avoid modern contraceptives. The dismissal for modern contraceptives co-exists with a strong stigma on abortion. As such even if women want to avoid unwanted pregnancies, they prefer using the traditional contraceptive method, regardless of their efficiency. Ferry, 36 years old from Umladkhur village argued,

> At no cost do I want any more children. So my husband ejaculates outside (giggles)...Otherwise I might also had to have many children like the other women in the village... There is no family planning in our village.. That's why women have so many children. Children are seen as gift from God, so nobody goes for abortion. If one aborts, she will be ridiculed and looked down upon by the villagers even though she might not be directly penalised.

In Umladkhur, a general narrative, especially from the lower-income group, was that continuous pregnancy had interrupted their work flow every year. Women left work while they were pregnant and returned to work after delivering the baby.

"I have 9 children from my ex-husband... he left me when I was pregnant with my youngest son...throughout my marriage with him I had to leave my smoked fish work each time I was pregnant and return to work after delivering the baby.. It was hard but I managed..." shared Amie (53 years old, Umladkhur village, West Jaintia hills).

Continuous pregnancies also forced women to leave work and take care of their children, especially after their husbands started earning well in the coal mines.

People interviewed were also aware that a significant proportion of the family income was spent for the maintenance of children and this is a problem in large families.

Stacy (25 years old from Wapung village) shared:

> Giving birth a lot of children has been a problem here...even my sister has 5 children you know. That has been a problem for us. I am the only person working now. Since the mining ban, my mother also has not been able to find much work. My mother was not the youngest daughter to my grand ma, so she did not inherit any land. But she did buy some with her own money. But now after the mining ban, the family's income has gone down. I have always advised my sister to use contraception, but she would not. She thinks using contraception is against God. On the top of that she had a bad husband who never cared. He left her recently. And now she is taking care of all the children alone. I pay for their school fee and clothes and other maintenance cost. But the funds fall short to maintain the house.

60-year-old Rita from Ladrymbai village also shared a similar perspective on children, which confirms that this religious stigma on contraception and childbirth has been a norm for many decades in Meghalaya. Being born in a poor family, Rita used to give all of her earning to her mother. After getting married, she had 7 children with her abusive husband who soon left her, and she was left alone to take care of her children. She struggled with acute financial crisis and frequent shortage of food and often skipped her own meal to feed her children. Being the only earning person with responsibility for her children, it was hard for her to balance paid work and care for her children. She would feed her children in the morning and leave for work. After arriving back home from work, she cooked them dinner. Each one of her 7 children had to drop out of school due to financial difficulties. On asking why she chose to have many children despite such abject poverty, Rita said,

"Nobody advised me then to not have many children, but I don't regret having many children either. Children are good, they come from God. No matter how many of them, I am fine."

Negative attitudes to contraception and abortion have exacerbated women's freedom of action and it underpins the rising rate of teenage pregnancy. The next section discusses a key change in attitudes that the older generation believes has also exacerbated this problem.

Sexuality, responsibility, and silence

Changing attitudes to sexuality amongst young women take place in a context where, while there is a greater freedom, there is also the continuation of older attitudes that link their access to information on safe abortion. Although the rate of teenage pregnancy has been increasing in Meghalaya after the coal boom, teenage pregnancy is not new to Meghalaya. The general narrative of the middle and older age group of women in the Jaintia hills that I interviewed spoke of being pregnant with their partners before they were formally married. The average age for marriage in the state being less than 20, these pregnancies were also teenage pregnancies, following which the women were married off with their partners. As such, although premarital sex was not celebrated, it was not prohibited either. However, the rate of teenage pregnancy was less in the past than it is currently since there was an idea of having responsible sex among the older generation, which is believed to be missing now.

> I don't think even today a traditional village like Nongtalang[14] yet knows of anything of modern marriages. But co-habitation was practised responsibly when the couples were mature enough to take sensible decisions. It is not like today where teenage pregnancy has become such a problem. Teenagers are misusing this freedom and have been suffering a lot because of it shared H. H. Mohrmen.
> (male, aged 45, Jowai, West Jaintia hills)

"We had fun in the field, but we never bypassed our tradition, we did not pose a problem to be controlled…today's children are all about fun but no responsibility" shared Bliss, 75 years old.

Dr. Joan Sullai (female, 60 Years, Jowai, West Jaintia hills), who is a physician and has been working on HIV prevention and supporting HIV-positive female sex workers in the Jaintia hills for many years, explained:

> We have greater freedom in our society. Women are everywhere, they maintain the business, run the family; they are very hardworking. If there is greater freedom, there is also greater responsibility. That's when sometimes this freedom becomes a burden. And this freedom is also misused. Because ours is an open society premarital sex has become very regular leading to lots of teenage pregnancies. Premarital sex was not encouraged according to tradition. Even today it is an open secret, but a secret yet. There is silence around this.

Silence on sex and sexuality is a pervasive feature in Meghalaya, so much so that the local language lacks any definite word on the genitalia (War and Albert, 2013). Factual knowledge remains minimal, moral dimensions receive paramount importance in discussions on sexuality where widely held Christian concepts of sin and guilt occupy the core of the discussions concerning on masturbation, premarital sex, abortion, and homosexuality (War and Albert, 2013).[15] The National Family Health Survey (NFHS) 2007 had also reported a stronger preference to discuss moral values in Family Planning Programs (95%) in Meghalaya than the use of condoms or contraception (51%) (War and Albert, 2013). A public vocabulary to talk about the sex organs without feeling hesitant is absent which poses a challenge in introducing health and sexuality education in the local dialect. The cultural emphasis for using decent and dignified language make this silence sustain as anything related to "sex" itself is considered indecent talk (War and Albert, 2013).

As the discussion throughout this chapter has revealed, the indigenous women in Meghalaya have relatively better freedom and choice in terms of dressing, choosing partners, sexual autonomy (when seen from a mainland and mainstream patrilineal Indian perspective). But the underlying moral structure where these choices are located emanate from the same sexist gendered terrain similar to that a patrilineal society, with frequent negative consequences for the women. For example, while on one hand sexual autonomy, stigma-free divorce, progressive marital arrangement characterises the Khasi/Jaintia woman, on the other hand, it also implies a lack of control by the woman on her body. This is a different dynamic of oppression where while on the surface the women could appear to have freedom and choice on her sexuality, on a deeper level the norms that grant these choices restrict a progressive possibility of her choices which is often reinforced through a silence on discussions concerning sex and sexuality, that ultimately means that women's freedom is illusory. Even though the shape of these stories and experiences have changed across different generations of women, the underlying dis-empowerment that underpins these experiences have not really changed. These contradictory gendered arrangements are woven together to produce this disempowerment in such a way that this dynamic of oppression has to be understood in its own matrilineal context which is different from the lens of understanding gender oppression in mainstream patrilineal societies. For example, War and Albert (2013) make an interesting observation in their study in Meghalaya that while majority of their respondents, including women, held women responsible for rape for dressing improperly, most of the respondent women themselves were dressed in, what might be termed as "provocative dress" in the rest of India. This observation further indicates how understanding the subtext of oppression of women in a matrilineal setting use the standards of understanding oppression in a typical patrilineal and patriarchal Indian mainstream culture. For women in Meghalaya, the sexual freedom they enjoyed in choosing their partners is overlaid by moral and patriarchal values which materially and emotionally disadvantage/devalue women as compared to men. For decades, the relative freedom of the women in a matrilineal, largely subsistence, economy has been undermined by a greater individual and cash economy. This has increased the economic power of men without increasing their responsibility in the family or for the maintenance of their children which, in turn, has increased the material burden on women as well as their risk of comparative disadvantage. Attitudes to contraception and abortion as well as the taboo on the discussion on sexuality also operate to increase the uncertainty of women's lives. It is also deepening the difference in the moral frameworks that are applied to men and women. Underpinning this framework is the idea of the self-sacrificing Khasi/Jaintia woman, and her counterpart, the sexually free woman who can be blamed for the failings of men, including their abandonment of partners and children and irresponsible sexual behaviour.

Notes

1 Mitali Chakravarty and Bapukan Choudhury. An Overview of Jaintia – a Unique Matrilineal tribe. Available at https://www.academia.edu/16196481/AN_OVERVIEW_OF_JAINTIAS_A_UNIQUE_MATRILINEAL_TRIBE (accessed in 20th August 2019).
2 Interview with Shylla, 72 years, Lumshlong, East Jaintia district.
3 See the section of "Conversion to Christianity" in Chapter 4.
4 However, the Unitarian church is an exception in this case because the Unitarian Church does not object to interreligious marriage or seeks conversion to Christianity for the marriage to be solemnised.
5 Interview with Rikil, 35 years old, Jowai, West Jaintia Hills.
6 Shillong is the capital of Meghalaya.
7 Interview with Rikil, 35 years old, West Jaintia district.
8 Rikil shared a case of the youngest daughter who had moved out of the house years ago, had to retake her responsibilities of taking care of the household property after her parents' death since her uncle and brothers were incapable of taking care of the family property by themselves.
9 Interview with Rikil, 35 years old, West Jaintia district.
10 National Family Health Survey-3. 2007. "International Institute for Population Sciences (IIPS) and Macro International." In National Family Health Survey (NFHS-3), 2005–2006: India: Volume I. Mumbai: IIPS.
11 The Shillong Times. 2012. Teen Pregnanct cause of High Fertily Rate in Meghalaya. Available at https://theshillongtimes.com/2012/03/23/teen-pregnancy-cause-of-high-fertility-rate-in-mlaya/ (accessed on 30th September 2019).
12 Shillong Times. January 2019. Teenage Pregnancy a cause of worry in State. Available at https://theshillongtimes.com/2019/01/15/teenage-pregnancy-a-cause-for-worry-in-state/ (accessed on 30th September 2019).
13 Ministry of Health and Family Welfare. 2014. District Level Household and Facility Survey DLHS 4 (2012–2013), Delhi, India.
14 Nongtalang is a dominantly Niamtre village in the Jaintia hills famous for its hold on traditional culture and hold on customs and values that continue to be practiced by the villagers.
15 The way in which Christian morals are interpreted here are not universal and may also be result of their integration with earlier traditional taboos that existed prior to Christianity.

CONCLUSION

During the years in which mining has dominated the lives of the people of Meghalaya, there have been major changes in gender relations. While these changes have been complex and multi-layered, they have overall led to a diminishing of women's place in society. Some of the processes that led to this outcome existed prior to the mining boom, but underwent a rapid acceleration as a result of this development. The matrilineal system was already being hollowed out by the pressure of knowledge of alternative systems that privileged men, and the gradual weakening of communal dependence on subsistence agriculture, and related trading activities. The role of the men, as matrilineal kinsmen, as fathers, and as husbands, was already being strengthened before the impact of the culture of mining. Men as matrilineal kinsmen had also played an important role in decision-making in the family and at the communal level. This role was gradually strengthening during the twentieth century. In addition to this, men also sought to strengthen their position as husbands and fathers. Women in this social structure experienced pressure from both sets of male relatives and it was their relationship to the ownership of land and the process of agricultural production that gave them both status and a certain amount of social freedom.

While women in Meghalaya have experienced the negative impact of mining, this has also been accompanied by a sense of empowerment for some women that they derive from the mining economy in terms of higher income, access to modern amenities, and consumption behaviour. These benefits are meeting the current needs of women living through a process of rapid urbanisation, a process that has meant the replacement of traditional survival needs. In Meghalaya, it is necessary to view the mine spaces not only as sites of masculine dominance but also as feminist spaces where women play active roles in supporting, resisting, and negotiating the base of a mining economy as suggested by Lahiri-Dutt (2012). Women have negotiated these changes that have been forced on them in complex ways.

Meghalaya's experiences of changing gender relations and masculine dispositions of the mining settlements contribute to the existing literature on gender and mining. In Meghalaya, a physical and gendered segregation

DOI: 10.4324/9781003149460-9

between the mineworkers and the residents, or between men and women, does not exist in the same way as it does in many mining locations internationally. The mining economy in Meghalaya attracted a huge number of migrant workers from other parts of India and neighbouring countries which has resulted in many cross-cultural marriages between the local indigenous women and male migrant labourers. Apart from marriages, the local indigenous mineworkers and the migrant mineworkers have closely intermingled which has to some extent produced a cultural fusion in the coal belts. However, this has had its negative side in anti-migrant conflicts. The relationship between the migrant population and the local population has been that of conflict and harmony and that has been instrumental in shaping the socio-cultural and political discourse of Meghalaya in an interesting insider–outsider discourse. The mining sites have not lost their social community fabric even though it has considerably changed from the sense of a traditional community in the past. As such, through its engagement with the nature of cultural fusion in Meghalaya, this offers newer insights into the idea of a mining settlement.

Also, Meghalaya has not experienced the phenomenon of sex-disaggregated public spaces that has been common to other mining areas. Women in Meghalaya did not have to fight for access to public spaces primarily because the idea of public space in Meghalaya has been historically feminised under customary laws of the region. Yet, women's access to public space has gradually decreased in functional terms as a result of mining, because women stopped going out for work when the men of the house started earning better incomes. This has led to a gradual decrease in women's mobility and had a greater effect on women of middle age than it had on the older women, who grew up in a dominantly traditional social structure, or younger women, who are benefiting from formal education.

Meghalaya also offers a different account on the heteronormative leadership of men in the family sphere which is different from the typical social structures of the rest of India as well as most mining communities internationally. Being a matrilineal society, women have always been an important stakeholder in the family governance where the men of the women's family have taken active leadership. As such, although men here too are the primary decision makers, their leadership is comparatively feminised compared to male leadership in a conventional patrilineal nuclear household. However, the introduction of the coal economy and exposure to urbanisation and other modernising forces have given rise to new debates in Meghalaya over the matrilineal social structure, which is informed by a gendered tug of war between men and women over the need and relevance of matrilineal structures in contemporary times.

Women in Meghalaya joined the mining workforce along with men, without facing any resistance from the men, as they were allocated with what was seen as the "soft mine work" as compared to men who took up the "tough and core" mining work and they were also paid less. This movement of women into mining support work was facilitated by the fact that women had always been the primary traditional working force in the family and community production processes. The female mining workforce in Meghalaya juggles between their roles as wives and mothers and this does not bring into question their femininity and feminine desirability.

With the mining economy taking over, the already-changing life preferences introduced by nascent urbanisation and modernisation in Meghalaya accelerated, changing the aspirations of people in terms of their desire to secure greater material benefits, over by an urbanised lifestyle. Though both men and women aspired to material benefits provided by mining alike, there is a difference in how men and women negotiated for these aspirations which informs the gendered implications of the social and cultural displacement in Meghalaya. Men sought more male power and privilege and included in this was a desire on the part of many men to do away with matrilineal system altogether. Another strand of male opinion wanted introduce significant modifications to the matrilineal structures in order to secure greater men's rights primarily as fathers and husbands as opposed to matrilineal kin.

Women's negotiations have been complex than that of men because for women, there was a negative trade-off between mining and their traditional rights. This is not to say that women had a real choice in securing their position in these changes, as it was not possible for them to benefit from mining while also ensuring their traditional status would continue. That is because the mining economy thrives on the destruction of nature, whereas women's traditional status was determined by their relationship with nature and its sustainability. This is also true for the whole traditional identity of the indigenous people in Meghalaya whose life was defined by their relationship with nature. As such mining taking over the traditional human–nature symbiotic relationship of the indigenous people and transforming it into an exploitative one meant not only the destruction of the basis of autonomy and identity for the women but also for the whole indigenous community. But what is significant about this transformation is that the men benefitted from this destructive nature of displacement on individual grounds by securing more male power. Women, on the other hand, did not have much to gain from this new situation, other than a rise in their cash income as compared to the past, and even if this dis-improved their comparative position with respect to the men who earned so much more. Mining destroyed the basis of the traditional fabric of the indigenous people, bringing individual benefits that encouraged the individual material and social pursuits of a "modern life," which overshadowed the disastrous loss of tradition and society as a whole.

This take-over by the mining economy with liberal ideas of individualism versus the traditional idea of collectivism is reflected in women's resistance to their lost status, where a majority of women too desire to secure personal advantage in terms of material benefits and social status under a monetised economy that they believe the traditional status did not have the scope to provide, even if it means lesser privileges than it provides to the men. Another reason for this surrender could also be attributed to the fact that money is seen as an ungendered entity which will benefit the household as a whole, irrespective of whether the man or the woman of the house earns it. Being a traditional agricultural society based on land administration, women are aware of the gendered nature of land and what it means in their gendered lives. But a monetised economy and the idea of money is a very new addition to the indigenous society, the gendered character of which and the way in which it changes culture was not understood. Women therefore were not critical of the monetised economy even though they are giving up their traditional rights on land and descent inheritance. Although women have been strongly seeking to protect matriliny and their rights under matriliny, their stand is not integrated with resistance to mining because they do not necessarily believe that mining will destroy matriliny. The loss of women's status is mostly seen as a logistical failure of their negotiation with the material structure of mining itself, whereas matriliny is still seen as a status quo that will endure. Other than individual material benefits and the fact that mining pulled the low-income group out of extreme poverty, the support for mining also comes from the reality that it has destroyed other economic activity leaving nothing else that can be done other than mining, since the land, rivers, and forests have been polluted. This is a very crucial feature of displacement where earning money becomes a desired objective, while mining wipes out all other traditional choices of a livelihood of the indigenous people.

This phenomenon of social and cultural displacement is informed by changes in ideologies concerning women's empowerment that is seen in the changing idea of how women have come to value their labour, leisure, and mobility across generations. For example, the idea of empowerment for the older generation was contained in the idea of choice and spaces for dissent that they enjoyed in terms of taking off from gendered duties, and in the fact that sexual division of labour was not extremely polarised. The idea of empowerment for the younger generation of women whereas is very western-ideal-inspired and learnt in the classroom, unlike their grandmothers who experienced it in the practices of their living experience. This also limits empowerment to a category of women who can access modern education as traditional forms of empowerment no longer exist. A lack of empowerment is experienced most strongly by the middle generation of women born in and around the mining boom, who neither had access to education as a form of empowerment nor could they hold onto the traditional idea of empowerment that was part of the matrilineal structures. This group of women was adversely affected by the deepening patriarchy in the region as a result of mining, and the increasingly polarised sexual division of labour and shrinking mobility for women that compelled them to give up on their traditionally women-dominated occupations. The educated section of younger women, on the other hand, has come to increasingly advocate for their rights in a way that modifies the traditional rights enjoyed by women, with western ideals that can be seen in their relationship preferences for modern education and occupational opportunities. Younger women are also more likely to support neo-local residences post marriage as opposed to the traditional matrilocal residence system, although they continue to support other matrilineal norms and values.

The social and cultural displacement introduced by mining also introduced different ideas of moralities into indigenous society, which have been part of a process of constantly negotiating, refining, and redefining the traditional moral fabric. As mining brought in a migrant workforce from different areas of India, Bangladesh, and Nepal, it led to a rise in cross-cultural marriages of the indigenous Khasi/Jaintia women with migrant men from these patrilineal societies. In the course of time, this established the idea of a "moral and ideal migrant" who is a good husband to his wife versus the immoral migrant man who will desert the indigenous women he married. However, the Khasi men escape this moral categorisation when they behave badly in this way because they are considered to have been corrupted by the mining wealth, and therefore, their behaviour is not considered to reflecting on their ethnic group, and thus excused.

For women, ideas of the "modern sex worker" have provided an antithesis to the "sacrificial ideal Khasi/Jaintia women" and with the rapid growth of a sex industry in the mining settlements, monogamy saw a shift to an ambiguous terrain of polygamous relationship where different wife-styling processes challenged conventional monogamous marriages and where women navigated through the idea of moral acceptability in complex ways.

As such, the discourse of social and cultural displacement in Meghalaya introduced by mining reveals a phenomenon shaped by differences, contradictions, and paradoxes where the indigenous society of Meghalaya collided with the mining economised Meghalaya, with all its social, political, cultural, geographic, and economic confrontations. It is this complex set of changes that was introduced by the mining displacement that offers interesting insights into the DID literature in general and also to the gender and mining literature, in particular. For example, the mining diaspora that this research has studied were not physically displaced in the literal sense of the term as the community did not have to move out of their land sacrificing their diasporic belonging; but the land they live on has gone through an extreme transformation in terms of ecological destruction and has become a completely different terrain altogether. In just a few years, the people discovered that it had resulted in an absolutely deteriorated ecosystem, broken socio-cultural structure, and a rapid disintegration of the indigenous tradition. As such, Meghalaya presents a very unique case where the people affected by mining displacement are constantly resettling themselves in a changing terrain in which this kind of a physical displacement has been a non-linear continuous process where people cannot choose how they want to resettle, as they are being engulfed by the mining economy. This provides a unique insight into the DID policy discourse that understands displacement only as a one-time event or at best as a sequence of linear events. The existing policy discourse around DID envisions resettlement and rehabilitation initiatives for displaced people in a clearly demarcated post-displacement scenario that is separated from the pre-displacement situation by time and space. The important question that arises here is that what would a compensation, resettlement, and rehabilitation policy look like in a situation like Meghalaya where neither monetary compensation nor a relocation/resettlement/rehabilitation plan designed in the conventional policy of DID is capable of addressing? This is a significant policy dilemma that policy makers might need to address.

Since a majority of the indigenous people were absorbed into the mining workforce and had started earning very high rates of income, the idea of monetary compensation to make up for the loss that the community social structure suffered under this form of displacement has become irrelevant, as is the idea of land resettlement, as most of the agricultural land of Meghalaya has already been polluted and rendered unusable by mining activities. Even if resettlement was possible it would mean the need for the people to move out of their villages and away from their social and cultural network. People have already faced a dislocation with relation to the coal economy. The indigenous population as miners and mine owners are making a better income than they would by being resettling in a different tract of agricultural land, where they would have to start to scratch. As such, the idea of any conventional, top-down approach of resettlement by legislations or compensation in cash or kind has a high risk of failure in cases like that of Meghalaya.

When it comes to legal security that advocates of just resettlement policies emphasises on, Meghalaya again poses as a unique case. As I have already discussed, the state of Meghalaya is a sixth schedule state under the constitution of India that recognises its right to self-governance. As such, the customary laws and the traditional land rights of the indigenous people are already protected under the sixth schedule, and, unlike many other indigenous tribal societies of India who lack legal recognition of CPRs, Meghalaya's system of commons is legally secured. Yet, it is this right of self-governance and right to indigeneity that has been used by the powerful, as well as the poor, to mine on their ancestral or common land, by arguing that they have the right to do what they choose on their land without any interference from external forces. This is where the case of Meghalaya goes beyond the "displacement is a development crisis" perspective in the DID literature that argues about the vested interests of dominant elites who design the development paradigms without caring for the marginalised people who pay the price for development. The idea of dominant elites becomes vague and layered in the context of Meghalaya since it is not only the powerful elite who benefited from mining. Rather, the poor and powerless indigenous people of the Jaintia hills with a long-standing history of family poverty became part of the mining elite when they discovered a mine deposit on their land. Once mining was banned, many of these individuals of these new elites went back to being poor as their money had been spent on consumerist aspiration. Monetisation being a very new addition to the traditional Meghalayan society, this rise and fall of the new elite has also been as much a reality, as is the idea of a stable dominant elite. As such, the case of Meghalaya offers newer insights into the idea of dominant elites versus the subaltern dichotomy, where the idea of the subaltern and the disadvantaged vis-à-vis. the making of traditional and insider and ruling elites are constantly changing and shifting in the intersection of tribal rights with the coal economy and other forces of urbanisation, modernisation, and capitalism. This points to the necessity of nuanced legislations that might be required to address such cases of extractive economies in self-governing states like that of Meghalaya, where neither an already "protected" tribal status has been fruitful in addressing the nuances of mining displacement nor is there any particular/polarised "elite" class group (needing regulations to be put under control) who exclusively represent the emerging capitalist interests in the coal economy in an indigenous land.

In Chapter 1, I discussed how existing gender and mining literature has engaged with the serious consequences that mining carries for indigenous women for its dominantly masculine character which is also the reason why work of gender in mining has been captured in detail unlike the general DID literature. This could also be probably because, the gendered implications of development projects such as dams, might not reveal their gendered nature as strongly as mining in the initial phase of displacement. Moreover, the strong policy focus of the DID literature that treats people as objects adds on to this invisibility of gender in the general displacement discourse. This is where the gap between the general DID literature and the gender and mining literature rests. The case of Meghalaya offers a situation where the gender nature displacement and a mining situation converge in such a way that a careful account of this context bridges the gap between the DID and the gender and mining literature. The magnitude of the physical spread of mining activities transformed almost the whole of East Jaintia hills of Meghalaya into a mining site, unlike any other context where mining or other extraction activities such as oil are limited to specific locations and finite spaces. The mining economy absorbed more than a majority of the population into its extraction work due to which the interactions between the mining landscape and the wider socio-cultural landscape of the region are spread out and intimately connected. In fact, this is a situation where mining and displacement go beyond just leaving impacts on the people. Mining has been integrated into the totality of life of the indigenous people from childhood to old age in which the whole community has become mining oriented.

This is the reason why the changes in gender relations in Meghalaya induced by mining displacement have been extremely layered and unfolds very differently than in a situation where there is a limited context for the extractive-industry. For example, while many indigenous women who were involved in women dominated traditional occupations like animal herding saw a sharp shutdown with the mining take over in Meghalaya, there were also women who did not necessarily have to give up on their traditional occupations, for example, the smoked fish workers, but these women were still deeply encapsulated by the mining economy in other ways. Not all smoked fish workers gave up smoking fish with the onset of mining. But the success of their smoked fish business was rendered dependent on the success of the mining economy. In fact, the more the mining economy prospered, the smoked fish business prospered despite the reality that mining had polluted the rivers and killed the local fish that the women had used for their business in the past. This left the women with no choice other than to depend on expensive imported fishes from other states of India to continue their business. At the same time, mining gave higher purchasing power to the buyers of the smoked fish which in turn increased the consumption of the traditionally famous smoked fish, and the higher income earned from smoked fish enabled the smoked fish women workers to continue to buy imported fish to keep their business going despite its increase in production cost. This is a cycle that goes beyond a gendered impact of mining on women to appropriating women's interests under the mining economy. As such, the case of Meghalaya offers a unique opportunity to the policy and literature discourse of DID to understand systematic changes in gender relation enforced by displacement in such a way that requires a focus on understanding the chain of these changes which cannot be captured or addressed solely by a conventional impact analysis framework but by a process analysis perspective.

Another distinct characteristic of this gendered transition in Meghalaya is that of gendered spaces. The geographical spread of the mining sites encompassed a majority of the Jaintia hills in Meghalaya which did not necessarily become extremely male-centric even though women's physical mobility was increasingly restricted with the loss of women-dominated traditional occupations. This is different from the American experience where mining spaces were getting increasingly masculine and male-centric where the men actively resisted women's access to the men-only spaces. In Meghalaya, there are women who continue to work as vegetable vendors and travel to the urban centres by public transport (unlike groups of women walking to the market together in the past) to sell their vegetables without having to face any active male aggression. So, the question of gendered public space in Meghalaya has to do more with changing women's mobility or shrinking women's mobility rather than the creation of exclusively masculine spaces. Many public spaces like forests (where women used to work in the past) continue to remain open to women even if not that many feel the need to visit them anymore.

The DID literature has been critiqued for treating the household as a homogeneous entity that fails to address that men's and women's household interests are not same, and that there are conflict of interests concerning the same between men and women/husbands and wives in the same household. As such this critique emphasises the need to understand household with heterogenous gendered interests which is essential for any policy planning to be able to cater to women's and men's interest in a displacement situation separately. The Meghalayan experience, however, goes beyond this argument of heterogeneity and unfolds newer ways of understanding homogeneity and heterogeneity in households. The mining economy in Meghalaya established money as a homogenising entity of the household even though the gendered interests of a household were or are not homogeneous. The idea of monetary income led men and women to the homogenous belief that the money earned from the mines would solve the problems and cater to the interests of men and women alike, and unlike land, money came to be viewed as an ungendered and neutral asset that could be equally used and accessed by both men and women. Hence, although on one hand men and women conflict over varied gendered interests in the administration of the household and society, there is a homogenising effect of money that brings men and women together to accumulate more wealth. But this insight of how money has been shaping the idea of homogenous and heterogeneous interests between men and women in the household and also the larger society, offers a breakthrough by questioning how could one understand homogeneity or heterogeneity in a situation like this? The Meghalayan experience uncovers that while it is true that the household is not a homogenous entity, it does not represent a gendered binary between homogenous and heterogeneous interest but rather a constant negotiation between the two. This understanding could be a significant insight into the existing DID policy and literature discourse in understanding the layers of gendered interests that play out in a household in a myriad of ways, which will require a very nuanced policy/plan/perspective to be able to address the same.

The idea of women's empowerment has been changing across generations of women in Meghalaya. With the coming in of the mining economy and with exposure to other forces of urbanisation and modernisation, the women in Meghalaya have been dislocated from the idea of empowerment that was ensured by their traditional rights under matriliny, while being offered other ideas of modern empowerment as service women in modern jobs, access to modern education, and white-collar job status. It is understood that these ideas of modern empowerment are very western centric, derived from a very different patrilineal western context of domination of women, which is not the same as the history of women's oppression in the traditional matrilineal society of Meghalaya. Taking this into consideration, how does one look into the modern idea of women's empowerment that is increasingly getting popular in Meghalaya, a belief in which is also shared by the indigenous women of today? Is this a case of empowerment or could it be interpreted as a different mode of internalisation of western patriarchy? A deeper understanding of this question can contribute to the polarised argument of internalisation of patriarchy in a displacement scenario that that been debated on by scholars such as Fernandes (2016) and Menon (1995). While Fernandes (2016) and Menon (1995) argued that the displacement process leads to an internalisation of patriarchal values by women themselves, Meghalaya offers an example of an internalisation of western feminist values which is also another form of patriarchy in itself. This could offer a layered lens of understanding "internalisation of patriarchy" which is not limited to a conventional understanding of gender roles of women in terms of their participation and visibility in a "private versus public domain" as is understood in western feminism but also capable in understanding "patriarchy disguised as empowerment" as the case of Meghalaya unfolds.

The approach of this research on understanding the complex ways in which gender has unfolded and operated in the totality of the lives of people in the mining areas of Meghalaya in North East India can be applied to and contribute to the discussion of understanding the ways gender operates under stress caused by extreme economic and social dislocation, not only in a DID situation but also in refugee communities and in conflict situations. This could help in understanding the idea of gendered transformation of spaces, gender roles, women's changing leadership and ideas of empowerment, gendered changes in the economy as it could unfold in a conflict situation or in the dislocation experienced by refugee communities. While this research does not claim that gendered experiences in other stress situation like conflict or refugee crisis would exactly unfold the way it has unfolded in the case of mining displacement in Meghalaya, it is most likely that an approach of keeping people's narratives as the centre of the of a gendered analysis, as this research has done, could unfold nuances of such changes experienced by people, women in particular, across different stages of their lives that a macro impact analysis framework of understanding women's experiences fails to capture.

BIBLIOGRAPHY

Aberlie, D. (1972). Matrilineal descent in cross cultural perspective, In Schneider, D & Gough, K (eds.). *Matrilineal Kinship*. Berkeley: University of California Pres, pp. 655–727.

Acker, J. (1990). Hierarchies, jobs, bodies: A theory of gendered organizations, *Gender and Society*, 4(2), pp. 139–158.

Adivasi (2006). Development displacement and rehabilitation, *Journal of the Scheduled Castes and Scheduled Tribe*, Research and Training Institute, Bhubaneswar, 6, pp. 1–49, 90–98.

Agarwala, T. (2019). *Citizenship Amendment Bill: Northeast Unifies for Bandh for the First Time*. [Online]. Available at: https://indianexpress.com/article/north-east-india/assam/northeast-assam-bandh-citizenship-bill-neso-5527506/ (Accessed on 24 May 2019).

Agency, S. N. (2013). *ILP is Not Helping Any State but Creates a Negative Impact on the Growth of the State: Dr Mukul*. [Online]. Available at: http://spnewsagency.com/ilp-is-not-helping-any-state-but-creates-a-negative-impact-on-the-growth-of-the-state-dr-mukul/ (Accessed on May 2019).

Agnihotri, A. (1998). The Orissa resettlement and rehabilitation of projects affected persons policy, 1994: Some critical issues, In Mohapatra, P., Ota, A. B. & Mohanty, R. N. (eds.). *Development Induced Displacement and Rehabilitation*. Bhubaneswar: Prachi Prakashan.

Ahmad, N. & Lahiri-Dutt, K. (2006). Engendering mining communities: Examining the missing gender concerns in coal mining displacement and rehabilitation in India, *Gender, Technology and Development*, 10(3), pp. 313–339.

Akhtara, A. (2010). *Nokma: The Powerless Woman Leader*. [Online]. Available at: https://www.videovolunteers.org/nokma-the-powerless-woman-leader/ (Accessed on April 2019).

Anderson, K. & Dana C. J. (1991). Learning to listen: Interview techniques and analyses, In Gluck, S. & Patai, D. (eds.). *Women's Words: The Feminist Practice of Oral History*. New York: Routledge Press, pp. 11–27.

Anon n.d. *Khasi Tribes*. [Online]. Available at: https://www.indianmirror.com/tribes/khasitribes.html (Accessed on April 2019).

Aragón, F. & Rud, J. (2012). *Mining, Pollution and Agricultural Productivity: Evidence from Ghana*. [Online]. Available at: https://www.researchgate.net/publication/254450492_Mining_Pollution_and_Agricultural_Productivity_Evidence_from_Ghana (Accessed on 20 June 2019).

Arun, S. (1999). Does land ownership make a difference? Women's roles in agriculture in Kerala, India, *Gender and Development*, 7(3), pp. 19–27.

Ashcroft, B., Griffiths, G. & Tiffin, H. (1989). *The Empire Writes Back*. London: Routledge.

Atkinson, R. (1995). The gift of stories, *Practical and Spritual Applications of Autobiography, Life Stories and Personal Mythmaking*. Westport, CT: Bergin and Garvey.

Ballard, C. & Banks, G. (2013). Resource wars: The anthropology of mining, *Annual Review of Anthropology*, 32, pp. 287–313.

Bamon, T. K. (2004). The English text: Establishing identity, *The IATEFL TTED SIG E-Newsletter*, https://ttedsig.iatefl.org/resources/e-newsletter/TheEnglishText.pdf

Banuri, T. (1990). Modernization and its discontents: A cultural perspective on the theories of development, In Marglin, F. A. & Marglin, S. A. (eds.). *Dominating Knowledge: Development, Culture and Resistance*. Oxford: Clarendon Press, pp. 73–101.

Bareh, H. (1967). *The History and Culture of the Khasi People*. Guwahati: Spectrum Publications.

Baruah, A. K. (2004). *Ethnic Conflict and Traditional Self Governing Institutuons: A study of Laitumkhrah Dorbar*. London: Crisis States Programme; London School of Economics and Political Science.

Basaiawmoit, E. R. (1987). An Attitude Study of the Matrilineal System and its Implications for Education, an unpublished thesis submitted for the degree of Doctor of Philisophy, Education Deptt., NEHU.

Basu, M. (2000). *Locating Gender; Feminist Perspective and Gender Approach in Development-Induced Displacement*. New Delhi: JNU.

Batra, V. (2013). *The History of the Indian State of Meghalaya*. [Online]. Available at: https://vedantbatra.wordpress.com/2013/02/18/the-history-of-the-indian-state-of-meghalaya/ (Accessed on April 2019).

Baviskar. A. (1995). *In the Belly of the River: Tribal Conflicts over Development in the Narmada Valley*. Delhi: Oxford University Press.

Beck, U., Bonss, W. & Lau, C. (2003). The theory of reflexive modernization: Problematic, hypotheses and research programme, *Theory, Culture & Society*, 20(2), pp. 1–33.

Behar, R. (1990). Rage and redemption: Reading the life story of a mexican marketing woman, *Feminist Studies*, 16(2), pp. 223–258.

Bell, E. (2007). *They Ask If We Eat Frogs: Garo Ethnicity in Bangladesh*. Singapore: ISEAS Publishing, International Institute for Asian Studies.

Bendix, R. (1967). Tradition and modernity reconsidered. *Comparative Studies in Society and History*, April, 9(3), pp. 292–346.

Benison, S. (1965). Reflections on oral history, *The American Archivist*, 28(1), pp. 71–77.

Benjamin, J. A. & Fancy, K. (1998). *The Gender Dimensions of Internal Displacement: Concept Paper and Annotated Bibliography*. New York: UNICEF.

Bennett, A. & Elman, C. (2007). Case study methods in the international relations subfield, *Comparative Political Studies*, 40(2), pp. 170–195.

Berger, M. T. & Guidroz, K. (eds.) (2009). *The Intersectional Approach: Transforming the Academy Through Race, Class, and Gender*. Chapel Hill: The University of North Carolina Press.

Berkes, F. (1999). *Sacred Ecology: Traditional Ecological Knowledge and Resource Management*. Philadelphia: Taylor and Francis.

Bhabha, H. (2004). *The Location of Culture*. London and New York: Routledge.

Bhattrai, R. (2007). *Open Borders, Closed Citizenships: Nepali Labor Migrants in Delhi*. Netherlands: Institute of Social Studies.

Bhaumik, Subir. (2003). Tripura's gumti dam must go, *The Ecologist Asia*, 11(1), Jan–March, pp. 84–89.

Bisht, T. C. (2009). Development-induced displacement and women: The case of the Tehri dam, India, *The Asia Pacific Journal of Anthropology*, 10(4), pp. 301–317.

Braidotti, R. (2002). *Metamorphoses: Towards a materialist theory of becoming*. Cambridge: Blackwell Publishers.

Braidotti, R. (2003). Becoming woman: Or sexual difference revisited, *Theory, Culture & Society*, 20(3), pp. 43–64.

Bryceson, D., Jønsson, J. & Verbrugge, H. (2013). Prostitution of partnership? Wifestyles in tanzanian artisanal gold mining settlements, *Journal of Modern African Studies*, 51(1), pp. 33–56.

Butler, J. (1990a). *Gender Trouble: Feminism and the Subversion of Identity*. New York: Routledge.

Butler, J. (1990b). Performative acts and gender constitution. In Case, S.-E. (ed.). *Performing Feminisms*. Baltimore: John Hopkins University.

Carastathis, A. (2014). The concept of intersectionality in feminist theory. *Philosophy Compass*, (9), pp. 304–314.

Carrin, M. & Guzy, L. (2012). *Voices from the Periphery: Subalternity and Empowerment in India*. London: Routledge India.

Casey, K. (1993). *Answer with my Life: Life Histories of Women Teachers Working for Social Change*. New York: Routledge.

Census of India 2011. *Meghalaya Population 2011–2021 Census*. [Online]. Available at: https://www.census2011.co.in/census/state/meghalaya.html#:~:text=Meghalaya%20Population%202011%20As%20per%20details%20from%20Census,male%20and%20female%20are%201%2C491%2C832%20and%201%2C475%2C057%20respectively (Accessed on February, 2019).

Cernea, M. (1993). Social science research and the crafting of policy on population resettlement. *Knowledge and Policy*, 6, pp. 176–200.

Cernea, M. (1997). The risks and reconstruction model for resettling displaced populations, *World Development*, 25(10), pp. 1569–1587.

Cernea, M. (1999). *Development's Painful Social Costs*. (Online). Available at: https://link.springer.com/chapter/10.1007/978-1-349-27248-8_1 (Accessed on June 2019).

Cernea, M. (2004). For a new economics of resettlement: A sociological critique of the compensation principle, *International Social Science Journal*, July, 55(175), pp. 37–45.

Cernea, M. M. & Guggenheim, S. (1993). *Anthropological Approaches to Resettlement: Theory, Policy and Practice*. Boulde: Westview Press.

Cernea, M. M. & Maldonado, J. K. (2018). *Challenging the Prevailing Paradigm of Displacement and Resettlement: Risks, Impoverishment, Legacies, Solutions*. Oxon and New York: Routledge.

Chacko, P. (1998). Matrilineal system: Some structural implication, In P. Chacko, (ed.). *Matriliny in Meghalaya: Tradition and Change*. New Delhi: Regency Publications, pp. 10–15.

Chakravarti T. (1991). The riang women of rural tripura: The participation in economic activities and social status', In Samanta, K. R. (ed.). *Rural Development in North East India: Perspectives, Issues and Experiences*. New Delhi: Uppal Publishing House, pp. 205–215.

Chatterjee, S. K. (1951). *The Indo-Mongoloids: Their Contribution to the History and Culture of India*. Calcutta: Royal Asiatic Society of Bengal.

Chatterji, S. K. (2014). *Kirata-Jana-Krti: The Indo-Mongoloids; Their Contribution to the History and Culture of India*. 4th edn. Calcutta: The Asiatic Society.

Chaube, S. K. (1973). *Hill Politics in North East India*. Calcutta: Orient Longman Limited.

Chinai, R. (2006). Coal calculations. *Frontline*, July, 14. Available at https://frontline.thehindu.com/other/article30210103.ece#! (Accessed on 17 November 2021)

Chodorow, N. (1978). *Reproducing Mothering*. Berkeley: University of California Press.

Chodorow, N. (1995). Family structure and feminine personality, In Tuana, N. & Tong, R. (eds.). *Feminism and Philosophy*. Boulder: Westview Press.

Chowdhry, G. (1995). Engendering development? Women in development (WID) in international development regimes. In: *Feminism/Postmodernism/Development*. London: Routledge, pp. 26–41.

Chowdhury, J. N. (1978). *The Khasi Canvas: A Cultural and Political History*. Shillong (Meghalaya): Jaya Chowdhury.

Collins, P. H. (1991). *Black Feminist Thought. Knowledge, Consciousness and the Politics of Empowerment*. London and New York: Routledge.

Colson, E. (1980). The resilience of matriliny: Gwembe and plateau tonga adaptations, In Cordell, L. & Beckerman, S. (eds.). *The Versatility of Kinship*. New York: Academic Press, pp. 364–366.

Colson, E. (1999). Engendering those uprooted by development, In D. Indra (ed.). *Engendering Forced Migration: Theory and Practice*. Oxford: Berghahn.

Crenshaw, K., Gotanda, N., Peller, G. & Thomas, K. (1995). *Critical Race Theory: The Key Writings that formed the Movement*. New York: The New Press.

Crenshaw, K. W. (1989). Demarginalizing the intersection of race and sex: A black feminist critique of antidiscrimination doctrine, feminist theory and antiracist politics, University of Chicago Legal Forum, 1989(1), pp. 139–167.

Crenshaw, K. W. (1991). Mapping the margins: Intersectionality, identity politics, and violence against women of color, *Stanford Law Review*, 43(6), pp. 1241–1299.

Cuvelier, J. (2014). Work and masculinity in Katanga's artisanal mines. *Africa Spectrum*, 49(2), pp. 3–26.

D'Souza, A. (2001). *Traditional System of Forest Conservation in North East India: The Angami Tribe of Nagaland*. Guwahati: North Eastern Social research Centre.

Das, M. (2001). *Changing Family System Among a Matrilineal Group in India*. Mumbai: Academia.edu.

Das, Madhumita. (n.d.). *Changing Family System Among a Matrilineal Tribe in India*. http://archive.iussp.org/Brazil2001/s10/S12_04_Das.pdf (Accessed on 1 May 2016)

Das, P. B. (2013). *Coexistence of Indigenous and Non-Indigenous People in Meghalaya*. (Online). Available at: https://meghalayatimes.info/coexistence-of-indigenous-and-non-indigenous-people-in-meghalaya/ (Accessed on April 2019).

Das, V. & Poole, D. (2004). *Anthropology in the Margins of the State*. Santa Fe: School of American Research Press.

Datta, R. (2015). A relational theoretical framework and meanings of land, nature, and sustainability for research with indigenous communities, *Local Environment*, 20(1), pp. 102–113.

Datta, S. (1996). *Socio Economic Structure of Urban Khasi Population in Meghalaya with Special Reference to Shillong Urban Agglomeration a Geographical Analysis*. (Online). Available at: http://shodhganga.inflibnet.ac.in/bitstream/10603/69529/12/12_chapter%204.pdf (Accessed on April 2019).

Davis, K. (2008). Intersectionality as buzzword: A sociology of science perspective on what makes a feminist theory successful, *Feminist Theory*, 9(1), pp. 67–85.

De Landa, M. (1999). Immanence and transcendence in the genesis of form, In Buchanan, I. (ed.). *A Deleuzian Century*. Durham NC: Duke University Press, pp. 119–134.

Deb, M. K. & Mahato, D. (2017). Understanding the politics around illegal migration from Bangladesh into Assam and Tripura, *Asian Journal of Research in Social Sciences and Humanities*, 7(9), pp. 222–234.

Deb, R. (2010). Knowledge, attitude and practices related to family planning methods among the Khasi tribes of East Khasi hills Meghalaya. *Anthropologist*, 12(1), pp. 41–45.

Debbarma, S. (2009). Refugee rehabilitation and land alienation in Tripura, In Fernandes, W. and Barbora, S. (eds.). *Land, People and Politics: Contest over Tribal Land in Northeast India*. Guwahati: North Eastern Social Research Centre and IWGIA, pp. 113–117.

Deka, M. (2013). *Women's Agency and Social Change: Assam and Beyond*. New Delhi: Sage Publications.

Deleuze, G. & Guattari, F. (1987). *A thousand plateaus: Capitalism and Schizophrenia*. Minneapolis: Minnesota University Press.

Deleuze, G. & Guattari, F. (2004). *L'Anti-Oedipe*. Paris: Minuit.

Dev, R. (2006). Narrative claims and identity impasse: The experiences of the nowhere people, In Bhattacharjee, S. & Dev, R. (eds.). *Ethnonarratives, Identity and Experience in North East India*. New Delhi: Anshah Publications, pp. 79–91.

Dhar, P. (2002). *Ethnic Unrest: in India and Her Neighbours*. New Delhi: Deep & Deep Publications.

Dias, A. (2012). *Development and its Human Cost*. New Delhi: Rawat Publications.

Dillard, C. (2008). When the ground is black, the ground is fertile: Exploring endarkened feminist epistemology and healing methodologies of the spirit, In Denzin, N. K., Lincoln, Y. S. & Smith, L. T. (eds.). *Handbook of Critical and Indigenous Methodologies*. Thousand Oaks: Sage Publications, pp. 227–291.

Directorate of Economics and Statistics (2004). Government of Meghalaya.

D'Souza, A. (2013). *Welfare of Children in Coal Mining areas of Meghalaya*. Guwahati: North Eastern Social Research Centre.

Dube, L. (1969). *Matriliny and Islam: Religion and Society in the Laccadives*. Delhi: National Publications.

Dube, L. (1996). Who gains from matriliny? Men, women and change on an Indian Island, In Palwiral, R. & Risseeuw, C (eds.). *Shifting Circles of Support: Contexualising Gender and Kinship in South Asia and Sub Saharan Africa*. New Delhi: Sage Publications, pp. 157–189.

Durkheim, E. (1933). *The Division of Labour in Society*. New York: Macmillan Publishers.

Dutta, P. (2016). *Matriliny and folk media a study of the Khasis of Meghalaya*. Tezpur: Shodhganga: A reservoir of Indian Thesis @INFLIBNET.

Dutt-Lahiri, K. (2012). Digging women: Towards a new agenda for feminist critiques of mining, *Gender, Place & Culture*, 19(2), pp. 193–212.

Dutt-Lahiri, K. (2016). *The Coal Nation: Histories Ecologies and Politics of Coal in India*. New York: Routledge.
Dwivedi, R. (2002). Models and methods in development-induced displacement, *Development and Change*, 33(4), pp. 709–732.
Eisenstadt, S. N. (1967). Israeli identity: Problems in the development of the collective identity of an ideological society. *The ANNALS of the American Academy of Political and Social Science*, 370(1), pp. 116–123.
Elmhirst, R. (2011) Introducing new feminist political ecologies, *Geoforum*, 42, pp. 129–132.
Ember, M. & Ember, C. (1971). The conditions favouring matrilocal residence. *American Anthropologist*, 73, pp. 571–594.
Engels, F. (1972). *The Origin of the Family, Private Property and the State*. New York: International Publishers.
Ennis, G., Tofa, M., Finlayson, M., (2014). Open for business but at what cost? Housing issues in boomtown Darwin. Australian Geographer, 45(4), pp. 447–464.
Escobar, A. (1996). Constructing nature: Elements for a poststructuralist political ecology, In Peet, R. & Watts, M. (eds.). *Liberation Ecologies: Environment, Development, Social Movements*. London: Routledge, pp. 46–68.
Escobar, A. (1999). After nature: Steps to an antiessentialist political ecology. *Current Anthropology*, 40(1), pp. 1–30.
Escober, A. (2011). Sustainability: Design for the pluriverse. *Development*, 54(2), pp. 137–140.
Evans, J. V. (2005). The moral state: Men, mining, and masculinity in the early GDR. *German History*, 23(3), pp. 354–370.
Fennell, S. & Arnot, M. (2008). Decentring hegemonic gender theory: The implications for educational research. *Compare: A Journal of Comparative and International Education*, 38(5).
Fernandes, W. (2001). Development induced displacement and sustainable development, *Social Change*, 31(1–2), pp. 87–103.
Fernandes, W. (2004). Rehabilitation policy for the displaced. *Economic and Political Weekly*, 39(12), pp. 1191–1193.
Fernandes, W. (2006). Development-induced Displacement: Impact on Tribals. Adivasi, 46(2), pp. 90–98.
Fernandes, W. (2009). Displacement and alienation from common property resources, In Mehta, L. (ed.). *Displaced by Development: Confronting Marginalisation and Gender Inustice*. New Delhi: SAGE Publications India Pvt Ltd, pp. 105–129.
Fernandes, W. (2011). Development-induced displacement in the era of privatisation, In Mathur, H. M. (ed.). *Resettling Displaced People: Policy and Practice in India*. 1st edn. New Delh: Routledge India.
Fernandes, W. & Bharali, G. (2011). *Uprooted for whose Benefit? Development-Induced Displacement in Assam 1947–2000*. Guwahati: NESRC.
Fernandes, W. & Naik, N. (2001). *Development-Induced Displacement in Goa 1965–1995: A Study on Its Extent and Nature*. New Delhi: Indian Social Institute & Panjim: INSAF.
Fernandes, W. Pereira & Khatso, V. (2007). *Customary Laws in North East India: Impact on Women*. New Delhi: National Commision on Women.
Fernandes, W. & Raj, A. S. (1992). *Development, Displacement and Rehabilitation in the Tribal Areas of Orissa*. New Delhi: Indian Social Institute.

Fernandes, W. et al. (2012). *Progress: At whose Cost? Development-Induced Displacement in West Bengal, 1947–2000*. Guwahati: NESRC.

Fernandes, W. et al. (2015). *Development Induced Displacement in Meghalaya* Guwahati. India: North Eastern Social Research Centre.

Fernandes, W. et al. (2016). *Development-Induced Displacement in Sikkim, 1975–2007 and Nagaland 1947–2007*. Guwahati: NESRC.

Flax, J. (1987). Postmodernism and gender relations in feminist theory, *Signs*, 2(4), pp. 621–643.

Fry, M. (2011). From crops to concrete: Urbanization, deagriculturalization, and construction material mining in central Mexico. *Annals of the Association of American Geographers*, 101(6), pp. 1285–1306.

Ganguly, T. E. (1999). 'Bottom-Up'. *Humanscape*, November, 6(11), pp. 10–12.

Gangwar, A. K. & Ramakrishnan, S. P. (1992). Agriculture and animal husbandry among the Sulungs and Nishis of Arunachal Pradesh, In Fernandes, W. (ed.). *National Development and Tribal Deprivation*. New Delhi: India Social Institute, pp. 100–128.

Gassah, L. (1998). *Traditional Institutions of Meghalaya: A Case Study of Doloi and His Administration*. New Delhi: Regency Publications.

George, S. & Sabelli, F. (1994). *Faith and Credit: The World Bank's Secular Empire*. London: Penguin Books.

Gheraddi, S. (1995). *Gender, Symbolism and Organizational Culture*. London: Sage.

Gherardi, S. & Poggio, B. (2002). Creating and recreating gender order in organizations. *Journal of World Business*, 36(3), pp. 245–259.

Giddens, A. (1991). *Modernity and Self-Identity: Self and Society in thę Ate Modern Age*. Stanford: Standford University Press.

Giddens, A. (1994). Living in a post-traditional society, In Beck, U., Giddens, A., & Lash, S. (eds.). *Reflexive Modernisation: Politics, Tradition and Aesthetics in the Modern Social Order*. Cambridge: Polity Press.

Gill, P. (ed.) (2013). *The Peripheral Centre*. 2nd edn. New Delhi: Zubaan.

Gilman, N. (2003). *Mandarins of the future: Modernisation Theory in Cold War America*. United States: The John Hopkins University Press.

Glasier, A., GuLmezoglu, A. M., Schmid, G. P., Moreno, C. G. & Van Look, P. F. A. (2006). Sexual and reproductive health: A matter of life and death, *The Lancet*, 368(9547), pp. 1595–1607.

Gluck, S. Berger. (2002). What's so special about women? Women's oral history, In Armitage, H. S., Hart, P. & Weathermon, K. (eds.). *Women's Oral History: The Frontiers Reader*. Lincoln, NE: University of Nebraska.

Gluck, S. Berger. (2008). Women's oral history: Is it so special?, In Charlton, L. T., Myers, E. L. & Sharpless, E. (eds.). *Thinking About Oral History: Theories and Applications*. New York: Alta Mira Press.

Goduka, I. N. (2000). African or indigenous philosophies; legitimizing spiritually centered wisdoms within the academy, In Higgs, P., Vakalisa, N. C. G., Mda, T.V., & Assie-Lumumba, N. T. (eds.). *African Voices in Education*. Lansdowne: Juta, pp. 63–83.

Goswami, U. (2010). Armed in Northeast: Special powers act or no act. *Peace and Conflict Review*, 4: p. 2.

Gough, K. (1972). The modern disintegration of matrilineal descent groups, In Schneider, D. & Gough, K. (eds.). *Matrilineal Kinship*. Allahabad: A. H. Wheeler and Co., pp. 631–652.

Grosz, E. (1994). A thousand tiny sexes: Feminism and rhizomatics, In Deleuze, G. (ed.). *TheTtheater of Philosophy*. New York: Routledge, pp. 187–210.

Guha, R. & Gadgil, M. (1996). What are forests for? in *Drafting a people's Forest Bill: The Forest Dweller-Social Activist Alternative*. Fernandes, W. (ed.). New Delhi: Indian Social Institute, pp. 33–67.

Gurdon, M. P. K. T. (1907). *The Khasis*. [Online]. Available at: https://archive.org/stream/in.ernet.dli.2015.276274/2015.276274.The-Khasis_djvu.txt (Accessed on 2019 April).

Gururaja, S. (2001). Gender dimensions of displacement, *Forced Migration Review*, 9, pp. 13–16.

Gusfield, J. R. (1967). Tradition and modernity: Misplaced polarities in the study of social change, *American Journal of Sociology*, January, 72(4), pp. 351–362.

Guy-Sheftall, B. (1995). *Words of Fire: An Anthology of African–American Feminist Thought*. New York: The New Press.

Haksar, N. (1998). Law and self management of tribal Societiesin North–East India, In Thomas, J. C. (ed.). *Dimensions of Displaced people in North East India*. New Delhi: Inter India Publications, pp. 161–192.

Haokip, T. (2012). Political integration of Northeast India: A historical analysis. *Strategic Analysis*, March, 36(2), pp. 304–314.

Haokip, T. (2013). Inter-ethnic relations in Meghalaya. *Asian Ethnicity*, 6 November, 15(3), pp. 302–316.

Heemskerk, M. (2000). *Gender and Gold Mining: The Case of the Ma- Roons of Suriname*. Ann Arbour: Michigan State University.

Heesterman, J. (1963). Tradition in Modern India. *Bijdragen: Tot de Taal-, Land-, en Volkenkund*, 119(3), pp. 237–253.

Hill, C. & Newell, K. (2009). *Women, Communities and Mining: The Gender Impacts of Mining and the Role of Gender Impact Assessment*. Carlton, Victoria: Oxfam Australia.

Hooks, B. (2000). *Feminist Theory: From Margins to Center*. 2nd edn. London: Pluto Press.

Hussain, M. (1987). Tribal Movements for Autonomous States in Assam. *Economic and Political Weekly*, 22(32), pp. 1329–1332.

Ingleheart, R. & Norris, P. (2003). *Rising Tide: Gender Equality And Cultural Change Around The World*. Cambridge: Cambridge University Press.

Ingold, T. (1996). Situating action. *Ecological Psychology*, 8(2), pp. 183–187.

Ingold, T. (2011). *Being Alive: Essays on Movement, Knowledge and Description*. London: Routledge.

International, M. R. G. (2017). *No Escape from Discrimination: Minorities, Indigenous Peoples and the Crisis of Displacement*. London: Minority Rights Group International.

Jayson Stanley (2004). Development-induced Displacement and Resettlement. Forced Migration Online Research Guide, Refugee Studies Centre, University of Oxford.

Joshi, H. (2004). *Meghalaya Past and Present*. New Delhi: Mittal Publications, pp. 229–232.

Kaarhus, R. (2010). Women's Land rights and land tenure reforms in Malawi: What difference does matriliny Make? *Forum for Development Studies*, 37(2), pp. 171–192.

Kanpur, R. (2004). *Development Economics and the Compensation Principle.* [Online]. Available at: https://onlinelibrary.wiley.com/doi/full/10.1111/1468-2451.5501003

Kapadia, K. M. (1966). The matrilineal family, In Kapadia K. (ed.). *Marriage and Family in India.* Bombay: Oxford University Press, pp. 336–354.

Karlsson, B. G. (2011). *Unruly Hills: A political Ecology of India's North East.* New York: Berghahn Books, p. 164.

Kikon, D. (2019). *Living with Oil and Coal: Resource Politics and Militarization in Northeast India.* Seattle: University of Washington Press.

Klubock, T. M. (1998). *Contested Communities: Class, Gender, and Politics in Chile's El Teniente Copper Mine.* Durham: Duke University Press.

Koeing, D. (1995). Women and resettlement, In Gallin, R, Ferguson, A. & Harper, J (eds.). *The Women and International Development Annual*, volume?. Boulder, Colorado: Westview, pp. 21–51.

Koian, R. *Women in patrilineal and matrilineal societies in Melanesia.* (Online). Available at: http://milda.aidwatch.org.au/sites/default/files/Rosa%20Koian.%20Women%20in%20patrilineal%20and%20matrilineal%20societies%20in%20Melanesia.pdf (Accessed on June, 2019).

Kothari, R. (1968). Tradition and modernity revisited. *Government and Opposition*, 3(3), pp. 273–293. doi:10.1111/j.1477-7053.1968.tb01292.x

Kotsdam, A. & Tolonen, A. (2016). African mining, gender, and local employment. *World Development*, 83, pp. 325–339.

Kreutzmann, H. (1998). From modernization theory towards the 'clash of civilizations': Directions and paradigm shifts in Samuel Huntington's analysis and prognosis of global development, *Geo Journal*, 46, pp. 255–265.

Kulischer, Eugene M. (1943). *The Displacement of Population in Europe.* International Labour Office, Studies and Reports, Series O (Migration), No. 8. Montreal International Labour Office, 1943. pp. ii, 171.

Kumar, S. & Mishra, A. J. (2018). Forced displacement: Impact on rural women in India. *ANTYAJAA: Indian Journal of Women and Social Change*, 19 June, 3(1), pp. 82–92.

Kurein (1980). Social factors and economic organisation of the traditional, small scale fishermen of India, *Social Action*, 15 September, 30(1), pp. 85–89.

Ladia O. D. V. (2004). *A critical analysis of the system of administration of justice in Meghalaya.*

Lahiri-Dutt, K. (2012). Digging women: Towards a new agenda for feminist critiques of mining, *Gender, Place and Culture: A journal of Feminist Geography*, 19(2), pp. 193–212.

Laird, T. (2004). A woman's world- Meghalaya, India, Matrilineal Culture http://lib.icimod.org/record/9474/files/3602.pdf (Accessed on 1 May 2016).

Lamin, H. (1995). *Economy and Society in Meghalaya.* New Delhi: Har Anand Publications.

Lapasam, S. B. (2016). Traditional political institutions in Jaintia Hills, In Lyngdoh, C. R. (ed.). *Revisiting Traditional Institutions in the Khasi Jaintia Hills.* Newscastle: Cambridge Scholars Publishing, pp. 97–101.

Latour, B. (2000). When things strike back: A possible contribution of "science studies" of the social science, *British Journal of Sociology*, 51(1), pp. 107–123.

Leonetti, D. L., Nath, D. C. & Hemam, N. S. (2007). Women's reproductive lives and the roles of their mothers and husbands among the matrilineal Khasi, *Current Anthropology*, 48(6), pp. 861–890.

Levi-Strauss, C. (1968). *The Savage Mind: The Nature of Human Society*. Chicago: Chicago University Press.

Lind, J. (2011). Democratization and stability in East Asia, *International Studies Quarterly*, 55, pp. 409–436.

Linstead, S. & Pullen, A. (2006). Gender as multiplicity: Desire, displacement, difference and dispersion, *Human Relations*, 59(9), pp. 1287–1310.

Lobo, L. & Shashikant, K. (2009). *Land Acquisition, Displacement and Resettlement in Gujarat 1947–2004*. New Delhi and California: Sage Publications.

Lozeva, S. & Marinova, D. (2010). Negotiating gender: Experience from Western Australian mining industry, *Journal of Economic and Social Policy*, 13(2). Available at https://www.researchgate.net/publication/49964877_Negotiating_Gender_Experience_from_Western_Australian_Mining_Industry (Accessed on 17 November 2021).

Yuba Raj Luintel (2014). Modernity and gender: A critique of modernization theory, *Himalayan Journal of Sociology & Anthropology*, 6, pp. 221–235.

Lyngdoh, C. R. & Gassah, L. S. (2003). Decades of inter-ethnic tension, *Economic and Political Weekly*, November–December, 38(48), pp. 5024–5026.

Lyngdoh, R. (1966). *Government and Politics in Meghlaya*. New Delhi: Sanchar Publishing House.

Lyngdoh, W. L. (2018). *Who will address income inequality in Meghalaya?* [Online]. Available at: http://www.theshillongtimes.com/2018/02/28/who-will-address-income-inequality-in-meghalaya/ (Accessed on 26 May 2019).

Madhavan, P. (2005). Ant people, *Eastern Panorama*, 14(6), 8–10.

Mahoney, J. (2010). After KKV: The new methodology of qualitative research, *World Politics*, 62, 120–147.

Mahy, P. (2011). Sex work and livelihoods: Beyond the 'negative impacts on women' in Indonesian mining, In Lahiri-Dutt, K. (ed.). *Gendering the Field: Towards Sustainable Livelihoods for Mining Communities*. Australia: Australia,Australian National University E Press, pp. 49–64.

Marak, B. & Bhatnagar, T. (2015). Sexual behaviours and condom use among young urban women in a town in northeast India: Implications for prevention and control of sexually transmitted infections, *Clinical Epidemiology and Global Health*, 3, pp. 43–48.

Marbaniang, I. (2009). *Meghalaya Legislative Assembly: The Role of the Opposition 1972–1988*. Shillong: North-Eastern Hill University

Mayes, R. & Pini, B. (2010). The 'Feminine revolution in mining': A critique, *Australian Geographer*, 41(2), pp. 233–245.

McCall, L. (2005). The complexity of intersectionality, *Signs*, 30(3), pp. 1771–1800.

McDowell, C. (ed.). (1997). *Understanding Impoverishment: The Consequence of Development Induced-Displacement*. Oxford: Berghahn.

McDuie-Ra, D. & Kikon, D. (2016). Tribal communities and coal in Northeast India: The politics of imposing and resisting mining bans, *Energy Policy*, 99, pp. 261–269.

McFarlane, J. A., Blackwell, B. D., Mounter, S. W., Grant, B. J., From agriculture to mining: The changing economic base of a rural economy and implications for development. *Economic Analysis and Policy* (2015), http://dx.doi.org/10.1016/j.eap.2015.11.012

Mehta, L. (2002). *The Double Bind: A Gender Analysis of Forced Displacement and Resettlement*. New Delhi: Institute of Development Studies & Action Aid, India.

Mehta, L. (ed.). (2009). *Displaced by Development; confronting Marginalisation and Gender Injustice*. New Delhi, California, UK, Singapore: Sage Publications.

Mehta, L. & Srinivasan, B. (2000a). 'Balancing Pains and gains: A perspective Paer on gender and Lage Dams', paper prepared for the Thematic review 1.1 *Social Impacts of Large Dams: Equity and Distributional Issues, World Commissions on Large Dams*.

Mehta, L. & Srinivasan, B. (2000b). Women facing Submergence: Displacement and resistance in Narmada, In Damodaran, V. & Unnitha, M. (eds.). *Identities, Nation, Global Culture*. New Delhi: Manohar.

Menon, G. (1995). The impact of migration on the work and tribal women's status, In Schenken-Sandbergen, L. (ed.). *Women and Seasonal Labour Migration*. New Delhi: Sage Publications, pp. 154–179.

Mishra, P. P. & Pujari, A. K. (2008). Impact of mining on agricultural productivity: A case study of the Indian state of Orissa. *South Asia Economic Journal*, 9(2), pp. 337–350.

Modi, R. (2004). Sardar sarovar oustees: coping with displacement, *Economic and Political Weekly*, 39(11), pp. 1123–1126.

Mohanty, C. T., Russo, A. & Torres, L. (eds.) (1991). *Third World Women and the Politics of Feminism*. Indianapolis: Indiana University Press.

Mohrmen, H. (2011). *Khasi Pnar: A Community in Transition*. [Online]. Available at: http://hhmohrmen.blogspot.com/2011/01/ (Accessed on April 2019).

Mohrmn, H. H. (2015). *Jaintia Hills in a Nutshell*. (Online). Available at: http://www.theshillongtimes.com/2015/03/16/jaintia-hills-in-a-nutshell/ (Accessed February 2019).

Mollet, S. & Faria, C. (2013). Messing with gender in feminist political ecology, *Geoforum*, 45, pp. 116–125.

Morgan, L. (1885). *Ancient Society*. Tuscon: University of Arizona Press.

Mukhim, P. (2000). *Giving Matriliny a Bad Name* (Accessed on 2019).

Mukhim, P. (2007a). Myths, tradition and identity: Women in matriliny", In Augustine, C. (ed.). *Matriliny in Transition: A Comparative Analysis*. New Delhi: Akansha Publishing House.

Mukhim, P. (2007b). Turbulence in the abode of clouds, In Saikia, J. (ed.). *Frontier in Flames*. New Delhi: Penguin Books India Private Limited.

Mukhim, P. (2009). "Khasi matrilineal society – challenges in the twenty-first century, In Abendroth, G. H. (ed.). *Societies of Peace-Matriarchies Past, Present and Future*. Canada: Inanna Publications and Education Inc.

Mukhim, P. (2013). *Sixth Schedule and Tribal Autonomy*. http://www.thestatesman.com/news/5573-sixth-schedule-and-tribal-autonomy.html (Accessed on 1 May 2016).

Mukhim, P. (2019). *Citizenship Bill: Why should the North East Bear the Burden?* ca. Available at: https://www.thequint.com/voices/opinion/citizenship-bill-north-east-ramifications-challenges (Accessed on May 2019).

Murdock, P. (1949). *Social Structure*. New York: Free Press.

Murphy, M. (1997). *Mining Cultures: Men, Women, and Leisure in Butte, 1914–1941*. Champaign: University of Illinois Press.

Mutolib, A., Yonariza, Mahdi & Ismono, H. (2016). Gender inequality and the oppression of women within minangkabau matrilineal society: A case study of the management of Ulayat forest land in Nagari Bonjol, Dharmasraya district, West Sumatra province, Indonesia, *Asian Women*, 32(3), pp. 23–49.

Nash, J. C. (2008). Re-thinking intersectionality, *Feminist Review*, 89, pp. 1–15.

Nayak, R. K. (2001). *History of Dudhi Estate District Mirzapur 1858–1950*. Uttar Pradesh: V. B. S. Purvanchal University.

New, J. R. et al. (2017). Levels and trends in contraceptive prevalence, unmet need, and demand for family planning for 29 states and union territories in India: A modelling study using the family planning estimation tool, *Lancet Glob Health*, March, 5, pp. 350–358.

Nnameka, O. (1997). Imag(in)ing knowledge, power and subversion in the margins, In Nnaemeka, O. (ed.). *The Politics of M(o)thering: Womanhood, Identity and Resistance in African Literature*. London: Routledge.

Nongbri, T. (2000). Khasi women and matriliny: Transformations in gender relations, *Gender, Technology and Development*, 4(3), pp. 359–395.

Nongkynrih, D. (2014a). Land relations in the tribal societies of Meghalaya: Changing patterns of land use and ownership, *Social Change and Development*, 12(2), pp. 1–20.

Nongkynrih, Deigracia. (2014b). *Land Relations in the Tribal Societies of Meghalaya: Changing patterns of land use and ownership*. http://www.okd.in/downloads/jr_14_july/Deigracia.pdf (Accessed on 1 May 2016).

Nongtdu, P. & Sahu, B. (2013). *Unorganised Coalmine Workers in Meghalaya*. New Delhi: Lakshi Publishers and Distributors.

Olkowski, D. (1999). *Gilles Deleuze and the Ruin of Representation*. Berkeley: University of California Press.

Oyewumi, O. (1998). DeConfounding gender: Feminist theorizing and western culture, *Signs*, 23(4), pp. 1049–1062.

Oyewumi, O. (2001). Ties that (un bind): Feminism, sisterhood and other foreign relations, *A Journal of Culture and African Women Studies*, 1(1). ISSN: 1530-5686 (online), https://www.africaknowledgeproject.org/index.php/jenda/article/viewArticle/25.

Pakyntein, V. (1999). Gender Preference in Khasi Society, In Subba, T. (ed.). *In Wonder That is Culture*. New Delhi: Mittal Publications, pp. 171–182.

Pakyntein, V. (2011). The Pnar trilogy: Explicating Pnar society and culture through the lahoo dance, *International Conference in St. Gallen on Matriarchal Politics: Insights from Matriarchal studies, perspectives on Matrarchal Politics*, Switzerland: Grand Opening of the Matri Archive, May 12–15, 2011.

Pandit, C. R. (2009). *Development-vs-Displacement of Tribal People in India, Problems and Prospects*. Delhi: Abhijeet Publications.

Parasuraman, S. (1993). *Impact of Displacement by Development Projects on Women in India*, ISS Working paper Series No. 159. Hague: Institute of Social Studies.

Parasuraman, S. (1996a). Development projects, displacement and outcomes for displaced: Two case studies. *Economic and Political Weekly*, 31(24), pp. 1529–1532. http://www.jstor.org/stable/4404277

Parasuraman, S. (1996b). Methodological issues in studies on resettlement and rehabilitation of project displaced people. *Indian Journal of Social Work*, 57, pp. 191–220.

Parasuraman, S. (1999). Development, displacement and resettlement in India: An overview. *The Development Dilemma*, pp. 35–36. Available at: https://link.springer.com/chapter/10.1007/978-1-349-27248-8_2

Parsons, T. (1940). An analytical approach to the theory of social stratification, *American Journal of Sociology*, May, 45(6), pp. 840–862.

Pathy, J. (1988). *Ethnic Minorities in the Process of Development*. Jaipur: Rawat Publications.

Patnaik, S. K., Das, B. & Mishra, A. B. (1987). Hirakud dam: Expectations and realities, In Pria (ed.). *People and Dams*. New Delhi: Society for Participatory Research in Asia, pp. 47–59.

Penz Peter, Drydyk Jay and Bose Pablo S. (2011). *Displacement by Development: Ethics, Rights and Responsibilities*. Cambridge: Cambridge University Press, p. 343, $31.99 (pbk), ISBN 9780521124645.

Phiri, K. M. (1983). Some changes in the matrilineal family system among the Chewa of Malawi since the nineteenth century, *The Journal of African History*, 24(2), pp. 257–274.

Phukan, S. (2006). *Ecossais*. Guwahati: Satyakam Phukan.

Picciotto, R., Van Wicklin, W. and Rice, E., (eds.). (2001). Involuntary resettlement: Comparative perspectives. New Brunswick and London: Transaction Publishers.

Poewe, K. (1989). *Religion, Kinship and Economy in Luapala, Zambia*. Lweiston, N.Y: Edwin Mellen Press.

Porsild, C. (2000). Mining Gender, *Gender & History*, July, 12(2), pp. 482–486.

Portelli, A. (2003). What makes oral history different, In Perks, R. and Thomson, A. (eds.). Oral History Reader. USA and Canada. Routledge.

Powewe, K. (1981). *Matrilineal Ideology: Male-Female Dynamics in Luapala, Zambia*. London: Academic Press.

Rao, V. & Hazarika, N. (1984). *A Century of Government and Politics in North East India*. New Delhi: S. Chand & Co.

Rao, V. V. (1975). *Development of Political and Social Institutions in the Garo Hills*. [Online]. Available at: http://shodhganga.inflibnet.ac.in/bitstream/10603/67610/7/07_chapter%203.pdf (Accessed on April 2019).

Rao, V. V., Hazarika, N. & Pakem, B. (1984). *A Century of Government and Politics in North East India*. Meghalaya: S. Chand & Co. Ltd, vol. 11, pp. 1874–1898.

Ravinder, D. (2004). 'Policy-induced displacement: A case of sheep and goat rearing communities in Andhra Pradesh' paper presented at *International Seminar on 'Development and Displacement: Afro-Asian Perspectives* organised by Department of Political Sciences and Regional Centre for Urban and environment Studies, Osmania University and Human Rights Education Programme, Dr. B. R. Ambedkar Open University, 27th and 28th November.

Ray, B. D. & Agarwal, S. P. (1996). *Reorganisations of North East India since 1947*. New Delhi: Concept Publishing Company.

Reddy, B. & Reddy M. (2007). Austro-asiatic tribes of Northeast India provide hitherto missing genetic link between South and Southeast Asia, *Plos One*, 2(11), pp. 1–12.

Rew, Alan, Fisher Elenor and Pandey Balaji. Policy Practices in Development Induced Displacement and resettlement, proceedings of the 10th World Congress of Rural Sociology, Rio De Jeneiro, August 200, pp. 1–19.

Richards, A. (1950). Some types of family structure amongst the Central Banter, In Radcliffe-Brown A. R. & D. Ford (ed.). *African Systems of Kinship and Marriage*. London: International African Institute by the Oxford University Press, pp. 207–251.

Robinson, W. (1841). *A Descriptive Account of Assam*. Delhi: Sanskaran Prakashak.

Rostow, W. W. (1960). *The Stage of Economic Growth*. London: Cambridge University Press.

Roy, S. (2017). *Political Economy of Land Governance and Women's Rights: The Case of Meghalaya*. Washington: World Bank, pp. 1–19.

Ruback, Timothy J. (2010). 'Let me tell the story straight on': Middlemarch, process tracing methods and the politics of narrative, *British Journal of Politics and International Relations*, 12, 477–497.

Rudolph, L. I. & Rudolph, S. H. (1967). *The Modernity of Tradition: Political Development in India*. Chicago: University of Chicago.

Ruwanpura, K. N. (2006). *Matrilineal Communities, Patriarchal Realities: A Feminist Nirvana Uncovered*. Michigan: University of Michigan Press.

Saavedra, C. M. & Nymark, E. D. (2008). Borderland-mestizaje feminism: The new tribalism, In Denzin, N. K., Lincoln, Y. S., & Smith, L. T. (eds.). *Handbook of Critical and Indigenous Methodologies*. Thousand Oaks: SAGE Publications Ltd, pp. 255–276.

Saikia, A. (2018). In *Meghalaya's Garo Hills, A Long Running Insurgency has Lost Steam but Peace Could be Elusive*. (Online). Available at: https://scroll.in/article/877026/in-meghalayas-garo-hills-a-long-running-insurgency-has-lost-steam-but-peace-could-prove-elusive (Accessed on 26 May 2019).

Sánchez, B. E. & Urueña, R. (2017) Colombian development-induced displacement – considering the impact of international law on domestic policy, *Groningen Journal of International Law*, 5(1), pp. 73–95.

Sandoval, C. (2000). *Methodology of the Oppressed*. Minneapolis: University of Minnesota Press.

Sangster, J. (1994). Telling our stories: feminist debates and the use of oral history. *Women's History Review*, 3(1), 5–28.

Sarma, K. (2010). Land ownership, administration and status of forests of Khasi Hills, *NeBIO*, 1(3), pp. 8–13.

Saxena, N. n.d. *Planning Commission of India*. (Online). Available at: http://planningcommission.nic.in/reports/articles/ncsxna/ncrural.pdf (Accessed on 26 May 2019).

Schneider, D. (1972). Some distinctive features of matrilineal descent groups, In David M. Schneider & Gough, K (eds.). *Matrilineal Kinship*. Allahabad: Wheeler and Co., pp. 8–27.

Schrijvers, J. & Postel-Coster, E. (1977). Minangkabau women: Change in a matrilineal society, *Archipel*, 13, pp. 79–103.

Scott, R. R. (2007). Dependent masculinity and political culture in pro-mountaintop removal discourse: Or, how I learned to stop worrying and love the dragline, *Feminist Studies*, 33(3), pp. 484–509.

Scudder, T. and Colson, E. (1982). From welfare to development: A conceptual framework for analysis of dislocated people, In Hansen, A. and Ohver-Smith, A. (eds.), *Involuntary Migration and Resettlement*, Boulder: Westview Press.

Sebastian, S. (2016). *What Led To The Decline Of The Matrilineal Society In Kerala?* (Online). Available at: https://sxpolitics.org/what-led-to-the-decline-of-the-matrilineal-society-in-kerala/16065 (Accessed on 5 August 2019).

Sen, Ilina. (1992). Mechanisation and the working class women. *Social Action*, 42(4, Oct.–Dec.), pp. 391–400.

Shacklock, G & Thorp, L. (2005). Life history and narrative approaches, In Somekh, B. & Lewin, C. (eds.). *Research Methods in the Social Sciences*. London: Sage Publications, pp. 156–163.

Shah, P. (2018). Healthcare in Meghalaya: An uphill battle. Observer Research Foundation. Available at https://www.orfonline.org/expert-speak/healthcare-meghalaya-uphill-battle/ (Accessed on15 November 2021).

Sharma, K. (1989). National Policies for Natural Resources Management, Marginalisation of Poor Rural Women' (Occasional Paper No 14), Centre for Women's Development Studies, New Delhi.

Sharma, M. (2004). *Critically Assessing Traditions: The Case of Meghalaya.* Crisis State Programme: Development Research Centre, Working Paper Series No. 1(Working Paper no. 52.).

Sheikh, A. U. R. (2009). Development induced displacement in Pakistan, In Basu, S. P. (ed.). *The Fleeing People of South Asia: Selections from Refugee Watch.* New Delhi: Anthem Press, pp. 183–186.

Singha, K. & Nayak, P. (2016). Economics, ethnicity and autonomy movements in Meghalaya, *Journal of Community Positive Practices*, 16(1), 37–55.

Sinha, A. C. (1990). *Northeast Frontier and the Nepalese Immigrants in Himalayan Environment and Culture.* Shimla: Indian Institute of Advanced Studies.

Sinha, K. (1970). *Meghalaya: Triumph of the Tribal Genius.* Delhi: Pub. Division of ISSD.

Smith, D., Krannich, R., Hunter, L., (2001). Growth, decline, stability, and disruption: A longitudinal analysis of social well–being in four western Australian communities. Rural Sociology, 66(3), pp. 425–450.

So, A. Y. (1990). *Social Change and Development: Modernisation, Dependency and World Systems theory.* USA: Sage Publications.

Spelmen, E. (1988). *Inessential Woman.* Boston: Beacon Press.

Spivak, G. C. (1988). Can the subaltern speak?, In Nelson, C. & Grossberg, L. (eds.). *Marxism and the Interpretation of Culture.* London: Macmillan.

Srinivasan, B. (1997). *In Defense of the Furute.* Mumbai: Vikas Adhyan Kendra.

Staples, M. (2017). *Gender Equality in Our Industry.* [Online]. Available at: http://www.mining.com/web/gender-equality-industry/

Sten, H. W. (1971). *The Meghalaya Year Book 1971.* Shillong: North East India News & Features Service.

Stephens, Julie. (2010). Our remembered selves: oral history and feminist memory, *Oral History*, 38(1), pp. 81–90.

Subba, T. B. (2008). Matriliny, reproductive health, and reproductive rights: An essay on the Khasis of Meghalaya, Northeast India. *European Bulletin of Himalayan Research*, 32(3), pp. 50–65.

Susman, I. W. (1964). History and the American intellectual: uses of a usable past, *American Quarterly*, 16(Part 2), p. 243.

Syiemlieh, D. R. (1989). *British Administration in Meghalaya Policy and Pattern.* New Delhi: Heritage Publishers.

Takyi, B. K. & Gyimah, S. O. (2007). matrilineal family ties and marital dissolution in Ghana. Journal of Family Issues, 28(5), pp. 682–705.

Tangvah, K. (2015). Religious beliefs and practices of the Pnars of Nangbah village in Jaintia Hills district, Meghalaya. *International Journal of Multidisciplinary Research and Development*, 2(1), pp. 250–257.

Tanius, M. (1983). Matrilineal society and family planning: A Minangkaban case study, In Wilfredo, F. A. & Alvarez, G. (eds.). *Population Change In.* Singapore: ISAS, pp. 358–390.

Terminski, B. (2012). Mining-induced displacement and resettlement: social problem and human rights issue (a global perspective). Link – http://indr.org/wp-content/uploads/2013/04/B.-Terminski-Mining-Induced-Displacement-and-Resettlement.pdf (Accessed on 28 November 2021).

Terminski, B. (2013). *Development-Induced Displacement and Resettlement: Theoretical Frameworks and Current Challenges*. Geneva: University of Geneva.

The Native Explorer, n.d. *Meghalaya*. (Online). Available at: http://nativeexplorer.co.in/meghalaya/ (Accessed on April 2019).

The Sixth Schedule of the Indian Constitution. (n.d.) https://www.mea.gov.in/Images/pdf1/S6.pdf (Accessed on 1 May 2016).

Thompson, P. (2003). The voice of the past, In Perks, R. & Thomson, A. (eds.). *The Oral history Reader*. London: Taylor & Francis e-Library, pp. 21–28.

Thomson, S. J. A. & Geddes, P. (1889). *The Evolution of Sex*. London: W. Scott.

Thukral, E. G. (1996). Development, displacement and rehabilitation: Locating gender, *Economic and Political Weekly*, 31(24), pp. 1500–1503.

Times, T. S. (2019). *Demand for ILP Back in Centre Stage in Meghalaya*. (Online). Available at: http://www.theshillongtimes.com/2019/02/12/demand-for-ilp-back-in-centre-stage-in-meghalaya/ (Accessed on 26 May 2019).

Timsina, S. R. (1992). *Nepali Community in India*. Darjeeling: Manak Publications.

Tripathy, P. S. (2009). Tribal displacement and deprivationin India, In Pandit, C. R. (ed.). *Development-vs-Displacement of Tribal People in India*. New Delhi: Abhijeet Publications, pp. 1–4.

Tuan, T. V. (2010). Meanings of sex, concepts of risk and sexual practices among migrant coal miners in Quang Ninh, Vietnam. *Culture, Health & Sexuality*, 12(S1), pp. S31–S40.

Vanclay Frank. (2017). Project-induced displacement and resettlement: From impoverishment risks to an opportunity for development?. *Impact Assessment and Project Appraisal*, 35(1), pp. 3–21. doi: 10.1080/14615517.2017.1278671

Vincent, K. (1978). *Socio-Economic Study of Bhoilymbong, A Village in Meghalaya*. Madras: Diocesan Press.

Wacquant, L. (1997). For an analytic of racial domination, In Davis, D. E. (ed.). *Political Power and Social Theory II*. Greenwich: Jai Press, pp. 221–234.

Wangari, E., Rocheleau, D. & Thomas-Slayter, B. (1996). *Feminist Political Ecology: Global Issues and Local Experiences*. London and New York: Routledge.

War, R. J. & Albert, S. (2013). Sexuality and 'silence' among Khasi youth of Meghalaya, Northeast India, *Culture, Health & Sexuality*, 15(S3), pp. S351–S364.

Watzlmaier, M. (2012). Cultural Impacts of Mining in Indigenous people's ancestral domains in the Philipines, *Forum South East Asia*, 5(2), pp. 335–344.

Weiner, M. (1983). The political demography of Assam's anti-immigrant movement, *Population and Development Review*, June, 9(2), pp. 279–292.

Whatmore, S. (2002). *Hybrid Geographies: Natures, Cultures, Spaces*. London: Routledge.

Whatmore, S. (2006). Materialist returns: practising culture geography in and for a more-than-human world, *Cultural Geographies*, 13(4), pp. 600–609.

Whitaker, C. S. (1970). The Politics of Tradition: Continuity and Change in Northern Nigeria, 1946–1966.

WLSA-Malawi & GIES-CR (2014). *Parallel Report to the United Nations Human Rights Committee*, Malawi: United Nations Human Rights Committee.

Women, U. (2017). *Gender and Equity Compact for the Energy and Mineral Development Sector* 2016/2017–2019/2020. (Online). Available at: http://www2.unwomen.org/-/media/field%20office%20africa/attachments/publications/2018/01/gender_and_equity_compact_energy_and_mineral_development.pdf?la=en&vs=3409 (Accessed on September 2018).

Wood, R. (2005). Hill tribes of Assam, In Sharma, S. K. & Sharma, U. (eds.). *Discovery of North East India*. New Delhi: Mittal Publications, pp. 181–182.

World Bank (2013). *Gender in Extractive Industries*. (Online). Available at: http://www.worldbank.org/en/topic/extractiveindustries/brief/gender-in-extractive-industries (Accessed on September 2018).

Zakaria, R. (2018). *If You Weren't Here Before 1971, You're Not a Citizen*. (Online). Available at: https://newrepublic.com/article/150350/werent-1971-youre-not-citizen (Accessed on May 2019).

Zanzani, S. (1997). *A Mine of Her Own: Women Prospectors in the American West 1850–1950*. Lincoln: University of Nebraska Press.

Appendix A

Sixth Schedule of the Indian Constitution (Articles 244-2 and 275-1) n.d. Available at, https://www.constitutionofindia.net/constitution_of_india/articles_244_2__and_275_1_/articles/Articles%20244(2)%20and%20275(1)%20%20 (Accessed on 10 August 2020).

PHOTOGRAPHS

Khasi women smoking fish. They are the last generation of women doing smoke fish in their families.

With the villagers of Umladkhur village, West Jaintia hills.

Enroute Ladymbai with 8 people onboard in a Maruti 800 used as a public transport.

Mine workers in a coal field near Ladrymbai, East Jaintia hills.

Coal stored on the roadside, East Jaintia hills.

Coal being loaded into a truck near Urium village, East Jaintia hills.

With the villagers in Urium village, East Jaintia hills.

Coal field in East Jaintia hills.

A woman washing clothes, somewhere in Ladrymbai.

INDEX

For Product Safety Concerns and Information please contact our EU
representative GPSR@taylorandfrancis.com
Taylor & Francis Verlag GmbH, Kaufingerstraße 24, 80331 München, Germany

www.ingramcontent.com/pod-product-compliance
Ingram Content Group UK Ltd.
Pitfield, Milton Keynes, MK11 3LW, UK
UKHW022020180926
475701UK00005B/938

* 9 7 8 0 3 6 7 7 1 1 2 8 3 *